Political and Social Science Journals

Political and Social Science Journals

A HANDBOOK FOR WRITERS AND REVIEWERS

ABC-Clio, Inc.

Santa Barbara, California   Oxford, England

Library of Congress Cataloging in Publication Data

Main entry under title:
Political and social science journals.

Includes index.
1. Political science—Authorship. 2. Social
sciences—Authorship. 3. Scholarly periodicals—
Authorship.
JA74.P62 1983   320'.0248 . 82-18455
ISBN 0-87436-026-9
ISBN 0-87436-037-4 (pbk.)

JA
74
.P62
1983

$24.85

9/84

10 9 8 7 6 5 4 3 2 1

94772

ABC-Clio, Inc.
2040 Alameda Padre Serra, Box 4397
Santa Barbara, California 93103

Clio Press Ltd.
55 St. Thomas Street
Oxford, OX1 1JG, England

Manufactured in the United States of America

Contents

Clio Guides to Publishing Opportunities

Acknowledgements

Grateful thanks are due to those journal editors who made this book possible by taking time from their busy schedules to complete and return the questionnaires that were sent to them. Dale R. Steiner, author of the ABC-Clio publication *Historical Journals: A Handbook for Writers and Reviewers*, advised on the design of questionnaires and organization of the book, and lent his wisdom and experience in writing for journals by preparing the sections of general advice to authors and reviewers. Lloyd W. Garrison, editor of ABC POL SCI, graciously supplied the special section on "Authors and the Law" and also gave much appreciated advice on the selection of journals. Helene Wright, assistant editor of ABC POL SCI, interrupted by frequent requests for information and advice, always gave both willingly. Terri Turner assisted with the long and difficult task of compiling and organizing data. Finally, John Wagner coordinated the entire project from beginning to end, gathered elusive bits of information, and edited the questionnaires.

Introduction

Scope

Political and Social Science Journals: A Handbook for Writers and Reviewers provides prospective authors with specific and current information on the editorial policies and procedures of journals accepting and publishing articles and reviews in political science, social science, and related disciplines. The *Handbook* attempts to identify recognized disciplines and sub-disciplines which fit into a broad, interdisciplinary social/political studies framework and to list only the best known and most widely recognized periodicals publishing within or across those fields. Containing over 440 English-language journals published throughout the world, the *Handbook* focuses on those found in the United States, Canada, and Great Britain. Besides journals with a general political or social science editorial focus, the *Handbook* also contains periodicals offering publishing opportunities in area studies, development studies, economics, government, history, law, international studies, peace studies, policy studies, public administration/management, urban studies, and other interrelated fields and sub-fields. Anyone preparing an article on a topic covering one or several of these fields will find the *Handbook* very useful.

In order to maximize the chances of publishing his or her article, an author must submit the article to a journal of suitable editorial focus and readership. Once such a journal has been found, the author will need to determine the specific editorial guidelines involved and tailor the submission accordingly. The *Handbook* can help in quickly and effectively completing both of these steps. Each entry in the *Handbook* provides that particular journal's editorial focus, as well as practical information concerning journal style and usage. By consulting the *Handbook*, an author will know what size manuscript the journal will accept, how many copies are required, the form and placement of notes, how to handle illustrations, and the style guide to follow. Since the entries were compiled from information supplied by the journal editors themselves, authors can be confident that carefully following the *Handbook* will bring their articles into conformity with the standards expected by the very people who will be considering their submitted manuscripts. Editors, on the other hand, can be assured of receiving more easily handled manuscripts which are consistent with the needs and guidelines of their journal. In addition to the individual entries, a special section of the *Handbook* offers general advice on writing, submitting, and resubmitting a manuscript.

For those writers seeking to begin or expand their book reviewing activity, a special section of the *Handbook* explores the purposes and techniques of reviewing. In addition, each entry offers current information on individual journal policies and requirements for reviewing.

Organization

The format of the *Handbook* entries reflects the questionnaire that was sent to and completed by journal editors. Although the entries are largely self-explanatory, a few remarks may be in order.

The heading "Subscription rate(s)" refers to the cost of a one-year subscription unless otherwise noted. Most rates are given in dollars, but again, exceptions are noted. The headings "Query" and "Abstract" denote journals requiring either one or both. A negative answer in either category does not mean that prior inquiry or an abstract is unwelcome, but rather that they are unnecessary. "Notes" gives the journal's preference in note placement, and "Blind referee" alerts the author to delete his or her name from the manuscript itself, since the journal prefers to conceal the author's identity from the reviewer. "Foreign languages" lists languages other than English that will be accepted for publication. The "Additional notes" section provides information on royalties and fees, simultaneous submissions, lag time between acceptance and publication, and any special features of the journal's review or publication processes.

The journal entries are arranged alphabetically by title, with journals having titles in more than one language listed under their English title. The Subject Index lists journals under the disciplines and sub-disciplines from which they will accept submissions.

Advice on Articles

WRITING AN ARTICLE

What Editors Look For

Prospective authors should be aware of the factors that influence an editor to publish or reject a particular manuscript. These factors should be understood and considered throughout both the composition and submission processes. The most important factors affecting a publishing decision are quality of presentation, suitability to the journal's readership, and degree of conformity to the journal's requirements of space and style. *Quality* is of prime importance. If an article is inaccurate, unclear, and lacking credibility, it will be rejected no matter how well its topic suits the journal's focus or its style conforms to the journal's style. Quality in physical appearance is also essential, and all manuscripts should be neatly and cleanly typed with only a minimum of corrections. *Suitability* means the subject of a manuscript falls within the editorial focus of the journal and would interest the journal's established readership. The editor of a journal dealing with African politics, society, and economics will not consider an article on urban expansion in the United States. Similarly, an extremely technical piece of great interest to professionals would not be welcomed by a journal aimed at the general public. The degree of *conformity* determines the amount of work an editor must perform to bring an article into alignment with the journal's particular needs and standards. A manuscript too long to be included without time-consuming editing and reorganization may well be rejected in favor of a shorter more easily handled article. A manuscript already following the same rules of style, punctuation, and note form and placement used by a particular journal is much more likely to receive a favorable response than one the editors must recast in style and usage.

Seek Criticism

Before any article is submitted to a journal, it should be made as lean and precise as possible. This tightening process is more effective if not conducted by the author alone. Discuss ideas with colleagues and knowledgeable friends; invite them to read and comment upon rough drafts. Whenever possible, test premises, research, and conclusions on an objective and knowledgeable audience. The little extra time this will take can reap rich rewards in useful criticism and be productive of a better article and improved chances of publication.

Literary Style

Articles should be written in clear, formal English. The style should not be stiff and cumbersome, but slang and professional jargon should be avoided. Words should be carefully chosen to reflect as precisely as possible the meaning to be conveyed. The necessity of each word used should be questioned, and unnecessary words or phrases should be eliminated or put more simply. *The Elements of Style* by William Strunk, Jr. and E.B. White, and *The Chicago Manual of Style* are good places to turn for assistance. For spelling and word division, consult *Webster's Third International Dictionary*, a volume recommended by many editors.

Introduction/title

The first few paragraphs of an article are the key to whether later paragraphs will ever be read. Editors realize that busy readers often skim the introduction before deciding to read an article in its entirety and therefore look for manuscripts with strong openings. The introduction should clearly and concisely state the topic and explain why that topic is worthy of an article. Authors should not assume that because the topic is important to them, it is also important to readers. The title of the article is also important. It should be informative, brief and, if possible, intriguing. Lengthy titles sometimes create space problems, and editors are grateful for any effort that the author's foresight spares them.

SELECTING A JOURNAL

What To Consider

Considerable care should be taken to select for submission those journals likely to be more receptive to the nature and subject of the article. List all the journals in the field that have an editorial focus and a readership that is compatible with the level of ideas and language contained in the article. Factors such as the size of the journal's circulation, its rate of acceptance, the length of time needed to reach a decision, and whether or not any payment is made to contributors should be used to narrow down the list. For most journals listed in the *Handbook*, payment consists of a few reprints of the article or several copies of the issue in which the work appears. Those offering monetary payment or requiring submission fees are clearly noted. An important but intangible and subjective factor in selecting journals for submission is prestige. All else being equal, publication in one journal is preferable to publication in another simply because the former carries more prestige and confers greater distinction on the author. Although the *Handbook* cannot assess a particular journal's prestige within its field, it can help ease the author through the rest of the journal selection process.

Publication of one article in a particular journal will not ensure acceptance of another article by the same journal. In any case, publication in more than one journal can strengthen an author's reputation for writing skill and breadth of knowledge and interest. The final decision on where to submit should not be made until the author has perused a copy or two of each of the journals to which the choice has been narrowed. Making certain that the article *is* really suited to these journals is worth a trip to the library.

Query

If the *Handbook* indicates a query is in order, send a letter to the editor describing the theme of the article, the major sources consulted, why the article is suited to that particular periodical, and whether it makes an original or unique contribution to the literature on the subject. Include a self-addressed, stamped envelope with the letter of inquiry. Although an author should never submit an article to more than one journal at a time, there is no reason to limit inquiries in such a manner. Waiting to send a second query until the first one is answered will only delay the quest for publication, should the initial inquiry eventually receive a negative response.

Style Guides

If a journal publishes its own style sheet, write for a copy (again, include a self-addressed, stamped envelope). This may be done in conjunction with a query. If the journal from which a style sheet is requested does not demand a query, it is wise to include one anyway with your request. It may give encouragement or spare a later rejection.

PREPARING THE MANUSCRIPT

Typing

All manuscripts submitted to journals should be typed. Use any standard, high quality, white bond paper, 8½ by 11 inches. Never use erasable, onionskin, or second-copy paper. Before beginning to type, clean the typewriter keys and replace worn ribbons. A pica typeface is easier to read and preferable to either elite or script. A double-spaced manuscript, including footnotes and quotations, facilitates editing as well as typesetting and should always be used. A few brief hand-written corrections per page are acceptable, provided they are done legibly and in ink, for neatness and readability is extremely important. Carelessly typed or otherwise messy manuscripts create unfavorable impressions and are less likely to be judged on the merits of the ideas they present or the knowledge they contribute.

By showing them consideration, the editors will be more favorably disposed toward the manuscript (or at least less prejudiced against it). Double-spacing and generous margins can create this favorable impression, and will leave room for editorial notations and corrections. The left side margin should be at least 1½ inches, and all others at least 1 inch.

All manuscripts should follow the editorial style of the journal to which they are submitted. If no specific style guide is indicated, use either the thirteenth edition of *The Chicago Manual of Style* or the second edition of the *MLA Style Sheet*.

Illustrations

All tables, graphs, charts, or maps drawn by or for the author should conform to the journal's standard format. Each should be clearly labeled and have its location within the manuscript clearly indicated. All illustrations should be placed on separate sheets or boards and should cite the source of the information they contain. Pictorial illustrations should be similarly labeled and identified. Permission for the use of any copyrighted illustration should be obtained from the copyright holders.

Identification

Reviewers who evaluate a manuscript without knowledge of the author's identity are known as blind referees. This system allows the article to be judged on its own merits rather than by the name or reputation of its author. The author's name should not appear anywhere on a manuscript, but the author's name and the manuscript title should be clearly stated in the accompanying cover letter. Some of the journals listed in the *Handbook* as not using blind referees in fact do so, but prefer to delete author's names themselves before forwarding manuscripts for review.

SUBMITTING THE MANUSCRIPT

Single Submission

Simultaneous submission (i.e., sending articles to more than one journal at a time) is unethical and can prove embarrassing should two journals accept the article. More to the point, the author might seriously damage his or her chances of future publication in some journals. Single submission can be both frustrating and time-consuming, especially if the article is rejected several times, but considerate treatment of editors is always in the author's best interest.

Copies

An author should usually send the original typescript of the manuscript; this assures editors that the manuscript is not under consideration elsewhere. Many journals require two, three, or more copies, so send crisp, clean carbon copies or photocopies with the original.

Cover letters/abstract

A cover letter which briefly introduces the article to an editor is useful, particularly if no abstract is submitted. The letter should briefly explain the topic of the article, why it is suited to that particular journal, and how it enlarges the understanding of the field. An abstract is a brief (often under 100 words) but concise summary outlining the thesis, argument, and conclusion of the article.

Mailing/postage

Never fold a manuscript. Mail it flat in a sturdy box or envelope, and leave the pages loose and unsecured by staples, clips, or binders. A self-addressed envelope will facilitate the return of a rejected manuscript or one in need of revision. Include sufficient postage to guarantee return but do not attach the stamps to the envelope; they may be returned if the article is accepted. Failure to include a return envelope and postage represents a real imposition and may cause a rejected manuscript to be thrown out rather than returned. Many editors are becoming quite flexible about return postage and original typescripts in an age of rising postal rates and decreasing duplication costs. Simply recopying a manuscript may be far less expensive than paying return postage. In view of this, it may be advisable to send copies instead of the original and forego return postage, provided the author explains in the cover letter that disposable copies are being submitted for the convenience of all concerned.

This makes particular sense if the article is sent to a journal outside the United States where return postage must be of that country's issue. Canadian editors are frequently frustrated by well-intentioned American authors who include return postage in United States stamps. This problem can be avoided by using International Reply Coupons, available at any post office in the United States for 65 cents. Editors in other countries can exchange these for the correct stamps at the rate of one coupon per ounce. Nonetheless, taking the time and effort to acquire and send the proper stamps is still most convenient for the editor. United States residents can obtain Canadian stamps by writing any Canadian post office and sending a money order made out to the Receiver-General of Canada. Be sure to include a self-addressed envelope and payment for return postage with the order.

United States postage may be obtained by writing any United States post office and including a money order payable to the Postmaster. First class rates, though higher, will insure the quickest delivery of the manuscript. Speed may not always be the primary consideration, but the longer the manuscript is in transit, the greater the risk of loss or damage.

WHAT HAPPENS NEXT?

Review/decision

The process by which articles are reviewed varies from journal to journal. A manuscript may be screened by one or two editors, or an entire editorial review board. Articles outside the focus of the journal are quickly rejected and returned. Sometimes, particularly in the case of smaller journals, the editor decides without reference to anyone else whether to accept or reject submitted material. In other cases, as with many scholarly journals aimed at professionals, editors enlist the services of one or more reviewers or referees selected for their expertise in the field. After weighing the referees' comments and recommendations, the editor decides whether or not to publish the article.

Time

The more people involved in the review process, the more time-consuming it becomes, especially for scholarly periodicals. Referees, engaged in their own research, writing, and teaching, have limited time and despite their best intentions may take longer in reviewing than intended. Decisions are particularly hard to reach in summer because so many scholars employed as reviewers depart the campus. If the normal length of review time indicated in the *Handbook* passes without response, the author is certainly within his or her rights to send a polite letter of inquiry to the editor. If done diplomatically, this should in no way affect the decision on the manuscript.

ACCEPTANCE AND REJECTION

Acceptance

Even after acceptance, important work remains to be done. Sometimes publication of an article is made contingent upon certain revisions. In such cases, complete the revisions as promptly as possible. If galley proofs are sent to the author, they should be read as carefully as possible and returned quickly. The author should always retain a full copy of the manuscript and all revisions to check against should the originals not be returned.

Rejection

Rejection is a considerably more common experience than acceptance, so it does not hurt to be prepared for it. Do not be discouraged. Rejection does not necessarily mean the manuscript is valueless. Sometimes editors or referees will criticize the manuscript and explain the decision to reject, but more often the author is left to discover and correct flaws and weaknesses on his or her own. Simply because one or two editors decided against publication of the manuscript does not mean it is unworthy of publication or in need of extensive revision. Opinions are only subjective and may not be shared by the editor or reviewers at another journal. Reconsider the article carefully and honestly and submit it again without revision if the research and writing still seem sound. Resubmit quickly; do not let discouragement stop the process. Even as the manuscript is initially sent off, the author should have a second journal in mind in case the article is rejected.

Revision

The most profitable way to make changes without undertaking full-scale revision is to rewrite the first paragaraph or two. The introduction can almost always be strengthened with further work; its importance cannot be stressed enough. Rejection means that a person or people with some expertise in the field detected apparent flaws in the work and it is possible that the article in its present form is not publishable. If that is indeed the case, major revision will be necessary. If the manuscript was returned with negative comments, the logical way to begin is to address those criticisms. Without benefit of the reviewers' comments, criticism should be sought from knowledgeable colleagues and friends. One major change that might prove beneficial is shortening the manuscript. Long articles, like long titles, may pose space problems for editors. Paring down the manuscript may improve it overall and make it more acceptable to an editor wrestling with a shortage of space.

Resubmission

As a general rule, resubmission to a journal which has already rejected the manuscript is unwise unless the editor has urged the author to do so. This is true even if the author has revised it extensively along the lines suggested by the journal's referees.

FOREIGN JOURNALS

The *Handbook* lists numerous political and social science journals published outside the United States and Canada. Since only journals publishing solely or primarily in English are listed, authors able to write in other languages have an even wider range of possible publishing opportunities. Dealing with journals in other countries can involve the expenditure of time and money which often varies in inverse proportion. Saving time costs money and saving money costs time. Surface mail is infamously slow; it would not be unusual for a query or manuscript to take three months just to travel from the United States to West Germany. Naturally, a reply would take just as long. Air mail is quicker, but the expense is much greater. International Reply Coupons are an absolute necessity for transacting business with an overseas journal. Before deciding to send a manuscript overseas, carefully weigh the importance of time and money spent in quest of publication.

FOR ADDITIONAL ADVICE

Barzun, Jacques, and Graff, Henry F. *The Modern Researcher*. Rev. ed. New York: Harcourt Brace Jovanovich, 1970.

Bernstein, Theodore M. *The Careful Writer: A Modern Guide to English Usage.* New York: Atheneum, 1965.

Cargill, Oscar, et al. *Publication of Academic Writing.* New York: Modern Language Association, 1966.

Cole, Richard L. *Introduction to Political Research.* New York: Macmillan, 1980.

Cortada, James W. "Publishing American Scholarship in Europe." *Scholarly Publishing,* vol. 5, no. 2 (January, 1974), 173–78.

Forscher, Bernard K. "The Role of the Referee." *Scholarly Publishing,* vol. 11, no. 2 (January, 1980), 165–69.

Harman, Eleanor. "On Seeking Permission." *Scholarly Publishing,* vol. 1, no. 2 (January, 1970), 188–92.

Kalvelage, Carl, and Segal, Morley. *Research Guide in Political Science.* 2d ed. Glenview, Ill: Scott, Foresman, 1976.

MacGregor, A.J. "Graphics Simplified: Choosing Illustrations." *Scholarly Publishing,* vol. 9, no. 3 (April, 1978), 270–79.

Mitchell, John H. *Writing for Professional and Technical Journals.* New York: John Wiley and Sons, 1968.

Modern Language Association of America. *MLA Handbook for Writers of Research Papers, Theses, and Dissertations.* New York: Modern Language Association, 1977.

_____*The MLA Style Sheet.* 2d ed. New York: Modern Language Association, 1970.

Mullins, Carolyn J. *A Guide to Writing and Publishing in the Social and Behavioral Sciences.* New York: John Wiley and Sons, 1977.

Rodman, Hyman "Some Practical Advice for Journal Contributors." *Scholarly Publishing,* vol. 9, no. 3 (April, 1978), 235–41.

_____and Mancini, Jay A. "Editors, Manuscripts, and Equal Treatment." *Research in Higher Education,* vol. 7 (1977), 369–74.

Shively, W. Phillips. *The Craft of Political Research.* 2d ed. Englewood Cliffs, N.J.: Prentice-Hall, 1980.

Skillin, Marjorie E., and Gay, Robert M., et al. *Words Into Type.* 3d ed. Engelwood Cliffs, N.J.: Prentice-Hall, 1974.

Strunk, William, Jr., and White, E.B. *The Elements of Style.* 3d ed. New York: Macmillan, 1979.

Turabian, Kate L. *A Manual for Writers of Term Papers, Theses, and Dissertations.* 4th ed. Chicago: University of Chicago Press, 1973.

United States Government Printing Office. *Style Manual.* Rev. ed. Washington, D.C.: United States Government Printing Office, 1973.

University of Chicago Press. *The Chicago Manual of Style.* 13th ed. Chicago: University of Chicago Press, 1982.

van Leunen, Mary-Claire. *A Handbook for Scholars.* New York: Alfred A. Knopf, 1978.

Westwood, John. *Typing for Print.* London: Pitman, 1976.

Authors and the Law

The rights and obligations of authors are set down in a bewildering array of statutes, cases, and court decisions. The Constitution simply empowered Congress to secure "for limited Times to Authors . . . the exclusive right to their respective Writings. . . ." (Article 1, Section 1, Clause 8). Since 1789 the legislation that amplifies that clause and defines the rights and liabilities accruing to literary property has become infinitely complex. The complexity is manageable when author and publisher agree to the terms of contract prior to publication—the author can always seek legal advice before selling, licensing, or transferring his or her rights and before assuming any risk or obligation. However, publication in "collective" works such as periodicals, journals, and magazines involves unwritten "trade customs" and terms of agreement that are implied, not specific. The laws that govern the public interest in the publishing process employ the following terms that are briefly defined here to emphasize a prospective author's "need to know." The references cited at the end of this section treat those terms in more definitive detail, but there is no substitute for legal counsel when more serious concerns arise.

Ad interim copyright   The Copyright Act of 1909 (amended in 1973) provided short-term protection of English-language materials published in collective works outside the United States. The Copyright Act of 1976 does not apply *ad interim* protection to such works published after June, 1977.

All Rights   Some journals require authors to transfer "all rights" (book rights, commercial rights, foreign rights, first serial rights, movie rights, translation rights, etc.) when an article is accepted for publication. Authors who plan to publish their material later, e.g., as part of a book, may want to avoid transfer of all rights.

All Rights Reserved   When this notice appears in a periodical it means that any use of the material published therein is prohibited without the consent of the copyright holder.

Author Warranties   By submitting an article for publication, an author implicitly guarantees that he or she is the author (owner) of the work submitted; that he or she has the right to license or copyright the work; that the work has not been licensed for publication elsewhere; that the work does not infringe another person's copyright (permission has been obtained to use, or quote, another copyrighted work); that the work does not libel, slander, defame, or invade the privacy of anyone; and that the author will indemnify, or hold harmless, the publisher, and bear the cost of any suit or litigation that ensues from the publication of the work. These guarantees appear to place an awesome legal burden on the author, but in reality the risks are minimal—providing the author prudently observes the provisions of the law. As a practical matter, the risks that accompany publication are ultimately shared by the publisher in most legal actions.

Collective Work   According to the Copyright Act of 1976, a collective work "is a work, such as a periodical issue, anthology, or encyclopedia, in which a number of contributions, constituting separate and independent works in themselves, are assembled into a collective whole." (Chapter 1, Section 101).

Copyright   The legal protection of literary property from unlicensed use; the owner is protected against any substantial copying of the work. (See also, Fair Use). Unpublished works are protected by common law, so authors are not required to secure copyright protection prior to submitting an article for publication (see *The Writer's Manual*, pp. 118–19 for a description of the "poor man's copyright"). Copyrightable material includes "original works of scholarship fixed in any tangible medium of expression. . . ." (Copyright Act of 1976, Chapter 1, Section 102). In general, the form of expression may be copyrightable, but ideas, concepts, discoveries, principles, historical facts, etc. are not. Copyright protection becomes statutory only after publication, with proper registration and appropriate notice (see the *Copyright Handbook*, Chapter 7). When an article is published in a periodical it is protected under the copyright held by the journal itself, and if an author later wants to sell the reprint or foreign rights, the copyright can be assigned to him or her. Authors may also retain the copyright in their own name by requiring the proper notice to be made on the first page of the article when it appears in print. There is no need for authors to become overly concerned with the need to ensure copyright protection. The editors of scholarly periodicals are generally knowledgeable concerning the authors' rights and obligations and only the most disreputable journals would deny them.

Copyright Clearance Center   The Copyright Clearance Center was established in 1977 to facilitate the growing need of users to photocopy printed information. The Center obtains permissions from the copyright holders and collects fees from users in response to a number of changes incorporated in the Copyright Act of 1976. The Center's users include academic libraries, colleges and universities, corporate libraries, government libraries, and other special library services.

Exclusive Rights   When a writer submits an article to a journal for publication it is customary to offer an "exclusive right" to publish the work. That offer entails the "first right of refusal" or, more simply, the "right to first publication" (in the United States and Canada). The editors of most scholarly periodicals deplore "simultaneous submissions," submitting an article to more than one editor at the same time. Except for certain periodicals that do not have overlapping circulations, the practice is considered unethical.

Fair Use   The Copyright Act of 1976 (Chapter 1, Section 107) specifically states that "the fair use of a copyrighted work for . . . scholarship, or research, is *not* an infringement of copyright." But, the law is moot with respect to the exact amount of material that can be copied without infringing the copyright holder's protection. Prior to quoting any published material, an author should read the law and, if there is any doubt, obtain permission before using copyrighted material. Fair use also includes an appropriate attribution, or credit, for the copyright holder.

First Serial Rights   This means the exclusive right to first-time North American publication. "Serial" refers to periodicals issued at regular intervals in numerical sequence.

Freedom of Information Act   Since 1967, citizens have had the right to obtain previously classified information from government agencies. Writers must send requests for disclosure of certain classes of information (classified national security matters, foreign affairs, and internal affairs of the agencies are excluded) to the cognizant agency and describe the records or information desired; the agency must decide within ten days whether to release the information requested.

Libel   Any false statement that tends to injure the reputation or damage the business or occupation of any person is libelous. Libel actions against an author must include evidence that the published material is defamatory (i.e., injures the reputation), that it applies to a person who can be identified, and that it must have been communicated to a third person (i.e., published). Authors have the right to make "fair comment" providing what they publish is factual (true), that the inferences drawn from those facts are reasonable and stated in good faith, and that the subject matter is of legitimate public interest (see *Writing and Selling Non-Fiction*, pp. 238–39).

Privacy   The individual's right to privacy (i.e., protection against public disclosure of private and embarrassing facts) frequently involves conflict with the publisher's traditional freedom of expression and First Amendment rights. Authors and publishers who "overstep . . . the obvious bounds and propriety" are liable to suit under the laws of tort (see *Law and the Writer*, Chapter 5, for a complete treatment).

Public Domain   Published works that have outlived their copyright life (the life of the author plus fifty years under the new law), and those published at public expense (by the Government Printing Office, for example) are in the public domain and not protected by copyright; they can be used or copied without permission. However, since authors are expected to warrant that they have not infringed copyright, it is their responsibility to ensure that quoted materials are actually in the public domain.

Second Serial Rights   These consist of the right to print an article after it has already been published in another periodical. Second serial rights also refer to the sale of part of a book to a journal after the book has been published regardless of whether the *first serial rights* were involved.

FOR ADDITIONAL ADVICE

Jacobs, Hayes B. *Writing and Selling Non-Fiction.* Cincinnati: Writer's Digest, 1967. See especially Chapter XVIII, "Boundaries of Freedom: The Writer and the Law," p. 237 ff.

Johnston, Donald F., ed. *Copyright Handbook.* 2d ed. New York: R.R. Bowker Company, 1982. This definitive work cites and indexes every facet of copyright law.

Polking, Kirk, ed. *Law and the Writer.* Cincinnati: Writer's Digest, 1978. This work is specifically intended to help writers "anticipate the most common legal mistakes . . . before you crank them out of your own typewriter." Chapters 15, 16, and 17 are of interest to professionals who desire to expense the cost of research and writing for state and federal income tax purposes and realize Social Security benefits.

Shulman, Joel J. *How to Get Published in Business and Professional Journals.* New York: AMACOM, 1980. Provides excellent guidelines concerning the preparation, marketing, and submission of articles to business and professional journals.

Wincor, Richard. *Literary Property.* New York: Clarkson N. Potter, Inc., 1967. One of several books by the same author that treat the rights, risks, warranties, payments, and protections of a writer, "a book for professionals."

The Writer's Manual. Palm Springs, Calif.: ETC Publications. The current edition of this *Manual* is an indispensable tool for anyone interested in writing for publication in any media.

Advice On Book Reviewing

WHY REVIEW?

Writing a book (or film or tape) review is a more readily accomplished alternative to authoring an article. Some review essays may attain the length of a full-size manuscript, but most book reviews run three pages or less. Obviously such a composition represents a considerable savings in time and effort over writing a full article. Also, research is limited to reading one or a few books rather than analyzing a variety of sources. The college instructor who is teaching classes, helping students outside of class, and working on committees often has little time to research and write books and articles, but can nonetheless demonstrate continuing intellectual activity by regularly writing reviews.

Reviewing books is also a means for expanding a personal library. Volumes sent to an individual for review usually become that person's property. Some reviewers see this activity as a means of imposing a degree of discipline upon their reading habits. Without the obligation to read and report upon books, they fear becoming too busy to remain well-read in their fields.

Book reviews also serve the interests of readers. Reviews assist readers in deciding whether or not to spend time or money on a book, and provide a means for keeping abreast of the flood of new literature in the field. Finally, a good review can be read and appreciated for its own sake by someone with no intention of ever picking up or reading the book in question. Such a review is, in its own way, as informative and valuable as a much lengthier article.

BECOMING A REVIEWER

Some journals only publish reviews written by a member of their in-house staff, but other journals maintain files of reviewers to whom they periodically assign books. Many journals are constantly seeking to expand their reviewer files. To become part of a file, simply consult the *Handbook* entry for a particular journal and see whether a special application form is required. If so, address a letter to the book review editor indicating interest in reviewing for the journal and requesting a form. In most cases, no such form is needed; a letter will suffice. The *Handbook* indicates the information each journal requires from prospective reviewers. Some journals may never reply, others may require a reviewer's services immediately and often. Be sensible and selective in applying to journals; special interest journals focus on specific subjects and only review books dealing with those subjects. A reviewer not interested or competent in Middle Eastern affairs should not apply to a journal which concentrates on that subject.

WRITING A REVIEW

A good book review must be interesting. A review is a creative composition and should not transcribe the book's table of contents or summarize its dustcover remarks. The conscientious reviewer seeks, in a few paragraphs, to bring a much longer work into focus through the application of his or her understanding of the subject of the book. The result is informative, whether the review itself is critical or laudatory. Informing readers is the principal purpose of a review, so bear in mind their interests and levels of expertise. They are more interested in a thoughtful evaluation of a book than in a display of the reviewer's cleverness, vitriol, or overstatement. A reviewer is as accountable as the author commented upon. All page numbers of passages quoted in the review should be clearly indicated.

POINTS TO COVER

Describe the author's purpose in writing the book, and his or her success in accomplishing that purpose. Assess the book's strengths and weaknesses and note whether one category overshadows the other. Placing a book in the context of other works on the same subject establishes its significance (or lack thereof). A few words about the author and his or her qualifications in the field may be in order. Has he or she written on the same subject before? How biased is the author in this work? How useful is the book for its readers? In reviewing a new edition of an old work, discuss the extent of revision from previous editions, and indicate whether the book continues to be of significance.

Spot-check the book for accuracy as to basic facts, quotations, and citations. Check the bibliography, index, and illustrations for quality and usefulness. Finally, check the book's overall physical appearance and the quality of the editing.

REVIEW FORM

Journals usually instruct their reviewers as to the form to be used for heading and signature. Those not given directions and authors of unsolicited reviews should check a copy of the journal in question for the desired form. An example of a standard heading is:

AUTHOR NAME (capitalized). <u>Title</u> (underlined to denote italic in print). Place of publication: publisher, <u>year</u>. Number of pages. Price.

Some journals require mention of any foreword, introduction, acknowledgements, notes, appendixes, bibliography, or indexes. The type and number of illustrations, and whether the book is available in cloth or paperback are also sometimes required. To know exactly what is required, look at reviews in the journal in question.

The reviewer's signature is more standardized:

<u>Institutional affiliation</u>   REVIEWER'S NAME
(underlined to denote italic in print)   (capitalized)

A FINAL NOTE

Conform to the length limitation imposed by the journal, and strictly observe the deadline for submitting the review. Usually only a few weeks are allowed between receipt of a book and return of its review. The timeliness of a book review often determines its value, so pay close attention to deadlines.

FOR ADDITIONAL ADVICE

Allen, Eliot D., and Colbrunn, Ethel B. *A Short Guide to Writing a Critical Review.* Rev. ed. Deland, Fla.: Everett-Edwards, 1975.

Drewry, John E. *Writing Book Reviews.* Westport, Conn.: Greenwood, 1974.

Gard, Wayne. *Book Reviewing.* Darby, Penn.: Folcroft, 1979.

Hoge, James O., and West, James L.W., III. "Academic Book Reviewing: Some Problems and Suggestions." *Scholarly Publishing,* vol. 11, no. 1 (October, 1979), 35-41.

Jones, Llewellyn. *How to Criticize Books.* New York: W.W. Norton and Co., 1928.

Kamerman, Sylvia E., ed. *Book Reviewing: A Guide to Writing Book Reviews for Newspapers, Magazines, Radio, and Television.* Boston: Writer, 1978.

Mullins, Carolyn J. *A Guide to Writing and Publishing in the Social and Behavioral Sciences.* New York: John Wiley and Sons, 1977, 231-37.

Wolper, R.S. " 'A Grass-Blade': On Academic Reviewing." *Scholarly Publishing,* vol. 10, no. 4 (July, 1979), 325-28.

Woodcock, George. "The Critic as Mediator." *Scholarly Publishing,* vol. 4, no. 3 (April, 1973), 201-9.

List of Abbreviations

Style Guides

AP — Associated Press, *AP Style Book*

APA — American Psychological Association, *Publication Manual of the American Psychological Association* (2d ed.)

EOS — Strunk, William, Jr., and E.B. White, *The Elements of Style* (3d ed.)

GPO — U.S. Government Printing Office, *Style Manual*

HLRA — Harvard Law Review Association, *A Uniform System of Citation: Forms of Citation and Abbreviation* (11th ed.)

MFW — Turabian, Kate L., *A Manual for Writers of Term Papers, Theses, and Dissertations* (4th ed.)

MLA — Modern Language Association, *MLA Style Sheet* (2d ed.)

MOS — University of Chicago Press, *The Chicago Manual of Style* (13th ed.)

NYT — *The New York Times Manual of Style and Usage: A Desk Book of Guidelines for Writers and Editors*

SAGE — Sage Publications, *Journal Editorial Style*

Abstracting and Indexing Services

ABC POL SCI — A Bibliography of Contents: Political Science and Government

Abstr Anthropol — Abstracts in Anthropology

Abstr Crim and Pen — Abstracts in Criminology and Penology

Abstr Mil Bibl — Abstracts of Military Bibliography

Abstr Pop Cult — Abstracts in Popular Culture

Abstr Soc Work — Abstracts for Social Workers

Acc Ind — Accountant's Index

Air Un Lib Ind — Air University Library Index to Military Periodicals

Alt Press Ind — Alternative Press Index

Amer Hist and Life — America: History and Life

Amer Hum Ind — American Humanities Index

Amer Stat Ind — American Statistics Index

Art Ind — Art Index

Aus PAIS — Australian Public Affairs Information Service

Bibl Ind — Bibliographic Index

Biol Abstr — Biological Abstracts

Bk Rev Ind — Book Review Index

BPI	Business Periodicals Index	Educ Admin Abstr	Educational Administration Abstracts
Br Hum Ind	British Humanities Index	Employ Rel Abstr	Employment Related Abstracts
Cal Per Ind	California Periodicals Index	Energy Abstr	Energy Abstracts
Can BIP	Canadian Business Periodicals Index	Environ Per Bibl	Environmental Periodicals Bibliography
Can Ind	Canadian Periodical Index	ERIC	Eric Clearinghouse
Cath Ind	Catholic Periodical and Literature Index	Eth Stud Bibl	Ethnic Studies Bibliography
Cath Ind Leg Per	Catholic Index of Legal Periodicals	Foreign Leg Per	Foreign Legal Periodicals
CCLP	Contents of Current Legal Periodicals	Geo Abstr	Geographical Abstracts
Child Devel Abstr	Child Development Abstracts	G Leg Per	Guide to Legal Periodicals
CIJE	Current Index to Journals in Education	Gov Ind	Government Index
		G Per Educ	Guide to Periodicals in Education
CIS Ind	Congressional Information Service Index	Hisp Amer Per Ind	Hispanic American Periodical Index
		Hist Abstr	Historical Abstracts
Comm Devel Abstr	Community Development Abstracts	Human Resour Abstr	Human Resources Abstracts
		Hum Ind	Humanities Index
Community Men Health Rev	Community Mental Health Review	IBR	Internationale Bibliographie der Rezensionen
Comput Rev	Computing Reviews		
CRIS	Combined Retrospective Index	IBZ	Internationale Bibliographie der Zeitschriftenliterature
Curr Cont	Current Contents		
Curr Cont Africa	Current Contents Africa	Ind Bk Rev Hum	Index to Book Reviews in the Humanities
Curr Ind J Educ	Current Index to Journals in Education	Ind Can Leg Per Lit	Index to Canadian Legal Periodical Literature
Curr Ind Leg Per	Current Index to Legal Periodicals	Ind Econ J	Index of Economic Journals
Curr Ind Stat	Current Index to Statistics	Ind Fed Tax Art	Index to Federal Tax Articles
Curr Law Ind	Current Law Index		
Curr Leg Per	Current Legal Periodicals	Ind For Leg Per	Index to Foreign Legal Periodicals
Curr Manage Lit	Current Management Literature	Ind Jew Per	Index to Jewish Periodicals
Econ Abstr	Economic Abstracts		

Soc Sci Ind	Social Sciences Index	Universal Ref Syst	Universal Reference System
Soc Work Res and Abstr	Social Work Research and Abstracts	Urb Aff Abstr	Urban Affairs Abstracts
SSCI	Social Science Citation Index	USPSD	United States Political Science Documents
Stand Per Dir	Standard Periodical Directory	Work Rel Abstr	Work Related Abstracts
Ulrich's Int Per Dir	Ulrich's International Periodicals Directory	Wom Stud Abstr	Women's Studies Abstracts

Directory of Journals

ACADEMY OF MANAGEMENT JOURNAL

Focus: all fields of management and administration
Institutional affiliation: Academy of Management
Editor: Thomas A. Mahoney
Editorial address:
School of Management
University of Minnesota
271 19th Avenue South
Minneapolis, MN 55455
Frequency: 4/year
Circulation: 7,500
Subscription rate(s): $24
Pages/issue: 230
Readership: academics, management professionals
Indexed/abstracted in: BPI, Psychol Abstr, SSCI, Work Rel Abstr

Manuscripts
Query: no
Abstract: yes, 50 words
Style guide: available on request
Preferred length: 10–15 pages
Number of copies: 3
Notes: end of manuscript
Blind referee: yes
Time to consider manuscript: 2 months
Proportion of manuscripts accepted: not given
Illustrations accepted: tables, graphs, charts
Foreign languages: no

Reviews
not applicable

Additional notes
Simultaneous submission is not permitted. Articles are published 1 year after acceptance. For brevity, tables should be combined or presented within the text whenever possible.

ADMINISTRATION AND SOCIETY

Focus: theoretical and empirical articles on administrative strategies, programs, and processes, within public organizations; as well as studies of intergroup, interorganizational, and organizational-environmental relationships and policy processes
Editor: John A. Rohr
Editorial address:
Center for Public Administration and Policy
Virginia Polytechnic Institute
Blacksburg, VA 24061
Frequency: 4/year
Circulation: not given
Subscription rate(s): domestic $20, foreign $24, institutional $42
Pages/issue: 125
Readership: scholars, business people, public administrators
Indexed/abstracted in: not given

Manuscripts
Query: no
Abstract: yes
Style guide: SAGE
Preferred length: 40 pages maximum
Number of copies: 4, double-spaced
Notes: end of manuscript
Blind referee: yes
Time to consider manuscript: 3–4 months
Proportion of manuscripts accepted: 5 percent
Illustrations accepted: tables, graphs, charts, drawings
Foreign languages: no

Reviews
Seeking reviewers: no
Unsolicited reviews accepted: no

Additional notes

Simultaneous submission is not permitted. Most articles appear 6–9 months after acceptance.

ADMINISTRATIVE SCIENCE QUARTERLY

Focus: organizational behavior and theory
Institutional affiliation: Cornell University, Graduate School of Business and Public Administration
Editors: Linda J. Pike, Karl E. Weick
Editorial address:
Malott Hall
Cornell University
Ithaca, NY 14853
Frequency: 4/year
Circulation: 5,300
Subscription rate(s): student $18.50, individual $20, institutional $40
Pages/issue: 180
Readership: academics, corporate executives and managers, government personnel
Indexed/abstracted in: BPI, PAIS, Psychol Abstr, SSCI, Sociol Abstr, Econ Abstr, Educ Admin Abstr, Int Polit Sci Abstr, Pers. Manage Abstr

Manuscripts

Query: no, but advisable
Abstract: yes, under 100 words
Style guide: available on request
Preferred length: 25–35 pages
Number of copies: 4
Notes: end of manuscript
Blind referee: yes
Time to consider manuscript: 3 months
Proportion of manuscripts accepted: 10 percent
Illustrations accepted: tables, graphs, charts
Foreign languages: no

Reviews

Book review editor: Samuel B. Bacharach
Address:
same as above

Seeking reviewers:
no
Unsolicited reviews accepted:
occasionally
Materials reviewed:
books
Length of review:
2–5 pages

Additional Notes

Simultaneous submission allowed only in special cases. Most articles published 3–4 months after acceptance.

AFRICA

Focus: Africa from a social sciences and humanities perspective
Institutional affiliation: International African Institute
Editor: submit to the Editor
Editorial address:
38 King Street
London WC2E 8JR
ENGLAND
Frequency: 4/year
Circulation: 2,000
Subscription rate(s): $45
Pages/issue: 120
Readership: academics
Indexed/abstracted in: ABC POL SCI, Hist Abstr

Manuscripts

Query: no
Abstract: yes, 250–400 words
Style guide: available on request
Preferred length: 6,500 words maximum
Number of copies: 2
Notes: end of manuscript
Blind referee: no
Time to consider manuscript: 4 months
Proportion of manuscripts accepted: not given
Illustrations accepted: tables, charts, drawings, camera-ready figures, maps
Foreign languages: French

Reviews
Book review editor: submit to the Review Editor
Address: same as above
Materials reviewed: books
Length of review: 1–3 pages

Additional Notes
Submit a brief biography with the manuscript. Simultaneous submission is not allowed. Articles are published 1 year after acceptance.

AFRICAN REVIEW: A JOURNAL OF AFRICAN POLITICS, DEVELOPMENT AND INTERNATIONAL AFFAIRS

Focus: current political, economic, and development issues in Africa
Institutional affiliation: Political Science Department, University of Dar es Salaam
Editor: submit to the Editors
Editorial address:
P.O. Box 35042
Dar es Salaam
TANZANIA
Frequency: 4/year
Circulation: 7,000
Subscription rate(s): individual $30, institutional $35
Pages/issue: 120
Readership: academics
Indexed/abstracted in: ABC POL SCI, Hist Abstr

Manuscripts
Query: no
Abstract: no
Style guide: see current issue or write for guidelines
Preferred length: 4,000–8,000 words
Number of copies: 2, double-spaced
Notes: end of manuscript
Blind referee: no
Time to consider manuscript: 2 months
Proportion of manuscripts accepted: not given

Illustrations accepted: not given
Foreign languages: no

Reviews
Book review editor: submit to the Editors
Address: same as above
Materials reviewed: books
Length of review: 10–20 pages for review articles

Additional notes
Include a brief biography with the manuscript. Simultaneous submission is not permitted. Articles are published 6 months after acceptance.

AFRICAN STUDIES

Focus: African government, society, and culture
Institutional affiliation: African Studies Institute
Editor: N. H. Wilson
Editorial address:
Witwatersrand University Press
1 Jan Smuts Avenue
2001 Johannesburg
South Africa
Frequency: 2/year
Circulation: 800
Subscription rate(s): individual 10 South African rands, institutional 20 South African rands
Pages/issue: 80
Readership: academics
Indexed/abstracted in: ABC POL SCI, Abstr Anthropol, SSCI, Soc Sci Ind

Manuscripts
Query: no
Abstract: no
Style guide: Oxford University Press Style Guide
Preferred length: 10–15 pages
Number of copies: 1, double-spaced
Notes: end of manuscript
Blind referee: no
Time to consider manuscript: 2 months
Proportion of manuscripts accepted: not given

Illustrations accepted: tables, charts, photos, drawings, maps
Foreign languages: Afrikaans, French, Portuguese

Reviews
Book review editor: N. H. Wilson
Address: same as above
Materials reviewed: books
Length of review: 1–2 pages

Additional notes
Simultaneous submission is permitted if editors are notified of such at the time of submission.

AFRICAN STUDIES REVIEW

Focus: interdisciplinary approach to African Studies
Institutional affiliation: African Studies Association, University of California, Los Angeles
Editor: R. Hunt Davis, Jr.
Editorial address:
Center for African Studies
470 GRI
University of Florida
Gainesville, FL 32611
Frequency: 4/year
Circulation: 3,500
Subscription rate(s): not given
Pages/issue: 150
Readership: academics (multidisciplinary)
Indexed/abstracted in: not given

Manuscripts
Query: no
Abstract: not required, but helpful
Style guide: MOS
Preferred length: 30–40 pages
Number of copies: 2, double-spaced
Notes: end of manuscript
Blind referee: yes
Time to consider manuscript: 1–2 months
Proportion of manuscripts accepted: not given
Illustrations accepted: tables, graphs, charts, photos, drawings
Foreign languages: no

Reviews
Book review editor: Mel Page
Address:
Department of History
Murray State University
Murray, KY 42071
Seeking reviewers: yes
Unsolicited reviews accepted: yes
How to apply: letter of inquiry
Include in application: professional degrees, institutional affiliation, areas of expertise, published works, foreign languages, current research
Materials reviewed: books, films, tapes
Length of review: 2–3 pages

Additional notes
Simultaneous submission is not permitted. Articles appear 1 year after acceptance.

AFRICAN URBAN STUDIES

Focus: urbanization in Africa
Institutional affiliation: African Studies Center, Michigan State University
Editor: Ruth Sims Hamilton
Editorial address:
African Studies Center
Michigan State University
East Lansing, MI 48824
Frequency: 3/year
Circulation: 600
Subscription rate(s): individual $8, institutional $12
Pages/issue: 80–100
Readership: academics, African specialists
Indexed/abstracted in: not given

Manuscripts
Query: no
Abstract: no
Style guide: MOS
Preferred length: 30 pages maximum
Number of copies: 2
Notes: end of manuscript
Blind referee: no
Time to consider manuscript: 2 months

Proportion of manuscripts
accepted: 60 percent
Illustrations accepted: tables,
graphs, charts, line illustrations
Foreign languages: French
(occasionally)

Reviews
Book review editor: Ruth Sims
Hamilton
Address: same as above
Seeking reviewers: no
Unsolicited reviews accepted: yes
How to apply: letter of inquiry
Include in application: professional
degrees, institutional affiliation, areas
of expertise, published works
Materials reviewed: books, films
Length of review: 5 pages maximum

AFRICA QUARTERLY

Focus: the politics, economics, and
history of Africa; Indo-African
relations
Institutional affiliation: Indian Council
for Cultural Relations
Editor: A. R. Basu
Editorial address:
Indian Council for Cultural Relations
Azad Bhavon
Indra prastha Estate
New Dehli–110002
INDIA
Frequency: 4/year
Circulation: 1,000
Subscription rate(s): $14.50
Pages/issue: 125
Readership: African specialists,
academics
Indexed/abstracted in: ABC POL
SCI, PAIS

Manuscripts
Query: no
Abstract: no
Style guide: none required
Preferred length: 10,000–12,000
words
Number of copies: 2, double-spaced
Notes: end of manuscript
Blind referee: no

Time to consider manuscript: 3
months
**Proportion of manuscripts
accepted:** not given
Illustrations accepted: tables,
graphs, charts
Foreign languages: no

Reviews
Book review editor: A. R. Basu
Address: same as above
Unsolicited reviews accepted: yes
Materials reviewed: books
Length of review: 2–6 pages

Additional notes
Simultaneous submission is not allowed.
Articles appear in 6 months.

AFRICA REPORT

Focus: African political, economic, and
cultural developments, especially in
relation to the U.S.
Institutional affiliation: The African
American Institute
Editor: Anthony J. Hughes
Editorial address:
833 United Nations Plaza
New York, NY 10017
Frequency: 6/year
Circulation: 10,000
Subscription rate(s): individual $15,
institutional $18
Pages/issue: 60
Readership: Americans with a
personal and/or professional interest
in African affairs
Indexed/abstracted in: January issue
of following year

Manuscripts
Query: yes
Abstract: no
Style guide: available on request
Preferred length: 2,500 words
Number of copies: 1, double-spaced
Notes: no notes
Blind referee: no
Time to consider manuscript: 1
month

Proportion of manuscripts
accepted: 20 percent
Illustrations accepted: tables,
graphs, charts, photos
Foreign languages: no

Reviews

Book review editor: Margaret C.
Novicki
Address:
same as above
Seeking reviewers: yes
Unsolicited reviews accepted: rarely
How to apply: letter of inquiry
Include in application: professional
degrees, institutional affiliation, areas
of expertise, published works,
current research, experience in and
of Africa
Materials reviewed: books
Length of review: negotiable

Additional notes

Articles should be written in a serious
but nonacademic style, and should
appeal to a reader with a general interest
in African affairs, and not necessarily
only to an interest in the field or region
under consideration. Before submitting
an article, send a letter of 200–400
words outlining the scope of the
proposed article and the author's
qualifications for writing it. Simultaneous
submission is not allowed. Most articles
appear 1 month after acceptance.
Royalties are negotiable, but usually are
$150 per article.

AFRICA TODAY

Focus: contemporary Africa
Institutional affiliation: University of
Denver
Editor: Edward A. Hawley
Editorial Address:
Graduate School of International
Studies
University of Denver
Denver, CO 80208
Frequency: 4/year
Circulation: not given

Subscription rate(s): student $9,
individual $12, institutional $18
Pages/issue: 80–110
Readership: academics, students,
others interested in Africa
Indexed/abstracted in: ABC POL
SCI, Amer Hist and Life, Hist Abstr,
Int African Bibl, PAIS, SSCI, Soc Sci
Ind

Manuscripts

Query: no
Abstract: no
Style guide: MOS
Preferred length: 2,000–6,000 words
Number of copies: 2
Notes: end of manuscript
Blind referee: yes
Time to consider manuscript: 3–9
months
Proportion of manuscripts
accepted: 20–25 percent
Illustrations accepted: tables,
graphs, charts, photos, drawings
Foreign languages: no

Reviews

Book review editor: George W. R.
Kalule
Address: same as above
Seeking reviewers: yes
Unsolicited reviews accepted: yes
How to apply: letter of inquiry
Include in application: profressional
degrees, institutional affiliation, areas
of expertise, published works
Materials reviewed: books, films
Length of review: 850 words

Additional notes

Simultaneous submission is not
permitted. Articles are published 3–12
months after acceptance.

ALTERNATIVES: A JOURNAL OF WORLD POLICY

Focus: global issues and problems
and the development of world
policies for solving those problems
Institutional affiliation: Center for the
Study of Developing Societies and
Institute for World Order

Editor: Saul H. Mendlovitz
Editorial address:
777 United Nations Plaza
New York, NY 10017
Frequency: 4/year
Circulation: not given
Subscription rate(s): individual $15,
institutional $30
Pages/issue: 125–150
Readership: academics
Indexed/abstracted in: ABC POL
SCI, Amer Hist and Life, Curr Cont,
Hist Abstr

Manuscripts
Query: no
Abstract: yes, 200 words maximum
Style guide: available on request
Preferred length: no preference
Number of copies: 3
Notes: end of manuscript
Blind referee: no
Time to consider manuscript: not
given
**Proportion of manuscripts
accepted:** not given
Illustrations accepted: tables,
graphs, charts, photos, drawings
Foreign languages: no

Reviews
not applicable

ALTERNATIVES: JOURNAL OF FRIENDS OF THE EARTH

Focus: socio-political aspects of
environmental issues
Institutional affiliation: Trent
University
Editor: Deborah J. Clarke
Editorial address:
Trent University
Peterborough, Ontario K9J 7B8
CANADA
Frequency: 4/year
Circulation: 3,000
Subscription rate(s): individual $10,
institutional $15
Pages/issue: 64–72

Readership: institutions (libraries,
government agencies, schools),
academics, general public
Indexed/abstracted in: Alt Press Ind,
Environ Per Bibl

Manuscripts
Query: no, but preferable
Abstract: no
Style guide: see latest issue for style
requirements
Preferred length: 3,000–6,000 words
Number of copies: 2 or 3
Notes: end of manuscript
Blind referee: no
Time to consider manuscript: 2
months
**Proportion of manuscripts
accepted:** varies
Illustrations accepted: tables,
graphs, charts, photos, drawings
Foreign languages: no

Reviews
Book review editor: Bill Ramp
Address:
same as above
Unsolicited reviews accepted: yes
How to apply: send review
Include in application: relevant and
well-written reviews published
regardless of author's previous
experience
Materials reviewed: books, films
Length of review: 350–700 words

Additional notes
In its Conserver Society Notes section,
Alternatives publishes short news items
of 200–300 words. Author may receive
20 reprints free. Simultaneous
submission is allowed if editors are
notified of such at the time of
submission. All articles appear within a
year of acceptance.

AMERICAN CITY AND COUNTY MAGAZINE

Focus: urban problems and issues and
possible solutions
Editor: W. L. Forestell

Editorial address:
Berkshire Common
Pittsfield, MA 01201
Frequency: 12/year
Circulation: 45,000
Subscription rate(s): $30
Pages/issue: 80–100
Readership: city administrators, planners, and other officials; academics
Indexed/abstracted in: RG, Ocean Abstr, Pollut Abstr

Manuscripts
Query: no
Abstract: no
Style guide: available on request
Preferred length: 500–1,000 words
Number of copies: 2
Notes: not given
Blind referee: no
Time to consider manuscript: 2–3 weeks
Proportion of manuscripts accepted: not given
Illustrations accepted: tables, graphs, charts, photos
Foreign languages: no

Reviews
not applicable

Additional notes
Simultaneous submission is not allowed. Articles are published within 6 months of acceptance.

THE AMERICAN ECONOMIC REVIEW

Focus: economic research, policy, analysis, and measurement
Institutional affiliation: American Economic Association
Editor: Robert W. Clower
Editorial address:
AER Editorial Office
University of California
Los Angeles, CA 90024
Frequency: 4/year
Circulation: 26,000

Subscription rate(s): student $15.50, nonstudent members $31–$43.40 depending on professional rank and income, institutional $100
Pages/issue: 160–180
Readership: economists, scholars in related disciplines
Indexed/abstracted in: BPI, PAIS, SSCI, Soc Sci Ind, Work Rel Abstr

Manuscripts
Query: no
Abstract: no
Style guide: available on request
Preferred length: 50 pages maximum
Number of copies: 3, double-spaced
Notes: end of manuscript
Blind referee: yes
Time to consider manuscript: 3–7 months
Proportion of manuscripts accepted: 15 percent
Illustrations accepted: tables, graphs, diagrams, charts, drawings
Foreign languages: no

Reviews
not applicable

Additional notes
Simultaneous submission is not permitted. Articles are published 1 year after acceptance. Each manuscript must be accompanied by a submission fee of $25 for AEA members and $50 for nonmembers.

AMERICAN HISTORICAL REVIEW

Focus: all fields of history
Institutional affiliation: American Historical Association
Editor: Otto Pflanze
Editorial address:
Ballantine Hall 721
Indiana University
Bloomington, IN 47405
Frequency: 5/year
Circulation: 23,000
Subscription rate(s): $35
Pages/issue: 360

Readership: academics, general public
Indexed/abstracted in: Hist Abstr, Amer Hist and Life, Hum Ind, RG, SSCI

Manuscripts
Query: no
Abstract: no
Style guide: MOS
Preferred length: 25–35 pages
Number of copies: 2
Notes: end of manuscript
Blind referee: yes
Time to consider manuscript: 1–3 months
Proportion of manuscripts accepted: 10 percent
Illustrations accepted: tables, graphs, charts, photos
Foreign languages: no

Reviews
Book review editor: Otto Pflanze
Address: same as above
Seeking reviewers: yes
Unsolicited reviews accepted: no
How to apply: write for special form
Include in application: professional degrees, institutional affiliation, areas of expertise, published works, foreign languages, current research
Materials reviewed: books
Length of review: 500–600 words

Additional notes
Simultaneous submission is not permitted. Articles appear 6–18 months after acceptance.

AMERICAN JOURNAL OF COMPARATIVE LAW

Focus: international comparative law
Institutional affiliation: American Association for the Comparative Study of Law
Editor: John G. Fleming
Editorial address:
Boalt Hall,
School of Law
University of California
Berkeley, CA 94720

Frequency: 4/year
Circulation: 2,000
Subscription rate(s): domestic $15, foreign $16.50
Pages/issue: 200
Readership: academics
Indexed/abstracted in: not given

Manuscripts
Query: no
Abstract: no
Style guide: see latest issue for style requirements
Preferred length: 30 pages maximum
Number of copies: 1
Notes: not given
Blind referee: not given
Time to consider manuscript: 1 month
Proportion of manuscripts accepted: not given
Illustrations accepted: tables, graphs, charts
Foreign languages: no

Reviews
Seeking reviewers: no
Unsolicited reviews accepted: no

Additional notes
Simultaneous submission is acceptable. The first 50 reprints are free. Articles published within 6 months of acceptance.

AMERICAN JOURNAL OF ECONOMICS AND SOCIOLOGY

Focus: seeks to promote a constructive synthesis in the social sciences and achieve solutions to the problems of American capitalism and democracy
Institutional affiliation: Francis Neilson Fund, Robert Schalkenbach Foundation
Editor: Will Lissner
Editorial address:
5 East 44th Street
New York, NY 10017
Frequency: 4/year

Circulation: 10,000.
Subscription rate(s): $10
Pages/issue: 112
Readership: academics, researchers in the social sciences
Indexed/abstracted in: all the leading American abstracting and indexing journals and agencies in the social sciences; major abstracting journals of the Soviet Union, France, and China

Manuscripts
Query: no
Abstract: yes, 150–200 words
Style guide: MLA
Preferred length: 5,000 words maximum
Number of copies: 2–4
Notes: end of manuscript
Blind referee: no
Time to consider manuscript: 1–3 months
Proportion of manuscripts accepted: 20 percent
Illustrations accepted: tables, graphs, charts, drawings
Foreign languages: no

Reviews
Book review editor: Will Lissner
Address: same as above
Seeking reviewers: no
Unsolicited reviews accepted: no
Materials reviewed: books, papers making an unusual contribution to the field are occasionally the subject of articles

Additional notes
Disciplinary studies are rarely published. The *Journal* emphasizes interdisciplinary research in the interest of realism, and does not duplicate the work of other publications. There is no requirement beyond total commitment to scientific method. The *Journal* is problem-oriented and stresses empirical verification. Theoretical articles are not published. Thorough documentation is required to facilitate the work of succeeding researchers. Reprints are available.

Simultaneous submission is not allowed. Accepted articles are published within 1 year.

AMERICAN JOURNAL OF INTERNATIONAL LAW

Focus: scholarly discussions, current developments, and judicial decisions concerning international law and economics
Institutional affiliation: The American Society of International Law
Editors: Oscar Schachter, Louis Henkin
Editorial address:
Columbia University
School of Law
Box 44
New York, NY 10027
Frequency: 4/year
Circulation: 8,500
Subscription rate(s): domestic $52, foreign $54.50
Pages/issue: 200
Readership: academics, diplomats, international law students, legal scholars
Indexed/abstracted in: not given

Manuscripts
Query: no
Abstract: no
Style Guide: HLRA
Preferred length: 10,000 words
Number of copies: 3
Notes: bottom of page
Blind referee: no
Time to consider manuscript: 4 months
Proportion of manuscripts accepted: not given
Illustrations accepted: tables, graphs, charts
Foreign languages: no

Reviews
Book review editor: Leo Gross
Address:
The Fletcher School of Law and Diplomacy
Tufts University
Medford, MA 02155

Seeking reviewers: no
Unsolicited reviews accepted: no
How to apply: letter of inquiry
Include in application: professional degrees, institutional affiliation, areas of expertise, foreign languages
Materials reviewed: books
Length of review: 400–600 words

Additional notes

Reprints are available. Simultaneous submission is not permitted. Articles appear within 4–6 months of acceptance.

AMERICAN JOURNAL OF JURISPRUDENCE

Focus: natural law and legal philosophy
Institutional affiliation: Notre Dame Law School
Editor: Aniela K. Murphy
Editorial address:
Notre Dame Law School
Notre Dame, IN 46556
Frequency: 1/year
Circulation: 1,000
Subscription rate(s): $9.50
Pages/issue: 225
Readership: academics, university libraries
Indexed/abstracted in: Twenty Year Index(1956–76)

Manuscripts

Query: no
Abstract: yes, 1 paragraph
Style guide: MLA
Preferred length: 40–50 pages
Number of copies: 3, double-spaced
Notes: end of manuscript
Blind referee: no
Time to consider manuscript: 2 months
Proportion of manuscripts accepted: 10 percent
Illustrations accepted: tables, graphs, charts
Foreign languages: no

Reviews

Book review editor Aniela K. Murphy
Address: same as above
Seeking reviewers: yes
Unsolicited reviews accepted: yes
How to apply: letter of inquiry
Include in application: professional degrees, institutional affiliation, areas of expertise, published works
Materials reviewed: books
Length of review: 10 pages

Additional notes

Simultaneous submission is not allowed.

THE AMERICAN JOURNAL OF LEGAL HISTORY

Focus: the history of American law and legal institutions; the development of legal doctrine
Institutional affiliation: Temple University
Editor: Diane C. Maleson
Editorial address:
Temple University School of Law
1719 North Broad Street
Philadelphia, PA 19122
Frequency: 4/year
Circulation: 1,650
Subscription rate(s): $12
Pages/issue: 100
Readership: academics, legal scholars and students, judges
Indexed/abstracted in: ABC POL SCI, Amer Hist and Life, Hist Abstr

Manuscripts

Query: no
Abstract: no
Style guide: none required
Preferred length: 20–25 pages
Number of copies: 1
Notes: end of manuscript
Blind referee: no
Time to consider manuscript: 3–5 months
Proportion of manuscripts accepted: not given
Illustrations accepted: use of illustrations very limited
Foreign languages: no

Reviews

Book review editor: Janet S. Loengard
Address: same as above
Seeking reviewers: yes
Unsolicited reviews accepted: no
How to apply: letter of inquiry
Include in application: professional degrees, institutional affiliation, areas of expertise, published works
Materials reviewed: books
Length of review: 1–2 pages

Additional notes

Simultaneous submission is not allowed. Articles appear 6 months after acceptance.

AMERICAN JOURNAL OF POLITICAL SCIENCE

Focus: political science, all subfields
Institutional affiliation: Midwest Political Science Association
Editor: Robert S. Erikson
Editorial address:
Department of Political Science
University of Houston
4800 Calhoun
Houston, TX 77004
Frequency: 4/year
Circulation: 3,000
Subscription rate(s): student and retired $8, professional $15, family $20, foreign add $2
Pages/issue: 200
Readership: academics
Indexed/abstracted in: not given

Manuscripts

Query: no
Abstract: yes
Style guide: MOS
Preferred length: 25 pages
Number of copies: 4
Notes: end of manuscript
Blind referee: yes
Time to consider manuscript: 2 months
Proportion of manuscripts accepted: 10 percent

Illustrations accepted: tables, graphs, charts
Foreign Languages: no

Reviews

Book review editor: Robert S. Erikson
Address: same as above
Materials reviewed: books

Additional notes

Simultaneous submission is not permitted. Articles are published 12–15 months after acceptance.

AMERICAN JOURNAL OF SOCIOLOGY

Focus: all areas of sociology, including perspectives from psychology, economics, statistics, anthropology, history, political science, and education
Institutional affiliation: University of Chicago
Editor: Edward O. Laumann
Editorial address:
1130 East 59th Street
Chicago, IL 60637
Frequency: 6/year
Circulation: 9,000
Subscription rate(s): student and ASA member $20, individual $25, institutional $40
Pages/issue: 250
Readership: academics
Indexed/abstracted in: ERIC

Manuscripts

Query: no
Abstract: yes
Style guide: MOS
Preferred length: 30–40 pages; comments, 1,500 words; research notes, 20 pages
Number of copies: 4
Notes: end of manuscript
Blind referee: yes
Time to consider manuscript: 3 months
Proportion of manuscripts accepted: 13–14 percent

Illustrations accepted: tables, graphs, charts, photos, drawings
Foreign languages: yes, translated at author's expense

Reviews
Book review editor: Paul M. Hirsch
Address:
   same as above
Seeking reviewers: yes
Unsolicited reviews accepted: yes
How to apply: letter of inquiry
Materials reviewed: books
Length of review: 800 words

Additional notes
A $10 submission fee is required. Simultaneous submission is not permitted. Articles appear 10 months after acceptance.

AMERICAN OPINION

Focus: political affairs
Editor: Scott Stanley, Jr.
Editorial address:
   395 Concord Avenue
   Belmont, MA 02178
Frequency: 11/year
Circulation: 35,000
Subscription rate(s): $18
Pages/issue: 112
Readership: general public
Indexed/abstracted in: Soc Sci Ind

Manuscripts
Query: yes
Abstract: no
Style guide: MOS
Preferred length: 2,000–3,000 words
Number of copies: 1
Notes: bottom of page
Blind referee: no
Time to consider manuscript: 2–3 months
Proportion of manuscripts accepted: 1 percent
Illustrations accepted: graphs, charts, photos
Foreign languages: no

Reviews
Book review editor: Medford Evans
Address:
   same as above
Seeking reviewers: no
Unsolicited reviews accepted: yes
How to apply: letter of inquiry
Include in application: professional degrees, institutional affiliation, areas of expertise, published works, current research
Materials reviewed: books
Length of review: 1,500 words

Additional notes
American Opinion seeks well researched, definitive studies of social, economic, political, and international problems written with verve and originality of style. Royalties paid at the rate of $25 per published page. Simultaneous submission is not permitted. Articles are published 2–3 months after acceptance.

THE AMERICAN POLITICAL SCIENCE REVIEW

Focus: political science and its major subfields
Institutional affiliation: University of Illinois
Editor: Dina A. Zinnes
Editorial address:
   University of Illinois
   50C Lincoln Hall
   702 S. Wright St
   Urbana, IL 61801
Frequency: 4/year
Circulation: 14,000
Subscription rate(s): single copy $5, subscription included in APSA membership dues
Pages/issue: 250–300
Readership: academics, practicing political scientists
Indexed/abstracted in: RG (before June 1953), Int Polit Sci Abstr, USPSD, Hum Ind, Soc Sci Ind

Manuscripts
Query: no
Abstract: yes

Style guide: MOS
Preferred length: 30 pages
Number of copies: 4
Notes: end of manuscript
Blind referee: yes
Time to consider manuscript: 4 months
Proportion of manuscripts accepted: ¼ percent
Illustrations accepted: tables, graphs, charts
Foreign languages: no

Reviews
Book review editor: Steven T. Seitz
Address: same as above
Seeking reviewers: yes
Unsolicited reviews accepted: no
How to apply: letter of inquiry
Include in application: professional degrees, institutional affiliation, areas of expertise, published works, current research
Materials reviewed: books
Length of review: 600 words

Additional notes
Simultaneous submission allowed if editors are informed at the time of submission. Accepted articles appear in 1 year.

AMERICAN POLITICS QUARTERLY

Focus: all fields of American politics (urban, state, and national)
Editor: Lee Sigelman
Editorial address:
Department of Political Science
University of Kentucky
Lexington, KY 40506
Frequency: 4/year
Circulation: 1,200
Subscription rate(s): individual $22, institutional $46
Pages/issue: 128
Readership: academics
Indexed/abstracted in: ABC POL SCI, Sage Urb Stud Abstr, Int Polit Sci Abstr, Sage Pub Admin Abstr, Human Resour Abstr, Eth Stud Bibl, PAIS, Curr Cont, SSCI, USPSD

Manuscripts
Query: no
Abstract: yes
Style guide: SAGE
Preferred length: 25–45 pages
Number of copies: 4, double-spaced
Notes: end of manuscript
Blind referee: yes
Time to consider manuscript: 4–5 weeks
Proportion of manuscripts accepted: 15 percent
Illustrations accepted: tables, graphs, charts
Foreign languages: no

Reviews
Book review editor: Lee Sigelman
Address: same as above
Materials reviewed: books

Additional notes
Simultaneous submission is not allowed. Reprints are available. Articles are published 6–9 months after acceptance.

AMERICAN QUARTERLY

Focus: American history and culture
Institutional affiliation: University of Pennsylvania, American Studies Association
Editor: Leila Zenderland
Editorial address:
Van Pelt Library CH
3420 Walnut Street
University of Pennsylvania
Philadelphia, PA 19104
Frequency: 5/year
Circulation: 5,500
Subscription rate(s): student $7.50, institutional $20
Pages/issue: 128
Readership: academics, academic libraries, general public
Indexed/abstracted in: not given

Manuscripts
Query: no
Abstract: no
Style guide: MLA
Preferred length: 30–35 pages

Number of copies: 2
Notes: no preference
Blind referee: yes
Time to consider manuscript: 3 months
Proportion of manuscripts accepted: 4 percent
Illustrations accepted: tables, graphs, charts, photos (no color)
Foreign languages: no

Reviews
Book review editor: Leo Ribuffo
Address:
George Washington University
Washington, DC 20006
Seeking reviewers: no
Unsolicited reviews accepted: occasionally
How to apply: letter of inquiry
Include in application: professional degrees, institutional affiliation, areas of expertise, published works, current research
Materials reviewed: not given
Length of review: 10–15 pages

Additional notes
Simultaneous submission is not permitted. Articles are published within 1 year of acceptance.

AMERICAN REVIEW OF CANADIAN STUDIES

Focus: interdisciplinary research on Canada and Canada–U.S. topics
Institutional affiliation: Association for Canadian Studies in the U.S.
Editor: William Metcalfe
Editorial address:
Department of History
Wheeler House
University of Vermont
Burlington, VT 05405
Frequency: 2–3/year
Circulation: 800
Subscription rate(s): individual $15, institutional $25
Pages/issue: 150
Readership: academics
Indexed/abstracted in: not given

Manuscripts
Query: no
Abstract: yes, 1 page
Style guide: MLA
Preferred length: 25 pages maximum
Number of copies: 2
Notes: end of manuscript
Blind referee: no
Time to consider manuscript: 2–3 months
Proportion of manuscripts accepted: not given
Illustrations accepted: tables, graphs, charts, photos, drawings
Foreign languages: French

Reviews
Book review editor: Victor Konrad
Address:
Canadian-American Center
Canada House
University of Maine
Orono, ME 04473
Seeking reviewers: yes
Unsolicited reviews accepted: no
How to apply: letter of inquiry
Materials reviewed: books
Length of review: negotiable

Additional notes
Avoid excessive length. English is preferred over jargon; remember the audience is interdisciplinary. Simultaneous submission is not permitted. Articles are published 3 months after acceptance.

AMERICAN REVIEW OF PUBLIC ADMINISTRATION

Focus: topics in public administration
Institutional affiliation: Park College
Editor: Jerzy Hauptmann
Editorial address:
Park College
Kansas City, MO 64152
Frequency: 4/year
Circulation: 750
Subscription rate(s): student $5, individual $12, institutional $20
Pages/issue: 100

Readership: academics, public administrators

Indexed/abstracted in: ABC POL SCI

Manuscripts
Query: no
Abstract: no
Style guide: none required
Preferred length: 2,000–3,000 words
Number of copies: 4
Notes: end of manuscript
Blind referee: yes
Time to consider manuscript: 3 months
Proportion of manuscripts accepted: 33 percent
Illustrations accepted: tables, graphs, charts, drawings
Foreign languages: no

Reviews
Book review editor: Jerzy Hauptmann
Address: same as above
Seeking reviewers: no
Unsolicited reviews accepted: no

Additional notes
Include a special cover page with the title, author, affiliation, and brief biographical paragraph.

AMERICAN SOCIOLOGICAL REVIEW

Focus: advancement of the discipline of sociology—theoretically, methodologically, substantively
Institutional affiliation: American Sociological Association
Editor: Sheldon Stryker
Editorial address:
Institute of Social Research
1022 East Third Street
Bloomington, IN 47405
Frequency: 6/year
Circulation: 14,000
Subscription rate(s): ASA member $10, individual $18, institutional $26
Pages/issue: 135

Readership: academics

Indexed/abstracted in: Soc Sci Ind, Psychol Abstr, Sociol Abstr, Soc Work Res and Abstr, Int Pol Sci Abstr, USPSD

Manuscripts
Query: no
Abstract: yes
Style guide: available on request
Preferred length: 30 pages maximum
Number of copies: 4
Notes: end of manuscript
Blind referee: yes
Time to consider manuscript: 3 months
Proportion of manuscripts accepted: 15 percent
Illustrations accepted: tables, graphs, charts, photos, drawings
Foreign languages: no

Reviews:
Book review editor: Sheldon Stryker
Address: same as above
Materials reviewed: books

Additional notes
Simultaneous submission is not allowed.

AMERICAN STUDIES

Focus: American society and culture; the literature, sociology, anthropology, and fine arts of the United States
Institutional affiliation: Midcontinent American Studies Association, Stephens College, University of Kansas
Editor: Stuart Levine
Editorial address:
University of Kansas
Lawrence, KS 66045
Frequency: 2/year
Circulation: 1,000
Subscription rate(s): individual $5, institutional $7
Pages/issue: 120
Readership: historians, social scientists
Indexed/abstracted in: not given

Manuscripts

Query: no
Abstract: yes, 2 copies
Style guide: MLA
Preferred length: 25 pages
Number of copies: 2
Notes: end of manuscript
Blind referee: yes
Time to consider manuscript: 1–5 months
Proportion of manuscripts accepted: 5 percent
Illustrations accepted: tables, graphs, charts, photos. (Authors pay part of the cost of printing up to $30)
Foreign languages: no

Reviews

Book review editor: Stuart Levine
Address: same as above
Seeking reviewers: yes
Unsolicited reviews accepted: no
Materials reviewed: books
Length of review: 50–100 words

Additional notes

Simultaneous submission is not allowed. Articles are published 6–12 months after acceptance.

THE ANNALS OF REGIONAL SCIENCE

Focus: location and interaction of economic activity, urban development, regional analysis, transportation studies, resource management, environmental impacts, land use planning, state and municipal finance, and other issues in regional science
Institutional affiliation: Western Washington University, Western Regional Science Association
Editor: Michael K. Mischaikow
Editorial address:
Department of Economics
Western Washington University
Bellingham, WA 98225
Frequency: 3/year
Circulation: 1,100

Subscription rate(s): $21
Pages/issue: 176
Readership: government ageices, consulting businesses, international organizations, economists, academics
Indexed/abstracted in: not given

Manuscripts

Query: no
Abstract: yes
Style guide: available on request
Preferred length: 20 pages
Number of copies: 3
Notes: bottom of page
Blind referee: no
Time to consider manuscript: 3–6 months
Proportion of manuscripts accepted: varies
Illustrations accepted: tables, graphs, charts, photos, drawings
Foreign languages: no

Reviews

Book review editor: Roger L. Burford
Address:
3189 CEBA Building
Louisiana State University
Baton Rouge, LA 70803
Seeking reviewers: yes
Unsolicited reviews accepted: yes
How to apply: letter of inquiry
Materials reviewed: books
Length of review: 2–3 pages

Additional notes

Simultaneous submission is not allowed. Most articles are published 8–10 months after acceptance.

ARAB STUDIES QUARTERLY

Focus: studies of Arab culture, history and institutions
Institutional affiliation: Association of Arab-American University Graduates and the Institute of Arab Studies
Editors: Edward W. Said, Fouad Moughrabi

Editorial address:
419 Hamilton Hall
Columbia University
New York, NY 10027
Frequency: 4/year
Circulation: not given
Subscription rate(s): individual $16,
institutional $35
Pages/issue: 100
Readership: academics
Indexed/abstracted in: Amer Hist
and Life, Hist Abstr

Manuscripts
Query: no
Abstract: no
Style guide: none required
Preferred length: 15–20 pages
Number of copies: 1
Notes: bottom of page
Blind referee: no
Time to consider manuscript: not
given
**Proportion of manuscripts
accepted:** not given
Illustrations accepted: tables,
graphs, charts
Foreign languages: no

Reviews
Book review editor: Mary Ellen
Lundsten
Address:
Box 10
Buffalo, MN 55313
Unsolicited reviews accepted: yes
Materials reviewed: books
Length of review: 20-page review
essays

Frequency: 4/year
Circulation: 2,000
Subscription rate(s): individual $20,
institutional $35
Pages/issue: 176
Readership: academics, professionals
Indexed/abstracted in: Sociol Abstr

Manuscripts
Query: no
Abstract: no
Style guide: MOS
Preferred length: 40 pages
Number of copies: 3
Notes: end of manuscript
Blind referee: yes
Time to consider manuscript: 3
months
**Proportion of manuscripts
accepted:** 15 percent
Illustrations accepted: tables,
graphs, charts
Foreign languages: no

Reviews
Book review editor: James Lewis
Address: same as above
Seeking reviewers: yes
Unsolicited reviews accepted: yes
How to apply: letter of inquiry
Include in application: professional
degrees, areas of expertise
Materials reviewed: books
Length of review: 1,250 words

Additional notes
Reprints are available. Simultaneous
submission is allowed. Articles appear
10–14 months after acceptance.

ARMED FORCES AND SOCIETY

Focus: military institutions, civil-military
relations, arms control and
peacekeeping, and conflict
management
Editor: Abby Beth Chack
Editorial address:
Social Science Building, Box 46
1126 East 59th Street
Chicago, IL 60637

ASIAN AFFAIRS: AN AMERICAN REVIEW

Focus: American policy in Asia (Japan
to Afghanistan); politics, economics,
and international relations of Asian
countries
Institutional affiliation: American-
Asian Educational Exchange
Editor: William Henderson

Editorial address:
555 Lake Street
St. James, NY 11780
Frequency: 6/year
Circulation: 1,000
Subscription rate(s): $30
Pages/issue: 60–70
Readership: general public, academics
Indexed/abstracted in: ABC POL SCI, Hist Abstr, PAIS

Manuscripts
Query: no
Abstract: no
Style guide: none required
Preferred length: 4,000–6,000 words
Number of copies: 1
Notes: end of manuscript
Blind referee: no
Time to consider manuscript: 6 weeks
Proportion of manuscripts accepted: 33 percent
Illustrations accepted: tables, graphs, charts, photos
Foreign languages: no

Reviews
Seeking reviewers: no
Unsolicited reviews accepted: no

Additional notes
Asian Affairs seeks policy-oriented discussion rather than research papers. Authors of accepted manuscripts receive a $250 honorarium. Simultaneous submission is permitted. Articles are published within 4 months of acceptance.

ASIAN PROFILE

Focus: all aspects of Asian studies
Institutional affiliation: Asian Research Service
Editor: submit to the Editor
Editorial address:
Asian Research Service
P.O. Box 2232, G.P.O.
HONG KONG
Frequency: 6/year

Circulation: not given
Subscription rate(s): individual $30, institutional $55
Pages/issue: 97
Readership: academics
Indexed/abstracted in: Hist Abstr, Amer Hist and Life

Manuscripts
Query: no
Abstract: yes, 150 words
Style guide: see current issue
Preferred length: 8,000 words maximum
Number of copies: 1
Notes: end of manuscript
Blind referee: yes
Time to consider manuscript: not given
Proportion of manuscripts accepted: not given
Illustrations accepted: tables, graphs, charts, photos, drawings, maps
Foreign languages: no

Reviews
Book review editor: submit to the Editor
Address: same as above
Materials reviewed: books
Length of review: 3–4 pages

Additional notes
Simultaneous submission is not permitted.

ASIAN SURVEY

Focus: contemporary Asian affairs
Institutional affiliation: University of California
Editors: Leo E. Rose, Robert A. Scalapino
Editorial address:
University of California Press
Berkeley, CA 94720
Frequency: 12/year
Circulation: 3,300
Subscription rate(s): student $17, individual $30, institutional $50
Pages/issue: 100

Readership: academics, general public
Indexed/abstracted in: ABC POL SCI, Hist Abstr

Manuscripts
Query: no
Abstract: no
Style guide: MOS
Preferred length: 30 pages
Number of copies: 2
Notes: bottom of page
Blind referee: yes
Time to consider manuscript: 6–8 weeks
Proportion of manuscripts accepted: 40–50 percent
Illustrations accepted: tables, graphs, charts, photos
Foreign languages: no

Reviews
Seeking reviewers: no
Unsolicited reviews accepted: no

Additional notes
Illustrations must be line copy only (no halftones) and camera-ready. Simultaneous submission is allowed. Articles are published 6–12 months after acceptance.

ASIAN THOUGHT AND SOCIETY: AN INTERNATIONAL REVIEW

Focus: intellectual and socio-political structures and changes
Institutional affiliation: State University of New York—Oneonta, Boston College, and University of Hong Kong
Editor: Ignatius J.H. Ts'ao
Editorial address:
State University of New York
Oneonta, NY 13820
Frequency: 3/year
Circulation: 450
Subscription rate(s): individual $15, institutional $30
Pages/issue: 110–120

Readership: academics
Indexed/abstracted in: ABC POL SCI, IBZ, IBR

Manuscripts
Query: no
Abstract: no
Style guide: MOS
Preferred length: 6,000 words
Number of copies: 3
Notes: bottom of page or end of manuscript
Blind referee: yes
Time to consider manuscript: 4–6 weeks
Proportion of manuscripts accepted: 33 percent
Illustrations accepted: tables, graphs, charts, photos, drawings
Foreign languages: French, German, Spanish

Reviews
Book review editor: Justus M. van der Kroef
Address: same as above
Seeking reviewers: yes
Unsolicited reviews accepted: yes
How to apply: letter of inquiry
Include in application: professional degrees, institutional affiliation, areas of expertise, published works, current research
Materials reviewed: books
Length of review: 1,000 words maximum

ASIA PACIFIC COMMUNITY: A QUARTERLY REVIEW

Focus: political, social, and economic issues and developments in East Asia and the Pacific region
Institutional affiliation: Asian Club
Editor: Hideo Ueno
Editorial address:
Suite 2302, World Trade Center Building
2-4-1 Hamamatsu-cho
Minato-Ku, Tokyo, JAPAN
Frequency: 4/year
Circulation: 6,000

Subscription rate(s): $24
Pages/issue: 130
Readership: academics
Indexed/abstracted in: SSCI

Manuscripts
Query: yes
Abstract: no
Style guide: see current issue or write for guidelines
Preferred length: no preference
Number of copies: 1
Notes: end of manuscript
Blind referee: no
Time to consider manuscript: not given
Proportion of manuscripts accepted: not given
Illustrations accepted: tables, photos
Foreign languages: no

Reviews
not applicable

THE ATLANTIC COMMUNITY QUARTERLY

Focus: problems and prospects for more effective cooperative action among the nations of the North Atlantic area, Australia, and Japan
Institutional affiliation: Atlantic Council of the United States, Inc.
Editor: Martha C. Finley
Editorial address:
1616 H Street, NW
Washington, DC 20006
Frequency: 4/year
Circulation: 2,500
Subscription rate(s): $15, foreign add $1
Pages/issue: 132
Readership: academics, general public, foreign readers
Indexed/abstracted in: Hist Abstr, Amer Hist and Life

Manuscripts
Query: no
Abstract: no
Style guide: none required
Preferred length: 5,000 words

Number of copies: 1
Blind referee: no
Time to consider manuscript: 2 months
Proportion of manuscripts accepted: not given
Illustrations accepted: tables, graphs, charts
Foreign languages: no

Reviews
Book review editor: Martha C. Finley
Address: same as above
Seeking reviewers: no
Unsolicited reviews accepted: no
Include in application: professional degrees
Materials reviewed: books

Additional notes
Simultaneous submission is permitted. Articles appear 4 weeks after acceptance.

AUSSENPOLITIK: GERMAN FOREIGN AFFAIRS REVIEW

Focus: current issues and developments in German and European foreign affairs
Editor: Heinrich Bechtoldt
Editorial address:
Schoene Aussicht 23
D-2000 Hamburg 76
FEDERAL REPUBLIC OF GERMANY
Frequency: 4/year
Circulation: 5,500
Subscription rate(s): 50 (West German marks)
Pages/issue: 105
Readership: political scientists
Indexed/abstracted in: ABC POL SCI, SSCI

Manuscripts
Query: no
Abstract: no
Style guide: see current issue or write for guidelines
Preferred length: no preference
Number of copies: 1
Notes: bottom of page

Blind referee: no
Time to consider manuscript: not given
Proportion of manuscripts accepted: not given
Illustrations accepted: not given
Foreign languages: there is a German edition

Reviews
Book review editor: Heinrich Bechtoldt
Address: same as above
Materials reviewed: books
Length of review: 1–2 pages.

AUSTRALIAN JOURNAL OF POLITICS AND HISTORY

Focus: international political and historical studies
Editor: submit to the Editor
Editorial address:
Department of History
University of Queensland
St. Lucia, 4067, Queensland
AUSTRALIA
Frequency: 3/year
Circulation: 1250
Subscription rate(s): $26 (in Australia)
Pages/issue: 140
Readership: political scientists, historians, other social scientists
Indexed/abstracted in: Curr Cont, Int Polit Sci Abstr, PAIS, SSCI

Manuscripts
Query: no
Abstract: no
Style guide: write for guidelines
Preferred length: no preference
Number of copies: 1
Notes: end of manuscript
Blind referee: no
Time to consider manuscript: not given
Proportion of manuscripts accepted: not given
Illustrations accepted: not given
Foreign languages: French, German

Reviews
Book review editor: Peter Loveday
Address: same as above
Materials reviewed: books
Length of review: 200–600 words

AUSTRALIAN OUTLOOK

Focus: international problems and issues
Institutional affiliation: Australian Institute of International Affairs
Editor: Ian Clark
Editorial address:
Department of Politics
University of Western Australia
Nedlands, W. A. 6009
AUSTRALIA
Frequency: 3/year
Circulation: 3,300
Subscription rate(s): $15 (in Australia)
Pages/issue: 60–80
Readership: political and social scientists
Indexed/abstracted in: Hist Abstr, Aus PAIS, Int Polit Sci Abstr

Manuscripts
Query: no
Abstract: no
Style guide: write for guidelines
Preferred length: 4,000–7,000 words
Number of copies: 1
Notes: end of manuscript
Blind referee: yes
Time to consider manuscript: not given
Proportion of manuscripts accepted: not given
Illustrations accepted: tables, graphs, charts
Foreign languages: German

Reviews
Book review editor: submit to Review Editor
Address:
Box E181 Post Office
Canberra, A.C.T. 2600
AUSTRALIA
Materials reviewed: books
Length of review: 2–3 pages

THE AUSTRALIAN QUARTERLY

Focus: the political, social, historical, economic, and scientific affairs of contemporary Australia
Institutional affiliation: Australian Institute of Political Science
Editor: submit to the Associate Editor
Editorial address:
Australian Institute of Political Science
32 Market Street
Sydney 2000
AUSTRALIA
Frequency: 4/year
Circulation: 4,000
Subscription rate(s): Australia $10, foreign $12 (Australian)
Pages/issue: 100–120
Readership: academics, general public
Indexed/abstracted in: SSCI, Aus PAIS

Manuscripts
Query: no
Abstract: yes, 100 words
Style guide: see current issue or write for guidelines
Preferred length: 5,000 words
Number of copies: 3, double-spaced
Notes: end of manuscript
Blind referee: no
Time to consider manuscript: not given
Proportion of manuscripts accepted: not given
Illustrations accepted: tables, graphs, charts, photos
Foreign languages: no

Reviews
not applicable

Additional notes
Simultaneous submission is not permitted. Manuscript should be submitted with a brief biography.

BEHAVIORAL SCIENCE

Focus: interdisciplinary articles and general systems science
Editor: Larry W. Dybala
Editorial address:
University of California
Santa Barbara, CA 93106
Frequency: 4/year
Circulation: 2,800
Subscription rate(s): individual $25, institutional $40
Pages/issue: 100
Readership: academics, general public (including engineers, social scientists, psychologists, mathematicians)
Indexed/abstracted in: Biol Abstr, Comput Rev, Psychol Abstr, SSCI, Sociol Abstr

Manuscripts
Query: no
Abstract: yes
Style guide: APA
Preferred length: 35 pages
Number of copies: 5
Notes: end of manuscript
Blind referee: not given
Time to consider manuscript: 6–8 months
Proportion of manuscripts accepted: 33 percent
Illustrations accepted: tables, graphs, charts, photos, drawings
Foreign languages: no

Reviews
Book review editor: Robert W. Bosserman
Address:
Systems Science Institute
University of Louisville
Louisville, KY 40292
Seeking reviewers: yes
Unsolicited reviews accepted: yes
How to apply: letter of inquiry
Include in application: professional degrees, institutional affiliation, areas of expertise, current research
Materials reviewed: books
Length of review: 5 pages, double-spaced.

Additional notes

Royalties are paid through the editorial office. Simultaneous submission is not allowed. Articles are published 9–12 months after submission. *Behavioral Science* is registered with the Copyright Clearance Center.

THE BLACK LAW JOURNAL

Focus: legal, social, political, and cultural issues that affect Blacks anc other people of color
Institutional affiliation: University of California, Los Angeles
Editor: Ronald S. Whitaker
Editorial address:
University of California
School of Law
405 Hilgard Avenue
Los Angeles, CA 90024
Frequency: 3/year
Circulation: 1500
Subscription rate(s): student $7.50, individual $12.50, institutional $25
Pages/issue: 175–200
Readership: students and those who work in the legal field
Indexed/abstracted in: Leg Per

Manuscripts

Query: no
Abstract: no
Style guide: HLRA
Preferred length: 20 pages
Number of copies: 2
Notes: end of manuscript
Blind referee: no
Time to consider manuscript: 3–4 weeks
Proportion of manuscripts accepted: 75 percent
Illustrations accepted: tables, graphs, charts, photos, drawings
Foreign languages: no

Reviews

Book review editor: Jacci Holmes Williams
Address: same as above
Seeking reviewers: yes
Unsolicited reviews accepted: yes

How to apply: letter of inquiry
Include in application: professional degrees, institutional affiliation, current research
Materials reviewed: books
Length of review: 6–12 pages

Additional notes

Simultaneous submission is not allowed. Publishing time after acceptance varies.

THE BLACK SCHOLAR

Focus: Black studies and research
Institutional affiliation: The Black World Foundation
Editor: Robert L. Allen
Editorial address:
P.O. Box 7106
San Francisco, CA 94120
Frequency: 6/year
Circulation: 15,000
Subscription rate(s): individual $16, institutional/libraries $24
Pages/issue: 80
Readership: academics, students, sociologists, poets, general public
Indexed/abstracted in: Alt Press Ind, ALA-Ethnic Materials Information Exchange Task Force, Psychol Abstr

Manuscripts

Query: no
Abstract: no
Style guide: MOS
Preferred length: 2,000–5,000 words
Number of copies: 1
Notes: end of manuscript
Blind referee: no
Time to consider manuscript: 2 months
Proportion of manuscripts accepted: not given
Illustrations accepted: tables, graphs, charts, photos, drawings
Foreign languages: no

Reviews

Book review editor: submit to the Book Review Editor
Address: same as above
Seeking reviewers: yes

Unsolicited reviews accepted: yes
How to apply: letter of inquiry
Materials reviewed: books, films
Length of review: 250–500 words

Additional notes

Payment is made in contributor's copies and a 1-year subscription. Simultaneous submission is not allowed. Publication time after acceptance varies.

B'NAI B'RITH INTERNATIONAL JEWISH MONTHLY

Focus: Jewish events, from political, cultural, and sociological perspectives.
Institutional affiliation: B'nai B'rith International
Editor: Marc Silver
Editorial address:
1640 Rhode Island Avenue NW
Washington, DC 20036
Frequency: 10/year
Circulation: 200,000
Subscription rate(s): $8
Pages/issue: 56
Readership: Jewish families
Indexed/abstracted in: Ind Jew Per

Manuscripts

Query: no
Abstract: no
Style guide: none required
Preferred length: 1,500–2,000 words
Number of copies: 1
Notes: end of manuscript
Blind referee: no
Time to consider manuscript: 2 weeks
Proportion of manuscripts accepted: 10 percent
Illustrations accepted: tables, graphs, charts, photos, drawings
Foreign languages: no

Reviews

Book review editor: Marc Silver
Address: same as above
Seeking reviewers: yes
Unsolicited reviews accepted: yes

How to apply: letter of inquiry
Include in application: institutional affiliation, areas of expertise, published works
Materials reviewed: books, films
Length of review: 300–500 words

Additional notes

Articles offering fresh insights into Middle East politics are welcomed. Israel is a prime subject for articles. Royalties are paid at the rate of 5 to 10 cents per word for first serial rights.

BOSTON COLLEGE INTERNATIONAL AND COMPARATIVE LAW REVIEW

Focus: international and comparative legal issues
Institutional affiliation: Boston College Law School
Editor: Peter R. Martin
Editorial address:
Boston College Law School
885 Centre Street
Newton Centre, MA 02159
Frequency: 2/year
Circulation: 450
Subscription rate(s): domestic $9, foreign $10
Pages/issue: 250
Readership: law libraries, law firms, corporations, government agencies, (both American and foreign)
Indexed/abstracted in: Leg Per, Curr Law Ind, CCLP

Manuscripts

Query: no
Abstract: no
Style guide: MOS, citations should follow HLRA
Preferred length: 5,000–10,000 words
Number of copies: 1
Notes: end of manuscript
Blind referee: no
Time to consider manuscript: 2–3 weeks
Proportion of manuscripts accepted: 10 percent

Illustrations accepted: tables, graphs, charts
Foreign languages: no

Reviews
Book review editor: Mark Romanesk
Address: same as above
Seeking reviewers: yes
Unsolicited reviews accepted: yes
How to apply: letter of inquiry
Include in application: professional degrees, institutional affiliation, areas of expertise, published works, current research
Materials reviewed: books
Length of review: 1,000–3,000 words

Additional notes
The *Review* circulates in 17 nations throughout the world.

BRITISH JOURNAL OF INDUSTRIAL RELATIONS

Focus: every aspect of industrial relations in Great Britain and overseas
Institutional affiliation: London School of Economics and Political Science
Editor: B. C. Roberts
Editorial address:
London School of Economics and Political Science
Houghton Street
Aldwych, London WC2A 2AE
ENGLAND
Frequency: 3/year
Circulation: 2,000
Subscription rate(s): $38
Pages/issue: 140
Readership: economists, labor relations specialists, other social scientists
Indexed/abstracted in: PAIS, Work Rel Abstr

Manuscripts
Query: no
Abstract: no
Style guide: available on request
Preferred length: 7,000–8,000 words

Number of copies: 2, double-spaced
Notes: end of manuscript
Blind referee: no
Time to consider manuscript: 2–4 months
Proportion of manuscripts accepted: not given
Illustrations accepted: tables, graphs, charts
Foreign languages: no

Reviews
Book review editor: S. R. Hill
Address: same as above
Materials reviewed: books
Length of review: 1–2 pages

Additional notes
Simultaneous submission is not permitted. Articles are published 3–9 months after acceptance.

BRITISH JOURNAL OF POLITICAL SCIENCE

Focus: all fields of political science
Editor: Ivor Crewe
Editorial address:
University of Essex
Wivenhoe Park
Colchester, Essex CO4 35Q
ENGLAND
Frequency: 4/year
Circulation: 1,100
Subscription rate(s): individual $57.50, institutional $99
Pages/issue: 120–130
Readership: political scientists
Indexed/abstracted in: SSCI, Soc Sci Ind, ABC POL SCI

Manuscripts
Query: no
Abstract: no
Style guide: available on request
Preferred length: 5,000–12,000 words
Number of copies: 3
Notes: end of manuscript
Blind referee: no
Time to consider manuscript: not given

**Proportion of manuscripts
  accepted:** not given
Illustrations accepted: tables,
  graphs, charts
Foreign languages: no

Reviews
Book review editor: John Gray
Address: same as above
Unsolicited reviews accepted: yes
How to apply: letter of inquiry
Materials reviewed: books

Additional notes
Simultaneous submission is not
permitted.

BULLETIN OF CONCERNED
ASIAN SCHOLARS

Focus: contemporary/modern Asia
  from an anti-imperialist, progressive,
  and independent viewpoint
Editor: Joe Moore
Editorial address:
  P.O. Box R
  Berthoud, CO 80513
Frequency: 4/year
Circulation: 2,100
Subscription rate(s): student/
  unemployed $15, domestic, $20,
  foreign $21, institutional $35
Pages/issue: 72
Readership: academics, activists,
  laypersons concerned about political
  and economic trends in Asia
Indexed/abstracted in: Alt Press Ind,
  Int Bibl Book Rev, Int Bibl Per Lit

Manuscripts
Query: no
Abstract: no
Style guide: MOS
Preferred length: 15,000 words
  maximum
Number of copies: 3
Notes: end of manuscript
Blind referee: no
Time to consider manuscript: 2–3
  months
**Proportion of manuscripts
  accepted:** not given

Illustrations accepted: tables,
  graphs, charts, photos, drawings
Foreign languages: no

Reviews
Book review editor: Joe Moore
Address: same as above
Seeking reviewers: yes
Unsolicited reviews accepted: yes
How to apply: letter of inquiry
Include in application: areas of
  expertise, published works, current
  research
Materials reviewed: books, films
Length of review: 1,000–2,500 words

Additional notes
Simultaneous submission is allowed.
Articles appear 6–9 months after
acceptance.

THE BULLETIN OF THE
ATOMIC SCIENTISTS

Focus: science and public affairs, with
  an emphasis on the threat of nuclear
  warfare
Institutional affiliation: Educational
  Foundation for Nuclear Science
Editor: Ruth Young
Editorial address:
  5801 South Kenwood
  Chicago, IL 60637
Frequency: 10/year
Circulation: 30,000
Subscription rate(s): individual
  $19.50, institutional $25
Pages/issue: 50
Readership: academics, scientists,
  politicians, others with an interest in
  the impact of nuclear warfare
Indexed/abstracted in: ABC POL
  SCI, Amer Hist and Life, Hist Abstr

Manuscripts
Query: no
Abstract: no
Style guide: MOS
Preferred length: 35,000 words
Number of copies: 2
Notes: end of manuscript
Blind referee: no

Time to consider manuscript: 3 months

Proportion of manuscripts accepted: 10 percent

Illustrations accepted: tables, graphs, charts, photos, drawings

Foreign languages: no

Reviews

Book review editor: Ruth Young

Address: same as above

Seeking reviewers: yes

Unsolicited reviews accepted: yes

How to apply: letter of inquiry

Include in application: professional degrees, institutional affiliation, areas of expertise, published works, current research

Materials reviewed: books, films

Length of review: 1,000 words maximum

Additional notes

Simultaneous submission is not allowed. Articles are published 1–4 months after acceptance.

THE BUREAUCRAT

Focus: professionalism in public administration

Institutional affiliation: Florida International University

Editor: Thomas W. Novotny

Editorial address:
P.O. Box 347
Arlington, VA 22210

Frequency: 4/year

Circulation: 5,000

Subscription rate(s): individual $18.50, institutional $29.50

Pages/issue: 64

Readership: federal government professionals, academics

Indexed/abstracted in: Human Resour Abstr, Sage Urb Stud Abstr, Urb Aff Abst, Sage Pub Admin Abstr, ABC POL SCI, Curr Cont, SSCI, USPSD

Manuscripts

Query: no

Abstract: no

Style guide: available on request

Preferred length: 20 pages

Number of copies: 3

Notes: end of manuscript

Blind referee: yes

Time to consider manuscript: 3 months

Proportion of manuscripts accepted: 20 percent

Illustrations accepted: tables, graphs, charts, photos, drawings

Foreign languages: no

Reviews

Book review editor: Norman Beckman

Address: same as above

Seeking reviewers: yes

Unsolicited reviews accepted: no

How to apply: letter of inquiry

Include in application: professional degrees, institutional affiliation, areas of expertise

Materials reviewed: books

Length of review: 5–10 pages

Additional notes

Simultaneous submission is permitted if editors are notified at the time of submission. Articles appear 6–9 months after acceptance.

BUSINESS HISTORY REVIEW

Focus: business enterprise throughout the world and its interaction with society

Institutional affiliation: Harvard Business School

Editor: Albro Martin

Editorial address:
215 Baker Library
Soldiers Field
Boston, MA 02163

Frequency: 4/year

Circulation: 2,500

Subscription rate(s): individual $15, institutional and foreign $20

Pages/issue: 150

Readership: academics, business people, government officials

Indexed/abstracted in: not given

Manuscripts

Query: no
Abstract: no
Style guide: MOS; also see *BHR*, Vol XLII (Autumn 1969), 388–91.
Preferred length: 20–30 pages
Number of copies: 3
Notes: end of manuscript
Blind referee: yes
Time to consider manuscript: 2–3 months
Proportion of manuscripts accepted: 20 percent
Illustrations accepted: camera-ready visuals, tables accepted only if vital to the text
Foreign languages: no

Reviews

Book review editor: Albro Martin
Address: same as above
Seeking reviewers: yes
Unsolicited reviews accepted: no
How to apply: letter of inquiry
Include in application: professional degrees, institutional affiliation, areas of expertise
Materials reviewed: books
Length of review: 400–600 words

Additional notes

Simultaneous submission is not allowed. Articles are published 12–15 months after acceptance.

CALIFORNIA JOURNAL

Focus: analysis of California politics and government
Institutional affiliation: The California Center
Editor: Ed Salzman
Editorial address:
1714 Capitol Avenue
Sacramento, CA 95814
Frequency: 12/year
Circulation: 20,000
Pages/issue: 36
Readership: California government officials, general public
Indexed/abstracted in: PAIS, Sage Urb Stud Abstr, Pub Issues Ind, Cal Per Ind

Manuscripts

Query: yes
Abstract: no
Style guide: none required
Preferred length: 2,000–3,000 words
Number of copies: 1
Notes: none
Blind referee: no
Time to consider manuscript: 1 week
Proportion of manuscripts accepted: 20 percent
Illustrations accepted: none
Foreign languages: no

Reviews

not applicable

Additional notes

The *Journal* is not an academic publication. Call or write before submitting manuscript.

CALIFORNIA LAW REVIEW

Focus: law—articles by professors, judges, and lawyers; student notes and comments on various aspects of law
Institutional affiliation: University of California, Berkeley
Editor: Carol Dillon
Editorial address:
14 Boalt Hall
School of Law
University of California
Berkeley, CA 94720
Frequency: 6/year
Circulation: 3,000
Subscription rate(s): U.S., Canada $20, foreign $24
Pages/issue: 200
Readership: professors of law, law libraries, students, judges, lawyers
Indexed/abstracted in: CCLP

Manuscripts

Query: no
Abstract: no
Style guide: MOS, citations should follow HLRA
Preferred length: no preference
Number of copies: 1

Notes: end of manuscript
Blind referee: no
Time to consider manuscript: 3–4 weeks
Proportion of manuscripts accepted: 7 percent
Illustrations accepted: sometimes
Foreign languages: no

Reviews
Book review editor: Edward L. Wolf
Address: same as above
Seeking reviewers: yes
Unsolicited reviews accepted: yes
How to apply: letter of inquiry
Include in application: professional degrees, institutional affiliation, areas of expertise
Materials reviewed: books

Additional notes
Previously published manuscripts are not accepted. If any part of the manuscript has been published before, or is to be published elsewhere, the author must include this information at the time of submission. Submitted manuscripts will not be returned unless accompanied by a self-addressed, stamped envelope. Royalties are negotiable. Simultaneous submission is allowed. Articles appear 2–6 months after acceptance.

CALIFORNIA MANAGEMENT REVIEW

Focus: management functions and practices
Institutional affiliation: University of California
Editor: Robert N. Katz
Editorial address:
Graduate School of Business Administration
350 Barrows Hall
University of California
Berkeley, CA 94720
Frequency: 4/year
Circulation: 4,400
Subscription rate(s): $15
Pages/issue: 95

Readership: active managers, scholars, teachers, and others concerned with management
Indexed/abstracted in: ABC POL SCI, Amer Hist and Life, BPI, Employ Rel Abstr, Hist Abstr, Manage Ind, PAIS

Manuscripts
Query: no
Abstract: no
Style guide: available on request
Preferred length: 2,500–7,500 words
Number of copies: 3
Notes: end of manuscript
Blind referee: no
Time to consider manuscript: 2 months
Proportion of manuscripts accepted: not given
Illustrations accepted: tables, graphs, charts, drawings
Foreign languages: no

Reviews
not applicable

Additional notes
Simultaneous submission is not allowed. Articles are published 6–9 months after acceptance.

CAMPAIGNS AND ELECTIONS: THE JOURNAL OF POLITICAL ACTION

Focus: advice to candidates and political organizations on running and winning political campaigns
Editor: Ann Siprelle
Editorial address:
National Press Building
Suite 602
Washington, DC 20045
Frequency: 4/year
Circulation: 2,000
Subscription rate(s): $48
Pages/issue: 75

Readership: political hopefuls, incumbents, corporations, academics, public interest groups, the politically aware
Indexed/abstracted in: PAIS

Manuscripts
Query: no
Abstract: no
Style guide: MOS
Preferred length: 2,500–5,000 words
Number of copies: 1
Notes: end of manuscript
Blind referee: no
Time to consider manuscript: 1 month
Proportion of manuscripts accepted: 50 percent
Illustrations accepted: tables, graphs, charts, photos, drawings
Foreign languages: no

Reviews
Book review editor: Tim Baldwin
Address:
400 South Zang Building
Suite 1319
Dallas, TX 75208
Seeking reviewers: no
Unsolicited reviews accepted: no
Materials reviewed: books

CANADIAN-AMERICAN SLAVIC STUDIES

Focus: humanities and social sciences devoted to Russian/Soviet and East European area studies
Institutional affiliation: Arizona State University
Editor: Charles Schlacks, Jr.
Editorial address:
Arizona State University
120 B McAllister
Tempe, AZ 85281
Frequency: 4/year
Circulation: 1,000
Subscription rate(s): $15
Pages/issue: 150
Readership: academics
Indexed/abstracted in: not given

Manuscripts
Query: no
Abstract: no
Style guide: MLA
Preferred length: 20–40 pages
Number of copies: 3
Notes: end of manuscript
Blind referee: no
Time to consider manuscript: 3 months
Proportion of manuscripts accepted: not given
Illustrations accepted: camera-ready tables, graphs, charts, photos
Foreign languages: French, German, Russian

Reviews
Book review editors: Allan Simel, Robert North
Address: same as above
Seeking reviewers: yes
Unsolicited reviews accepted: yes
How to apply: letter of inquiry
Include in application: areas of expertise, published works, foreign languages
Materials reviewed: books
Length of review: 600 words

Additional notes
Simultaneous submission is not permitted. Articles appear 3–6 months after acceptance.

CANADIAN ETHNIC STUDIES/ ETUDES ETHNIQUES AU CANADA

Focus: interdisciplinary studies of the ethnicity, immigration, intergroup relations, and cultural life of ethnic groups in Canada
Institutional affiliation: Research Centre for Canadian Ethnic Studies, University of Calgary
Editors: James Frideres, Anthony Raspovich
Editorial address:
University of Calgary
Calgary, Alberta T2N 1N4
CANADA

Frequency: 2–3/year
Circulation: 975
Subscription rate(s): individual $15, institutional $20
Pages/issue: 250
Readership: academics, librarians, high school teachers and administrators
Indexed/abstracted in: not given

Manuscripts
Query: yes
Abstract: yes
Style guide: MLA
Preferred length: 15–20 pages
Number of copies: 3
Notes: end of manuscript
Blind referee: no
Time to consider manuscript: 4–6 months
Proportion of manuscripts accepted: 33 percent
Illustrations accepted: tables, graphs, charts, photos
Foreign languages: French

Reviews
Book review editor: Herman Ganzevoort
Address: same as above
Seeking reviewers: yes
Unsolicited reviews accepted: yes
How to apply: letter of inquiry
Include in application: areas of expertise, foreign languages, current research
Materials reviewed: books, films, novels, translations
Length of review: 750 words maximum

Additional notes
Simultaneous submission is not permitted. Articles appear within 6 months of acceptance.

CANADIAN JOURNAL OF AFRICAN STUDIES/REVUE CANADIENNE DES ETUDES AFRICAINES

Focus: African studies (social sciences, humanities, health)
Institutional affiliation: Canadian Association of African Studies/ Association canadienne d'études africaines
Editors: Joel W. Gregory, Bogumil Jewsiewicki, Richard Stren
Editorial address:
Department of Geography
Carleton University
Ottawa, Ontario K1S 5B6
CANADA
Frequency: 3/year
Circulation: 1,100
Subscription rate(s): $30 (Canadian)
Pages/issue: 200
Readership: academics
Indexed/abstracted in: Int Polit Sci Abstr, ABC POL SCI, Hist Abstr, Abstr Anthropol, Sociol Abstr, RADAR, Universal Ref Syst, Curr Cont Africa

Manuscripts
Query: no
Abstract: yes
Style guide: MOS
Preferred length: 3,000–6,000 words or shorter for research notes
Number of copies: 3
Notes: end of manuscript
Blind referee: yes
Time to consider manuscript: 4 months
Proportion of manuscripts accepted: 5–10 percent
Illustrations accepted: tables, graphs, charts, drawings
Foreign languages: French

Reviews

Book review editor: Joel W. Gregory
Address:
départment de démographie
Université de Montreal
C.P. 6128
succursale A
Montreal, Quebec H3C 3J7
CANADA
Seeking reviewers: occasionally
Unsolicited reviews accepted: occasionally
How to apply: letter of inquiry
Include in application: professional degrees, institutional affiliation, areas of expertise, published works, foreign languages, current research
Materials reviewed: books
Length of review: 750 words; 1,250–1,500 for review articles of 2 or more books

CANADIAN JOURNAL OF DEVELOPMENT STUDIES/ REVUE CANADIENNE D'ETUDES DU DEVELOPPEMENT

Focus: interdisciplinary approach to all fields of development studies
Editors: Maxime A. Crener, Ozay Mehmet
Editorial address:
Institute for International Cooperation
University of Ottawa
190 Laurier East
Ottawa, Ontario K1N 6N5
CANADA
Frequency: 2/year
Circulation: not given
Subscription rate(s): individual $10, institutional $15
Pages/issue: 250
Readership: academics
Indexed/abstracted in: ABC POL SCI

Manuscripts

Query: no
Abstract: yes, 100 words maximum
Style guide: available on request

Preferred length: 25 pages
Number of copies: 3, double-spaced
Notes: end of manuscript
Blind referee: yes
Time to consider manuscript: not given
Proportion of manuscripts accepted: not given
Illustrations accepted: tables, graphs, charts
Foreign languages: French

Reviews

Book review editor: William D. Ward
Address: same as above
Materials reviewed: books
Length of review: 2–3 pages

CANADIAN JOURNAL OF POLITICAL AND SOCIAL THEORY/REVUE CANADIENNE DE THEORIE POLITIQUE ET SOCIALE

Focus: contemporary expressions of cultural theory and political analysis of the dynamics of advanced industrial societies
Editor: Arthur Kroker
Editorial address:
Department of Political Science
Concordia University
7141 Sherbrooke Street West
Montreal, Quebec H4B 1M8
CANADA
Frequency: 3/year
Circulation: 1,500
Subscription rate(s): student $10, individual $15, institutional $25, $3 extra if outside Canada
Pages/issue: 120–220
Readership: academics
Indexed/abstracted in: ABC POL SCI, Int Polit Sci Abstr, Sociol Abstr, Alt Press Ind, Can Ind

Manuscripts

Query: no
Abstract: no
Style guide: MOS

Preferred length: 25 pages
Number of copies: 3
Notes: end of manuscript
Blind referee: no
Time to consider manuscript: 4–6 weeks
Proportion of manuscripts accepted: 7 percent
Illustrations accepted: charts, photos, drawings
Foreign languages: French

Reviews

Book review editor: David Cook
Address:
Room 219, Simcoe Hall
University of Toronto
Toronto, Ontario M5S 1A1 CANADA
Seeking reviewers: yes
Unsolicited reviews accepted: no
How to apply: letter of inquiry
Include in application: institutional affiliation, areas of expertise, published works, foreign languages, current research
Materials reviewed: books
Length of review: 20 pages

Additional notes

The *Journal* uses only review essays.

CANADIAN JOURNAL OF POLITICAL SCIENCE/REVUE CANADIENNE DE SCIENCE POLITIQUE

Focus: political science, with emphasis on Canada
Institutional affiliation: Wilfrid Laurier University Press
Editor: John C. Courtney
Editorial address:
Department of Economics and Political Science
University of Saskatchewan
Saskatoon, Saskatchewan
S7N 0W0
CANADA
Frequency: 4/year
Circulation: not given
Subscription rate(s): not given
Pages/issue: 224

Readership: academics
Indexed/abstracted in: ABC POL SCI, Arts and Hum Cit Ind, Curr Cont, IBR, IBZ, Ind Can Leg Per Lit, Int Polit Sci Abstr, PAIS, Sociol Abstr, USPSD

Manuscripts

Query: no
Abstract: yes, 250 words
Style guide: available on request
Preferred length: 30 pages
Number of copies: 3
Notes: end of manuscript
Blind referee: no
Time to consider manuscript: 9 weeks
Proportion of manuscripts accepted: 20 percent
Illustrations accepted: tables, graphs, charts
Foreign languages: French

Reviews

Book review editor: David Smith
Address: same as above
Seeking reviewers: yes
Unsolicited reviews accepted: no
How to apply: letter of inquiry
Include in application: professional degrees, institutional affiliation, areas of expertise, published works, current research
Materials reviewed: books, documents
Length of review: 700 words

CANADIAN PUBLIC ADMINISTRATION/ ADMINISTRATION PUBLIQUE DU CANADA

Focus: structures, processes, and outcomes of public policy and public management related to executive, legislative, judicial, and quasijudicial functions in the municipal, provincial, and federal spheres of government
Institutional affiliation: Institute of Public Administration of Canada
Editor: W.D.K. Kernaghan

Editorial address:
897 Bay Street
Toronto, Ontario M5S 1Z7
CANADA
Frequency: 4/year
Circulation: 4,000
Subscription rate(s): $40
Pages/issue: 45
Readership: academics, public servants, general public
Indexed/abstracted in: Can Ind, PAIS, Int Polit Sci Abstr, Pub Admin Abst, Index of Abstracts (Indian Institute of Public Administration); Ind Can Leg Per Lit, Human Resour Abstr

Manuscripts
Query: no
Abstract: yes
Style guide: see current issue or write for guidelines
Preferred length: 20–30 pages
Number of copies: 3, double-spaced
Notes: end of manuscript
Blind referee: yes
Time to consider manuscript: 2–3 months
Proportion of manuscripts accepted: 30 percent
Illustrations accepted: tables, graphs, charts
Foreign languages: French

Reviews
Book review editors: V.S. Wilson, R. Bolduc
Address: same as above
Seeking reviewers: yes
Unsolicited reviews accepted: yes
How to apply: letter of inquiry
Materials reviewed: books
Length of review: 3–4 pages

Additional notes
Simultaneous submission is not permitted. Articles are published 3 months after acceptance.

CANADIAN PUBLIC POLICY/ ANALYSE DE POLITIQUES

Focus: public policy in Canada
Institutional affiliation: University of Guelph
Editor: A. Scott
Editorial address:
Room 039
Arts Building
University of Guelph
Guelph, Ontario N1G 2W1
CANADA
Frequency: 4/year
Circulation: 2,400
Subscription rate(s): student $14, individual $20, institutional $30
Pages/issue: 128–144
Readership: academics, government officials, business executives
Indexed/abstracted in: Can BPI, Can Ind, Curr Cont, Human Resour Abstr, Ind Can Leg Per Lit, Int Polit Sci Abstr, J of Econ Lit, PAIS, Sage Pub Admin Abstr, Sage Urb Stud Abstr, SSCI, Sociol Abstr

Manuscripts
Query: no
Abstract: yes
Style guide: MOS
Preferred length: 20–25 pages
Number of copies: 4, double-spaced
Notes: bottom of page
Blind referee: yes
Time to consider manuscript: 3 months
Proportion of manuscripts accepted: 23 percent
Illustrations accepted: tables, graphs, charts
Foreign languages: French

Reviews
Book review editor: Douglas Auld
Address: same as above
Seeking reviewers: yes
Unsolicited reviews accepted: yes
How to apply: letter of inquiry
Include in application: professional degrees, institutional affiliation, areas of expertise, published works, foreign languages, current research

Materials reviewed: books, government documents
Length of review: 500 words maximum

Additional notes
Simultaneous submission is not allowed. Articles are published 3 months after acceptance.

CANADIAN REVIEW OF AMERICAN STUDIES

Focus: American society, culture, history, and the arts; interdisciplinary studies of the Americas; Canadian-American cultural relations
Institutional affiliation: Canadian Association for American Studies
Editor: submit to the Editors
Editorial address:
Department of English
University of Manitoba
Winnipeg, Manitoba RT3 2N2
CANADA
Frequency: 3/year
Circulation: 600
Subscription rate(s): institutional $12, members $15
Pages/issue: not given
Readership: academics
Indexed/abstracted in: Hist Abstr, Amer Hist and Life, SSCI, MLA, Abstr Pop Cult

Manuscripts
Query: no
Abstract: no
Style guide: MLA
Preferred length: 3,000–10,000 words
Number of copies: 2
Notes: end of manuscript
Blind referee: no
Time to consider manuscript: 3–8 weeks
Proportion of manuscripts accepted: not given
Illustrations accepted: photos, drawings
Foreign languages: French

Reviews
Book review editor: submit to the Editors
Address: same as above
Unsolicited reviews accepted: rarely
Materials reviewed: books
Length of review: review essays of 10–15 pages

Additional notes
Simultaneous submission is not permitted. Articles are published 9–12 months after acceptance.

CANADIAN REVIEW OF STUDIES IN NATIONALISM

Focus: nationalism and cognate topics
Institutional affiliation: University of Prince Edward Island
Editor: Andrew Robb
Editorial address:
University of Prince Edward Island
Charlottetown, P.E.I. C1A 4P3
CANADA
Frequency: 2/year plus annotated bibliography
Circulation: 500
Subscription rate(s): student $5, all others $9
Pages/issue: 160
Readership: academics
Indexed/abstracted in: ABC POL SCI

Manuscripts
Query: no
Abstract: no
Style guide: MOS
Preferred length: 25–35 pages
Number of copies: 2
Notes: end of manuscript
Blind referee: yes
Time to consider manuscript: 1–3 months
Proportion of manuscripts accepted: 25 percent
Illustrations accepted: tables, graphs, charts
Foreign languages: French, German

Reviews

Book review editor: Reginald C. Stuart
Address: same as above
Seeking reviewers: yes
Unsolicited reviews accepted: no
How to apply: letter of inquiry
Include in application: professional degrees, institutional affiliation, areas of expertise, published works, foreign languages, current research
Materials reviewed: books
Length of review: 900 words

Additional notes

Royalties are paid. Simultaneous submission is not accepted. Articles are published 6–18 months after acceptance.

CANADIAN SLAVONIC PAPERS

Focus: Soviet Union and Eastern Europe
Institutional affiliation: Canadian Association of Slavists
Editor: R. C. Elwood
Editorial address:
256 Paterson Hall
Carleton University
Ottawa, Ontario K1S 5B6
CANADA
Frequency: 4/year
Circulation: 1,000
Subscription rate(s): student $7.50, members $17
Pages/issue: 150
Readership: academics
Indexed/abstracted in: not given

Manuscripts

Query: no
Abstract: yes, after acceptance
Style guide: available on request
Preferred length: 35 pages maximum
Number of copies: 2
Notes: end of manuscript
Blind referee: no
Time to consider manuscript: 3 months

Proportion of manuscripts accepted: 25 percent
Illustrations accepted: camera-ready tables, graphs, charts
Foreign languages: French

Reviews

Book review editor: J. L. Black
Address: same as above
Seeking reviewers: yes
Unsolicited reviews accepted: no
How to apply: special form
Include in application: institutional affiliation, areas of expertise, foreign languages
Materials reviewed: books
Length of review: 500 words

Additional notes

Simultaneous submission is not allowed. Articles appear within 1 year of acceptance.

CARIBBEAN QUARTERLY

Focus: interdisciplinary journal concerned with the culture, politics, society, economics, and life of the Caribbean region
Institutional affiliation: Department of Extra-Mural Studies, University of the West Indies
Editors: Rex M. Nettleford, Janet Lia Terry
Editorial address:
Department of Extra Mural Studies
University of the West Indies
P.O. Box 42
Mona, Kingston 7
JAMAICA
Frequency: 4/year
Circulation: 1,500
Subscription rate(s): $22
Pages/issue: 100
Readership: social scientists and students interested in the Caribbean region
Indexed/abstracted in: not given

Manuscripts

Query: no, but advisable
Abstract: yes

Style guide: available on request
Preferred length: 10,000 words maximum
Number of copies: 2
Notes: end of manuscript
Blind referee: yes
Time to consider manuscript: 6–12 months
Proportion of manuscripts accepted: not given
Illustrations accepted: tables, photos
Foreign languages: no

Reviews
Book review editor: submit to the Editors
Address: same as above
Materials reviewed: books
Length of review: 2,000 words maximum

Additional notes
Simultaneous submission is permitted if editors are notified of such at the time of submission. Articles are published 2 years after acceptance. A brief biography should accompany each submission.

CARIBBEAN REVIEW

Focus: the culture and ideals of the Caribbean and Latin America
Editor: Barry B. Levine
Editorial address:
   Florida International University
   Tamiami Trail
   Miami, FL 33199
Frequency: 4/year
Circulation: 2,000
Subscription rate(s): United States $12, Caribbean, Latin America, and Canada $18, elsewhere $24
Pages/issue: 68
Readership: general public, academics
Indexed/abstracted in: Amer Hist and Life, Hisp Amer Per Ind, Hist Abstr, USPSD

Manuscripts
Query: no
Abstract: no
Style guide: see current issue
Preferred length: no preference
Number of copies: 1
Notes: not given
Blind referee: no
Time to consider manuscript: not given
Proportion of manuscripts accepted: not given
Illustrations accepted: photos, drawings, maps
Foreign languages: no

Reviews
The *Review* publishes a listing of current books on the Caribbean and Latin America.

CARIBBEAN STUDIES

Focus: interdisciplinary journal of Caribbean studies, focusing on the social sciences and humanities
Institutional affiliation: Institute of Caribbean Studies, University of Puerto Rico, Rio Piedras Campus
Editor: submit to the Editor
Editorial address:
   P.O. Box BM
   University Station
   Rio Piedras, Puerto Rico 00931
Frequency: 4/year
Circulation: 1,200
Subscription rate(s): individual $16, institutional $25
Pages/issue: 140
Readership: social scientists and students interested in the Caribbean area
Indexed/abstracted in: Hist Abstr, Amer Hist and Life

Manuscripts
Query: no
Abstract: yes, 250 words
Style guide: MOS
Preferred length: 25–30 pages
Number of copies: 3, double-spaced
Notes: end of manuscript

Blind referee: no
Time to consider manuscript: 6
months
**Proportion of manuscripts
accepted:** not given
Illustrations accepted: tables, figures
Foreign languages: Spanish, French

Reviews
Book review editor: submit to the
Editor
Address: same as above
Materials reviewed: books
Length of review: 3–4 pages

Additional notes
Simultaneous submission is not
permitted. Articles appear 1 year after
acceptance.

THE CATO JOURNAL

Focus: applied public policy
Institutional affiliation: Cato Institute
Editor: Robert L. Formaini
Editorial address:
747 Front Street
San Francisco, CA 94111
Frequency: 2/year
Circulation: not given
Subscription rate(s): $10
Pages/issue: 300
Readership: academics
Indexed/abstracted in: ABC POL
SCI, Amer Hist and Life, Hist Abstr

Manuscripts
Query: no
Abstract: no
Style guide: available on request
Preferred length: 10–15 pages
Number of copies: 2
Notes: bottom of page
Blind referee: no
Time to consider manuscript: not
given
**Proportion of manuscripts
accepted:** not given
Illustrations accepted: tables,
graphs, charts
Foreign languages: no

Reviews
not applicable

Additional notes
Articles should focus on specific issues
in public policy rather than on general
theory.

CENTERPOINT: A JOURNAL OF INTERDISCIPLINARY STUDIES

Focus: interdisciplinary articles in the
sciences, social sciences, and
humanities
Institutional affiliation: City University
of New York and Queens College
Press
Editor: Akiva Kaminsky
Editorial address:
33 West 42nd Street
New York, NY 10036
Frequency: 2–4/year
Circulation: 1,000
Subscription rate(s): individual $10,
institutional $14
Pages/issue: 96
Readership: scholars, libraries
Indexed/abstracted in: not given

Manuscripts
Query: yes
Abstract: yes, on acceptance
Style guide: MLA or MOS
Preferred length: 8–12 pages
Number of copies: 3
Notes: end of manuscript
Blind referee: no
Time to consider manuscript: 3–6
months
**Proportion of manuscripts
accepted:** 15–20 percent
Illustrations accepted: tables,
graphs, charts, photos
Foreign languages: Spanish, French,
German, Italian

Reviews
Book review editor: Toni Kamins
Address: same as above
Seeking reviewers: yes
Unsolicited reviews accepted: no

How to apply: letter of inquiry
Include in application: professional
degrees, institutional affiliation, areas
of expertise, published works,
foreign languages, current research
Materials reviewed: books, films
Length of review: 300 words

THE CHINA QUARTERLY

Focus: China since 1949
Institutional affiliation: Contemporary
China Institute
Editor: Brian Hook
Editorial address:
School of Oriental and African
Studies
Malet Street
London WC1E 7HP
ENGLAND
Frequency: 4/year
Circulation: 4,700
Subscription rate(s): $30
Pages/issue: 160
Readership: academics
Indexed/abstracted in: ABC POL SCI

Manuscripts
Query: no
Abstract: no
Style guide: available on request
Preferred length: 8,000–10,000 words
Number of copies: 3, double-spaced
Notes: not given
Blind referee: no
Time to consider manuscript: 2–8
weeks
Proportion of manuscripts
accepted: not given
Illustrations accepted: tables,
graphs, charts, maps
Foreign languages: no

Reviews
Book review editor: Brian Hook
Address: same as above
Materials reviewed: books
Length of review: 2–3 pages

Additional notes
Simultaneous submission is not
permitted. Articles appear 3–12 months
after acceptance.

THE CITIZEN

Focus: a conservative view of the civil
rights revolution
Institutional affiliation: Citizens
Councils of America
Editors: Medford Evans, George W.
Shannon
Editorial address:
Box 1675
Jackson, MS 39205
Frequency: 12/year
Circulation: 10,000
Subscription rate(s): $10
Pages/issue: 32
Readership: general public,
universities, public officials,
lawmakers, teachers
Indexed/abstracted in: not given

Manuscripts
Query: yes
Abstract: no
Style guide: none required
Preferred length: 4–8 pages
Number of copies: 1, double-spaced
Notes: end of manuscript
Blind referee: no
Time to consider manuscript: 4–6
weeks
Proportion of manuscripts
accepted: 50 percent
Illustrations accepted: charts,
photos, maps
Foreign languages: no

Reviews
Book review editor: George W.
Shannon
Address: same as above
Seeking reviewers: no
Unsolicited reviews accepted: no
How to apply: letter of inquiry
Include in application: areas of
expertise, published works
Materials reviewed: books
Length of review: 4 pages maximum

Additional notes
Contributors should familiarize
themselves with publication by
examining several issues.

CITY AND TOWN

Focus: urban and municipal affairs; coverage is local, state, and national with emphasis on pertinent congressional actions
Institutional affiliation: Arkansas Municipal League
Editor: Harry J. Hamner
Editorial address:
P.O. Box 38
North Little Rock, AR 72115
Frequency: 10/year
Circulation: 6,000
Subscription rate(s): $15
Pages/issue: 28
Readership: academics, public officials at all levels of government, press, business people

Manuscripts
Query: no
Abstract: no
Style guide: MFW
Preferred length: 2,000 words maximum
Number of copies: 1
Notes: end of manuscript
Blind referee: no
Time to consider manuscript: 1 month
Proportion of manuscripts accepted: 50 percent
Illustrations accepted: tables, graphs, charts, photos, drawings
Foreign languages: no

Reviews
Book review editor: Harry J. Hamner
Address: same as above
Seeking reviewers: no
Unsolicited reviews accepted: yes
Include in application: professional degrees, institutional affiliation, areas of expertise, published works, foreign languages, current research
Materials reviewed: books
Length of review: 1,500 words maximum

Additional notes
Submitted manuscripts should be brief and strictly relevant to municipal affairs and urban problems.

COALITION CLOSE-UP

Focus: foreign and military policy
Institutional affiliation: Coalition for a New Foreign and Military Policy
Editor: Cynthia Washington
Editorial address:
120 Maryland Avenue, NE
Washington, DC 20002
Frequency: 4/year
Circulation: 13,000–15,000
Subscription rate(s): $20
Pages/issue: 12–16
Readership: general public, social activists, lobbyists
Indexed/abstracted in: Pub Issues Ind

Manuscripts
Query: yes
Abstract: yes
Style guide: MFW
Preferred length: 5–8 pages
Number of copies: 2
Notes: bottom of page
Blind referee: no
Time to consider manuscript: 1 month
Proportion of manuscripts accepted: 10 percent
Illustrations accepted: tables, graphs, charts, photos, drawings
Foreign languages: no

Reviews
Book review editors: Gene Carroll, Howard Morland
Address: same as above
Seeking reviewers: no
Unsolicited reviews accepted: no
Materials reviewed: books, films, tapes, slide shows, filmstrips

Additional notes
Coalition Close-Up does not do formal reviews, only short blurbs in the "New Resources " section.

CO-EXISTENCE

Focus: an international, interdisciplinary journal for the comparative study of politics, sociology, economics, and law
Editor: submit to the Editors
Editorial address:
9/11 Southpark Terrace
Glasgow G12 8LQ
SCOTLAND
Frequency: 2/year
Circulation: not given
Subscription rate(s): institutional £20
Pages/issue: 125
Readership: social scientists
Indexed/abstracted in: ABC POL SCI, Hist Abstr, Amer Hist and Life

Manuscripts
Query: no
Abstract: no
Style guide: available on request
Preferred length: no preference
Number of copies: 1
Notes: end of manuscript
Blind referee: no
Time to consider manuscript: not given
Proportion of manuscripts accepted: not given
Illustrations accepted: tables, graphs, charts
Foreign languages: French, German, Italian, Russian

Reviews
Book review editor: submit to the Editors
Address: same as above
Materials reviewed: books
Length of review: 2–3 pages

COLUMBIA JOURNAL OF TRANSNATIONAL LAW

Focus: public and private international law; comparative and foreign law
Institutional affiliation: Columbia University School of Law
Editors: John A. Bick, J. Clark Kelso, Neil E. McDonell
Editorial address:
Columbia University School of Law
435 West 116th Street, Box 8
New York, NY 10027
Frequency: 3/year
Circulation: 1,000
Subscription rate(s): domestic $18, foreign $19
Pages/issue: 200
Readership: scholars, attorneys in the field of transnational law
Indexed/abstracted in: Per Guide Leg Lit

Manuscripts
Query: no
Abstract: no, but helpful
Style guide: HLRA
Preferred length: 40 pages
Number of copies: 2, triple-spaced
Notes: end of manuscript,
Blind referee: no
Time to consider manuscript: 2–4 weeks
Proportion of manuscripts accepted: 10–15 percent
Illustrations accepted: tables, graphs, charts, photos, drawings
Foreign languages: no

Reviews
Book review editor: Victoria Bjorklund
Address: same as above
Seeking reviewers: yes
Unsolicited reviews accepted: yes
How to apply: letter of inquiry
Include in application: professional degrees, institutional affiliation, areas of expertise, published works
Materials reviewed: books
Length of review: 15 pages

Additional notes
Accuracy and clarity are crucial. A $50 royalty is paid for republication of the article elsewhere. Book reviews are signed. Simultaneous submission is not permitted. Articles appear 2–12 months after acceptance.

COLUMBIA LAW REVIEW

Focus: scholarly articles of professional interest by academic authors and practicing lawyers; notes and comments by students
Institutional affiliation: Columbia University School of Law
Editors: Susan Charles, Richard Hahn
Editorial address:
435 West 116th Street
New York, NY 10027
Frequency: 8/year
Circulation: 4,000
Subscription rate(s): $28
Pages/issue: 200
Readership: academics, law firms
Indexed/abstracted in: not given

Manuscripts
Query: no
Abstract: no
Style guide: HLRA, GPO
Preferred length: no preference
Number of copies: 1
Notes: end of manuscript
Blind referee: no
Time to consider manuscript: 2–3 weeks
Proportion of manuscripts accepted: 5 percent
Illustrations accepted: tables, graphs, charts, photos, drawings
Foreign languages: no

Reviews
Book review editor: Daniel Troy
Address: same as above
Seeking reviewers: yes
Unsolicited reviews accepted: yes
How to apply: letter of inquiry
Include in application: professional degrees, institutional affiliation, published works
Materials reviewed: books
Length of review: 3,500–6,500 words

Additional notes
Simultaneous submission is allowed.
Publication time after acceptance varies.

COMMON MARKET LAW REVIEW

Focus: serves as a medium for the understanding and implementation of community law within the Common Market; also serves to promote and disseminate legal thinking on legal matters within the community
Editor: submit to the Editors
Editorial address:
Europa Institute
Hugo de Grootstraat 27
2311 XK Leyden
THE NETHERLANDS
Frequency: not given
Circulation: 1,700
Subscription rate(s): $90
Pages/issue: 153
Readership: lawyers, legal scholars, academics
Indexed/abstracted in: Foreign Leg Per

Manuscripts
Query: no
Abstract: no
Style guide: see current issue or write for guidelines
Preferred length: 3,000–10,000 words
Number of copies: 2
Notes: end of manuscript
Blind referee: yes
Time to consider manuscript: 8–12 weeks
Proportion of manuscripts accepted: not given
Illustrations accepted: not given
Foreign languages: no

Reviews
Book review editor: submit to the Editors
Address: same as above
Materials reviewed: books
Length of review: 3–4 pages

Additional notes
Simultaneous submission is not allowed.
Articles should be submitted with a covering letter and a brief biography.

COMPARATIVE POLITICAL STUDIES

Focus: issues of general theoretical and/or empirical interest for comparative research in politics
Editor: James A. Caporaso
Editorial address:
Graduate School of International Studies
University of Denver
Denver, CO 80208
Frequency: 4/year
Circulation: 2,000
Subscription rate(s): individual $22, institutional $46
Pages/issue: 130
Readership: academics in political science and sociology
Indexed/abstracted in: Int Polit Sci Abstr, Sage Urb Stud Abstr, Sociol Abstr, ABC POL SCI, Human Resour Abstr, Eth Stud Bibl, PAIS, Curr Cont, SSCI, Universal Ref Syst, Soc Sci Ind, USPSD

Manuscripts
Query: no
Abstract: yes
Style guide: SAGE
Preferred length: 25–35 pages
Number of copies: 3
Notes: end of manuscript
Blind referee: yes
Time to consider manuscript: 2–3 months
Proportion of manuscripts accepted: 25 percent
Illustrations accepted: tables, graphs, charts, drawings
Foreign languages: no

Reviews
Seeking reviewers: no
Unsolicited reviews accepted: no

Additional notes
Manuscripts should focus on issues relating to comparative, cross-national research. Most published manuscripts are based on systematic, empirical research, but some essays are also published.

COMPARATIVE POLITICS

Focus: comparative analysis of political institutions and behavior
Institutional affiliation: Political Science Program of the City University of New York
Editor: Ruth Davis
Editorial address:
City University of New York
Graduate Center
33 West 42nd Street
New York, NY 10036
Frequency: 4/year
Circulation: not given
Subscription rate(s): individual $15, institutional $25
Pages/issue: 128
Indexed/abstracted in: ABC POL SCI, Hist Abstr, Amer Hist and Life, USPSD, Int Polit Sci Abstr, PAIS, Soc Sci Ind

Manuscripts
Query: no
Abstract: no
Style guide: MOS
Preferred length: 30–35 pages maximum; research notes 20 pages maximum
Number of copies: 3
Notes: end of manuscript
Blind referee: yes
Time to consider manuscript: not given
Proportion of manuscripts accepted: not given
Illustrations accepted: tables, graphs, charts
Foreign languages: no

Reviews
Book review editor: Ezra Suleiman
Address:
Department of Politics
Princeton University
Princeton, NJ 08544
Seeking reviewers: yes
Unsolicited reviews accepted: no
How to apply: letter of inquiry
Include in application: professional degrees, institutional affiliation, areas of expertise, published works
Materials reviewed: books

Additional notes

Simultaneous submission is not allowed. Most articles are published 1 year after acceptance.

COMPARATIVE STRATEGY

Focus: political, military, and economic perspectives of international strategic issues
Editor: Richard B. Foster
Editorial address:
SRI International
1611 North Kent Street
Rosslyn Plaza
Arlington, VA 22209
Frequency: 4/year
Circulation: 1,000
Subscription rate (s): $48
Pages/issue: 100
Readership: professionals, academics, graduate students
Indexed/abstracted in: Abstr Mil Bibl, Int Polit Sci Abstr, Mon List Sel Art, Curr Cont, SSCI, USPSD

Manuscripts

Query: not given
Abstract: yes, 150 words maximum
Style Guide: MOS, HLRA for legal articles
Preferred length: no preference
Number of copies: 3
Notes: not given
Time to consider manuscript: not given
Proportion of manuscripts accepted: not given
Illustrations accepted: tables, graphs, charts, photos, drawings
Foreign languages: no

Reviews

Book review editor: Richard B. Foster
Address: same as above
Materials reviewed: books

Additional notes

Simultaneous submission is not permitted. Article titles should be kept brief, 6–12 words if possible.

COMPARATIVE STUDIES IN SOCIETY AND HISTORY

Focus: original research into the problems of change and stability in human societies through time or in the contemporary world
Institutional affiliation: Cambridge University Press
Editor: Raymond Grew
Editorial address:
Department of History
University of Michigan
Ann Arbor, MI 48109
Frequency: 4/year
Circulation: 2,500
Subscription rate(s): student $16, individual $25, institutional $49
Pages/issue: 160–180
Readership: social scientists
Indexed/abstracted in: ABC POL SCI, Amer Hist and Life, Hist Abstr

Manuscripts

Query: yes
Abstract: no
Style guide: available on request
Preferred length: 10,000–12,000 words
Number of copies: 2
Notes: end of manuscript
Blind referee: no
Time to consider manuscript: 3–6 months
Proportion of manuscripts accepted: 12 percent
Illustrations accepted: tables, graphs, photos, drawings
Foreign languages: no

Reviews

Book review editors: Aram A. Yengoyon, Geoff Eley, Sylvia Thrupp
Address: same as above
Seeking reviewers: yes
Unsolicited reviews accepted: no
How to apply: letter of inquiry
Include in application: professional degrees, institutional affiliation, areas of expertise, published works, current research
Materials reviewed: books
Length of review: 600–800 words, review essays 8–10 pages

Additional notes

Contributors will receive 50 offprints of articles published. Simultaneous submission is not allowed. Articles are published 6–18 months after acceptance.

COMPARATIVE URBAN RESEARCH

Focus: an international, interdisciplinary journal, of news and ideas devoted to facilitating communication among scholars and others interested in the study of urbanization and urban areas throughout the world
Institutional affiliation: University of Maryland
Editor: William John Hanna
Editorial address:
College of Human Ecology
University of Maryland
College Park, MD 20742
Frequency: 2/year
Circulation: 800
Subscription rate(s): individual $8, institutional $13
Pages/issue: 140
Readership: academics
Indexed/abstracted in: Int Bibl Soc Sci, USPSD, SAGE Urb Stud Abstr, Universal Ref Syst, Abstr Anthropol, Int Polit Sci Abstr

Manuscripts

Query: no
Abstract: no
Style guide: available on request
Preferred length: 20–50 pages
Number of copies: 3, double-spaced
Notes: end of manuscript
Blind referee: yes
Time to consider manuscript: 3–4 months
Proportion of manuscripts accepted: 25 percent
Illustrations accepted: tables, graphs, charts, photos, drawings
Foreign languages: no

Reviews

Book review editor: William John Hanna
Address: same as above
Seeking reviewers: no
Unsolicited reviews accepted: no
Materials reviewed: books
Length of review: 1,000–2,000 words

Additional notes

Narrowly focused empirical research reports are not accepted for publication. Manuscripts offering new theoretical approaches are especially sought. Simultaneous submission is not permitted. Articles are published within 1 year of acceptance.

CONFLICT: ALL WARFARE SHORT OF WAR

Focus: conflicts short of formal war, including guerrilla warfare, insurgency, revolution, unconventional warfare, terrorism, and nonphysical conflicts
Editor: George K. Tanham
Editorial address:
The Rand Corporation
2100 M Street, NW
Washington, DC 20037
Frequency: 4/year
Circulation: 1,000
Subscription rate(s): $60
Pages/issue: 100
Readership: professionals, academics, graduate students
Indexed/abstracted in: Abstr Mil Bibl, Amer Hist and Life, Curr Cont, Hist Abstr, Int Polit Sci Abstr, Morr List Sel Art, Pub Admin Abstr, SSCI, USPSD

Manuscripts

Query: not given
Abstract: yes, 150 words maximum
Style Guide: MOS, HLRA for legal articles
Preferred length: no preference
Number of copies: 3
Notes: not given
Blind referee: not given

Time to consider manuscript: not given

Proportion of manuscripts accepted: not given

Illustrations accepted: tables, graphs, charts, photos, drawings

Foreign languages: no

Reviews

Book review editor: George K. Tanham

Address: same as above

Materials reviewed: books

Additional notes

Simultaneous submission is not permitted. Article titles should be kept brief, 6–12 words if possible.

CONGRESS AND THE PRESIDENCY

Focus: the presidency and Congress; national policy-making

Institutional affiliation: Center for Congressional and Presidential Studies, The American University

Editors: Jeff Fishel, Susan Webb Hammond

Editorial address:
Center for Congressional and Presidential Studies
The American University
Washington, DC 20016

Frequency: 2/year

Circulation: 600

Subscription rate(s): individual $10, institutional $12

Pages/issue: 100–125

Readership: academics

Indexed/abstracted in: ABC POL SCI, Amer Hist and Life, Hist Abstr, Int Polit Sci Abstr

Manuscripts

Query: no

Abstract: no

Style guide: available on request

Preferred length: 20–40 pages

Number of copies: 3

Notes: end of manuscript

Blind referee: no

Time to consider manuscript: 3 months

Proportion of manuscripts accepted: 15 percent

Illustrations accepted: tables, graphs, charts

Foreign languages: no

Reviews

Book review editor: Roger H. Davidson

Address: same as above

Seeking reviewers: yes

Unsolicited reviews accepted: no

How to apply: letter of inquiry

Include in application: professional degrees, institutional affiliation, areas of expertise, published works, current research

Materials reviewed: books

Length of review: 500–1,000 words

CONGRESS MONTHLY

Focus: political, social, economic, and cultural issues of interest to the Jewish community

Institutional affiliation: American Jewish Congress

Editor: Nancy Miller

Editorial address:
15 East 84th Street
New York, NY 10028

Frequency: 8/year

Circulation: 30,000

Subscription rate(s): $5

Pages/issue: 24

Readership: educated Jewish, politically, culturally active, but popular, audience

Indexed/abstracted in: Ind Jew Per

Manuscripts

Query: no

Abstract: no

Style guide: none required

Preferred length: 1,000 words

Number of copies: 1

Notes: end of manuscript

Blind referee: no

Time to consider manuscript: 6–8 weeks

**Proportion of manuscripts
accepted:** less than 10 percent
Illustrations accepted: tables,
graphs, charts, photos, drawings
Foreign languages: French, translated
at author's expense

Reviews
Book review editor: Nancy Miller
Address: same as above
Seeking reviewers: yes
Unsolicited reviews accepted: yes
How to apply: send review or
telephone
Include in application: institutional
affiliation, areas of expertise,
published works, current researach
Materials reviewed: books, films,
museum shows
Length of review: 750–1,000 words

Additional notes
Read the magazine first. Even if an
article is well-researched and well-written
it will not be accepted if it is too far
afield from the magazine's subject and
purpose. Please do not fold manuscripts
When in doubt as to style, check the
New York Times Style Book.

CONSERVATIVE DIGEST

Focus: conservative political and social
issues
Institutional affiliation: The Viguerie
Company
Editor: Susan Longyear
Editorial address:
7777 Leesburg Pike
Falls Church, VA 22043
Frequency: 12/year
Circulation: 65,000
Subscription rate(s): $15
Pages/issue: 48
Readership: general public
Indexed/abstracted in: not given

Manuscripts
Query: yes
Abstract: no
Style guide: none required
Preferred length: 1,000 words

Number of copies: 1
Notes: bottom of page
Blind referee: no
Time to consider manuscript: 3
weeks
**Proportion of manuscripts
accepted:** 1 percent
Illustrations accepted: tables,
graphs, charts, photos, drawings
Foreign languages: no

Reviews
Book review editor: Frank Gannon
Address: same as above
Seeking reviewers: yes
Unsolicited reviews accepted: yes
How to apply: letter of inquiry
Materials reviewed: books, films
Length of review: 850 words

CONTEMPORARY FRENCH
CIVILIZATION

Focus: interdisciplinary studies of
French-speaking cultures throughout
the world
Editor: Bernard J. Quinn
Editorial address:
Department of Languages
University of South Alabama
Mobile, AL 36688
Frequency: 3/year
Circulation: 900
Subscription rate(s): domestic $12,
Canada and overseas $14
Pages/issue: 130
Readership: academics
Indexed/abstracted in: ERIC

Manuscripts
Query: no
Abstract: no
Style guide: MLA
Preferred length: 20 pages maximum
Number of copies: 3
Notes: end of article
Blind referee: no
Time to consider manuscript: 6
months
**Proportion of manuscripts
accepted:** not given

Illustrations accepted: tables, graphs, charts
Foreign languages: French

Reviews
Book review editor: Pierre Aubéry
Address:
Department of Modern Languages
and Literatures
Amherst Campus
State University of New York
Buffalo, NY 14260
Seeking reviewers: yes
Unsolicited reviews accepted: yes
How to apply: not necessary
Materials reviewed: books
Length of review: 3 pages maximum, 4–8 pages for review articles

Additional notes
Simultaneous submission is not permitted. Articles are published 6 months after acceptance.

CONTRIBUTIONS TO ASIAN STUDIES

Focus: scholarly analyses of Asian societies and cultures, past and contemporary, from the diverse standpoints of scholars in all the social sciences and humanities
Institutional affiliation: Canadian Association for South Asian Studies
Editor: K. Ishwaran
Editorial address:
Department of Sociology and
Anthropology
York University
Toronto, Ontario M3J 1P3
CANADA
Frequency: 2/year
Circulation: not given
Subscription rate(s): $16
Pages/issue: 150
Readership: academics
Indexed/abstracted in: not given

Manuscripts
Query: no
Abstract: no
Style guide: available on request

Preferred length: 15–20 pages
Number of copies: 2
Notes: end of manuscript
Blind referee: no
Time to consider manuscript: 1–2 months
Proportion of manuscripts accepted: not given
Illustrations accepted: tables, graphs, charts, photos, drawings, maps
Foreign languages: no

Reviews
not applicable

Additional notes
Simultaneous submission is not allowed. Articles are published 1 year after acceptance.

COOPERATION AND CONFLICT: NORDIC JOURNAL OF INTERNATIONAL POLITICS

Focus: international political and economic issues
Institutional affiliation: Nordic Cooperation Committee for International Politics
Editor: Christer Jönsson
Editorial address:
Department of Political Science
University of Lund
P.O. Box 5131
S-22005 Lund
SWEDEN
Frequency: 4/year
Circulation: 600
Subscription rate(s): individual $17, institutional $22
Pages/issue: 70–80
Readership: academics
Indexed/abstracted in: Int Polit Sci Abstr, ABC POL SCI, Hist Abstr, CRIS

Manuscripts
Query: no
Abstract: no

Style guide: see current issue or write for guidelines
Preferred length: no preference
Number of copies: 2
Notes: end of manuscript
Blind referee: no
Time to consider manuscript: not given
Proportion of manuscripts accepted: not given
Illustrations accepted: tables, graphs, charts
Foreign languages: no

Reviews
not applicable

CORNELL INTERNATIONAL LAW JOURNAL

Focus: public and private international law
Institutional affiliation: Cornell University Law School
Editor: Robert C. Kirsch
Editorial address:
Cornell International Law School
Cornell Law School
Myron Taylor Hall
Ithaca, NY 14853
Frequency: 2/year
Circulation: 800
Subscription rate(s): domestic $7.50, foreign $9
Pages/issue: 400
Readership: legal professionals and students, academics
Indexed/abstracted in: Leg Per, Foreign Leg Per, SSCI

Manuscripts
Query: no
Abstract: not given
Style guide: HLRA
Preferred length: 15–25 pages
Number of copies: 1
Notes: end of manuscript
Blind referee: no
Time to consider manuscript: 3 weeks
Proportion of manuscripts accepted: not given

Illustrations accepted: not given
Foreign languages: no

Reviews
Book review editor: Robert C. Kirsch
Address: same as above
Materials reviewed: books

Additional notes
Simultaneous submission is permitted. Articles are published 4 months after acceptance.

CORNELL LAW REVIEW

Focus: legal studies
Institutional affiliation: Cornell University
Editors: Ernest Schmider, Sharyl Walker
Editorial address:
Myron Taylor Hall
Cornell Law School
Ithaca, NY 14853
Frequency: 6/year
Circulation: 3,500
Subscription rate(s): $18
Pages/issue: 225
Readership: legal professionals and students
Indexed/abstracted in: Leg Per, SSCI, PAIS

Manuscripts
Query: no
Abstract: no
Style guide: none required
Number of copies: 1
Notes: bottom of page
Blind referee: no
Time to consider manuscript: 2–4 weeks
Proportion of manuscripts accepted: 3.5 percent
Illustrations accepted: tables, graphs, charts
Foreign languages: no

Reviews
Book review editor: Mark Sugino
Address: same as above
Seeking reviewers: yes

Unsolicited reviews accepted: yes
How to apply: letter of inquiry
Include in application: professional degrees, institutional affiliation, areas of expertise, published works
Materials reviewed: books

THE CRISIS: A RECORD OF THE DARKER RACES

Focus: the status of civil rights and race relations in the United States and abroad
Institutional affiliation: National Association for the Advancement of Colored People
Editor: Chester A. Higgins, Sr.
Editorial address:
1790 Broadway
New York, NY 10019
Frequency: 10/year
Circulation: 115,000
Subscription rate(s): domestic $6, foreign $7
Pages/issue: 50
Readership: general public, academics
Indexed/abstracted in: Amer Hist and Life, Amer Hum Ind, CIJE, Hist Abstr, Ind Per Negroes, Soc Sci Ind

Manuscripts
Query: no
Abstract: no
Style guide: none required
Preferred length: 1,500–2,000 words
Number of copies: 1
Notes: not given
Blind referee: no
Time to consider manuscript: 3–4 weeks
Proportion of manuscripts accepted: not given
Illustrations accepted: tables, photos, drawings, maps
Foreign languages: no

Reviews
Book review editor: Chester A. Higgins, Sr.
Address: same as above

Materials reviewed: books, films, records
Length of review: 3–5 pages

Additional notes
Simultaneous submission is not allowed. Articles are published 3 months after acceptance.

CRITIQUE: A JOURNAL OF SOVIET STUDIES AND SOCIALIST THOUGHT

Focus: the Soviet Union and Eastern Europe; the development of Marxist thought
Editor: submit to the Editor
Editorial address:
31 Cleveden Road
Glasgow G12 OPH
SCOTLAND
Frequency: 2/year
Circulation: 5,000
Subscription rate(s): $7
Pages/issue: 150–170
Readership: academics
Indexed/abstracted in: Hist Abstr

Manuscripts
Query: no
Abstract: no
Style guide: see current issue or write for guidelines
Preferred length: 10,000 words maximum
Number of copies: 3
Notes: bottom of page
Blind referee: no
Time to consider manuscript: 3 months
Proportion of manuscripts accepted: not given
Illustrations accepted: tables, graphs, charts
Foreign languages: no

Reviews
Book review editor: submit to the Editor
Address: same as above
Materials reviewed: books
Length of review: 3–5 pages

Additional notes

Simultaneous submission is not permitted. Articles are published within 1 year of acceptance.

CRITIQUE: SOUTHERN CALIFORNIA PUBLIC POLICY AND ADMINISTRATION

Focus: public administration; local government
Institutional affiliation: Center for Public Policy and Administration, California State University, Long Beach
Editor: William C. Manes
Editorial address:
Center for Public Policy and Administration
California State University
1250 Bellflower Boulevard
Long Beach, CA 90840
Frequency: 4/year
Circulation: sponsoring organizations, students, libraries, cities
Subscription rate(s): $10
Pages/issue: 40
Readership: professionals, academics in public administration
Indexed/abstracted in: PAIS

Manuscripts

Query: no
Abstract: no
Style guide: available on request
Preferred length: 1,000–10,000 words
Number of copies: minimum 1, prefer 6
Notes: not given
Blind referee: no
Time to consider manuscript: 1 month
Proportion of manuscripts accepted: over 50 percent
Illustrations accepted: tables, graphs, charts, photos, drawings
Foreign languages: no

Reviews

Book review editor: Harry L. Huggins
Address: same as above
Seeking reviewers: yes

Unsolicited reviews accepted: yes
How to apply: letter of inquiry
Include in application: areas of expertise
Materials reviewed: books
Length of review: 1,000 words minimum

CUBAN STUDIES/ESTUDIOS CUBANOS

Focus: contemporary Cuba
Institutional affiliation: Center for Latin American Studies, University of Pittsburgh
Editor: June S. Belkin
Editorial address:
Center for Latin American Studies
University of Pittsburgh
Pittsburgh, PA 15260
Frequency: 6/year
Circulation: 1,000
Subscription rate(s):   individual $8, institutional $16
Pages/issue: 140
Readership: academics, students, others interested in Cuba
Indexed/abstracted in: ABC POL SCI, Amer Hist and Life, Hist Abstr

Manuscripts

Query: no
Abstract: no
Style guide: MLA
Preferred length: 40 pages maximum
Number of copies: 2
Notes: end of manuscript
Blind referee: no
Time to consider manuscript: 6–8 weeks
Proportion of manuscripts accepted: 25 percent
Illustrations accepted: tables, graphs, charts
Foreign languages: Spanish

Reviews

Book review editor: Harold D. Sims
Address: same as above
Seeking reviewers: yes
Unsolicited reviews accepted: yes
How to apply: letter of inquiry

Include in application: professional degrees, institutional affiliation, areas of expertise, published works, foreign languages, current research
Materials reviewed: books
Length of review: 2–3 pages

Additional notes

Simultaneous submission is not permitted. Articles are published 4–6 months after acceptance.

CURRENT HISTORY

Focus: political science, economics, current events
Editor: Carol L. Thompson
Editorial address:
RR1, Box 132
Furlong, PA 18925
Frequency: 9/year
Circulation: 30,000
Subscription rate(s): $20
Pages/issue: 48
Readership: academics
Indexed/abstracted in: ABC POL SCI, RG, Amer Hist and Life, Hist Abstr, PAIS, SSCI

Manuscripts

Query: yes
Abstract: no
Style guide: MOS
Preferred length: 5,000 words
Number of copies: 1
Notes: bottom of page
Blind referee: no
Time to consider manuscript: 2 months
Proportion of manuscripts accepted: not given
Illustrations accepted: tables, graphs, charts
Foreign languages: no

Reviews

Seeking reviewers: no
Unsolicited reviews accepted: no

Additional notes

No unsolicited manuscripts. Prospective authors should write or telephone.

CURRENT MUNICIPAL PROBLEMS

Focus: identify problems facing local governments and suggest solutions by examining the experience of one or more cities, counties, school boards, or other local governments
Editor: Byron S. Matthews
Editorial address:
2303 South Florence Avenue
Tulsa, OK 74114
Frequency: 4/year
Circulation: 800
Subscription rate(s): $69
Pages/issue: 125
Readership: local officials, attorneys, managers, others interested in local government
Indexed/abstracted in: not given

Manuscripts

Query: no
Abstract: no
Style guide: none required
Preferred length: no established guidelines
Number of copies: 1
Notes: end oi manuscript
Blind referee: no
Time to consider manuscript: varies
Proportion of manuscripts accepted: not given
Illustrations accepted: tables

Reviews
not applicable

Additional notes

Decision to accept an article is based on the article, not on the reputation of the author. If you work with or advise local governments, you may know of a subject that would make a timely article. What is a new trend or idea? What is being done in one locality that would be effective other places, if others could learn of it through your article? Present facts and ideas that work, not abstract theory. Avoid extensive footnotes.

CURRENT RESEARCH ON PEACE AND VIOLENCE

Focus: actual world problems are discussed from a peace research perspective
Institutional affiliation: Tampere Peace Research Institute
Editor: Tapio Varis
Editorial address:
Hämeemk 136A
P.O. Box 447 B
33101 Tampere 10
FINLAND
Frequency: 4/year
Circulation: 1,000
Subscription rate(s): individual $12.50, institutional $14
Pages/issue: not given
Readership: academics, journalists, peace activists
Indexed/abstracted in: Curr Cont, SSCI, Sociol Abstr, Int Polit Sci Abstr

Manuscripts
Query: no
Abstract: yes
Style guide: available on request
Preferred length: 15–25 pages
Number of copies: 2
Notes: not given
Blind referee: no
Time to consider manuscript: 1–12 weeks
Proportion of manuscripts accepted: not given
Illustrations accepted: tables, graphs, charts, diagrams
Foreign languages: no

Reviews
Book review editor: Tapio Varis
Address: same as above
Materials reviewed: books

Additional notes
Simultaneous submission is permitted. Articles are published 2–4 months after acceptance.

DENVER JOURNAL OF INTERNATIONAL LAW AND POLICY

Focus: international law and policy
Institutional affiliation: University of Denver, College of Law
Editor: Gina L. Swets
Editorial address:
200 West 14th Avenue
Denver, CO 80203
Frequency: 3/year
Circulation: 1,000
Subscription rate(s): student $10, domestic $15, foreign $18
Pages/issue: 175
Readership: law libraries, law firms, corporations, academics
Indexed/abstracted in: Curr Ind Leg Per, Curr Law Ind, Ind Fed Tax Art, Ind For Leg Per, Leg Per, Int Polit Sci Abstr, Law Review Digest, CCLP, PAIS

Manuscripts
Query: no
Abstract: yes
Style guide: GPO
Preferred length: 20–50 pages
Number of copies: 2
Notes: end of manuscript
Blind referee: no
Time to consider manuscript: 3 weeks
Proportion of manuscripts accepted: 10 percent
Illustrations accepted: tables, graphs, charts, photos, drawings
Foreign languages: no

Reviews
Book review editor: Gina L. Swets
Address: same as above
Seeking reviewers: yes
Unsolicited reviews accepted: yes
How to apply: letter of inquiry
Include in application: professional degrees, institutional affiliation, areas of expertise, published works, foreign languages, current research
Materials reviewed: books
Length of review: 10 pages

Additional notes
Simultaneous submission is not allowed. Articles are published 3 months after acceptance.

THE DEVELOPING ECONOMIES

Focus: an international and interdisciplinary forum for social science studies of developing countries
Institutional affiliation: Institute of Developing Economies
Editor: submit to the Secretary
Editorial address:
Institute of Developing Economies
42 Ichigaya-Hommura-chō
Shinjuku-ku, Tokyo 162
JAPAN
Frequency: 4/year
Circulation: 1,400
Subscription rate(s): $16
Pages/issue: 115
Readership: social scientists
Indexed/abstracted in: SSCI

Manuscripts
Query: no
Abstract: no
Style guide: see current issue or write for guidelines
Preferred length: 10,000 words maximum
Number of copies: 2
Notes: bottom of page
Blind referee: no
Time to consider manuscript: not given
Proportion of manuscripts accepted: not given
Illustrations accepted: tables, graphs, charts
Foreign languages: no

Reviews
Book review editor: submit to the Secretary, Institute of Developing Economies
Address: same as above

Materials reviewed: books
Length of review: see current issue or write for guidelines

DEVELOPMENT AND CHANGE

Focus: interdisciplinary approach to problems and issues of development
Institutional affiliation: Institute of Social Studies, The Hague
Editor: submit to the Editors
Editorial address:
251 Badhuisweg
2509 LS
The Hague
NETHERLANDS
Frequency: 4/year
Circulation: not given
Subscription rate(s): individual $22.50, institutional $50.40
Pages/issue: 150
Readership: social scientists
Indexed/abstracted in: ABC POL SCI, Curr Cont

Manuscripts
Query: no
Abstract: no
Style guide: available on request
Preferred length: 7,000 words
Number of copies: 1
Notes: end of manuscript
Blind referee: no
Time to consider manuscript: 3 months
Proportion of manuscripts accepted: not given
Illustrations accepted: tables, graphs, charts, drawings
Foreign languages: no

Reviews
not applicable

Additional notes
Simultaneous submission is not permitted. Articles are published 1 year after acceptance.

DIPLOMATIC HISTORY

Focus: American foreign policy, all periods

Institutional affiliation: Society for Historians of American Foreign Relations

Editor: Warren I. Cohen

Editorial address:
Department of History
Michigan State University
East Lansing, MI 48824

Frequency: 4/year

Circulation: 950

Subscription rate(s): nonmembers $30

Pages/issue: 100–110

Readership: academics, society members, libraries

Indexed/abstracted in: Hist Abst, Amer Hist and Life

Manuscripts
Query: no
Abstract: no
Style guide: MLA
Preferred length: 30 pages maximum
Number of copies: 3
Notes: end of manuscript
Blind referee: yes
Time to consider manuscript: 3–4 months
Proportion of manuscripts accepted: 20 percent
Illustrations accepted: tables, charts, maps
Foreign languages: no

Reviews
Book review editor: Warren I. Cohen
Address: same as above
Seeking reviewers: no
Unsolicited reviews accepted: yes
Materials reviewed: books
Length of review: 10 to 15–page review essays

Additional notes
Simultaneous submission is allowed. Articles are published 3 months after acceptance.

DISSENT

Focus: expositional and analytical articles on social and political subjects with general emphasis on a radical viewpoint

Institutional affiliation: Foundation for the Study of Independent Social Ideas, Inc.

Editors: Irving Howe, Michael Walzer

Editorial address:
521 Fifth Avenue
New York, NY 10017

Frequency: 4/year

Circulation: 7,500

Subscription rate(s): student $9, individual $12, institutional $17, foreign (including Canada) add $2

Pages/issue: 128

Readership: general public, academics

Indexed/abstracted in: Alt Press Ind

Manuscripts
Query: yes,
Abstract: no
Style guide: MOS
Preferred length: 5,000 words maximum
Number of copies: 2
Notes: end of manuscript
Blind referee: no
Time to consider manuscript: 6 weeks
Proportion of manuscripts accepted: 5 percent
Illustrations accepted: tables
Foreign languages: no

Reviews
Book review editor: Joseph Clark
Address:
same as above
Seeking reviewers: no
Unsolicited reviews accepted: no
How to apply: letter of inquiry
Materials reviewed: books
Length of review: 1,000 words

Additional notes
Manuscripts are not returned unless accompanied by a self-addressed, stamped envelope. Read a few issues of *Dissent* before trying to write for it.

EAST CENTRAL EUROPE

Focus: humanities and social sciences
pertaining to the German
Democratic Republic, Poland,
Czechoslovakia, Hungary, and the
Habsburg Empire
Institutional affiliation: Arizona State
University
Editor: Charles Schlacks, Jr.
Editorial address:
Arizona State University
120 B McAllister
Tempe, AZ 85281
Frequency: 2–4/year
Circulation: 500
Subscription rate(s): $12
Pages/issue: 130–160
Readership: academics, diplomats,
East European specialists
Indexed/abstracted in: not given

Manuscripts
Query: no
Abstract: no
Style guide: MLA
Preferred length: 20–30 pages
Number of copies: 3
Notes: end of manuscript
Blind referee: no
Time to consider manuscript: 3
months
**Proportion of manuscripts
accepted:** not given
Illustrations accepted: tables,
graphs, charts, photos
Foreign languages: French, German,
Russian

Reviews
Book review editor: Charles
Schlacks, Jr.
Address: same as above
Seeking reviewers: yes
Unsolicited reviews accepted: no
How to apply: letter of inquiry
Include in application: areas of
expertise
Materials reviewed: books
Length of review: 600–800 words

Additional notes
Simultaneous submission is not
permitted. Articles are published 3–6
months after acceptance.

EAST EUROPEAN
QUARTERLY

Focus: East European civilization,
politics, and economics
Institutional affiliation: University of
Colorado
Editor: Stephen Fischer-Galati
Editorial address:
Box 29, Regent Hall
University of Colorado
Boulder, CO 80309
Frequency: 4/year
Circulation: 800
Subscription rate(s): $12
Pages/issue: 128
Readership: academics, general
public
Indexed/abstracted in: not given

Manuscripts
Query: no
Abstract: no
Style guide: none required
Preferred length: 15–25 pages
Number of copies: 1
Notes: no preference
Blind referee: no
Time to consider manuscript: 4
weeks
**Proportion of manuscripts
accepted:** 60 percent
Illustrations accepted: tables,
graphs, charts, photos
Foreign languages: French, German,
Italian

Reviews
Book review editor: Stephen Fischer-
Galati
Address: same as above
Seeking reviewers: yes
Unsolicited reviews accepted: yes
How to apply: letter of inquiry
Include in application: professional
degrees, institutional affiliation, areas
of expertise, foreign languages

Materials reviewed: books
Length of review: 1,000–1,500 words maximum

Additional notes
Simultaneous submission is permitted. Articles are published 2 years after acceptance.

ECONOMIC DEVELOPMENT AND CULTURAL CHANGE

Focus: the problems of economic development and cultural change
Institutional affiliation: University of Chicago Press
Editor: Lia Green
Editorial address:
1130 East 59th Street
Chicago, IL 60637
Frequency: 4/year
Circulation: 4,000
Subscription rate(s): student $22, individual $27.50, institutional $50
Pages/issue: 230
Readership: academics
Indexed/abstracted in: ABC POL SCI, Amer Hist and Life, Hist Abstr

Manuscripts
Query: no
Abstract: no
Style guide: available on request
Preferred length: 20–35 pages
Number of copies: 2
Notes: end of manuscript
Blind referee: no
Time to consider manuscript: 3–6 months
Proportion of manuscripts accepted: 5 percent
Illustrations accepted: tables, graphs, charts
Foreign languages: no

Reviews
Book review editor: Lia Green
Address: same as above
Seeking reviewers: yes
Unsolicited reviews accepted: no
How to apply: letter of inquiry

Include in application: professional degrees, institutional affiliation, areas of expertise, published works, current research
Materials reviewed: books
Length of review: 3,000 words

Additional notes
Manuscripts should include footnotes, not references. Simultaneous submission is not allowed. Articles are published 12–18 months after acceptance.

EMORY LAW JOURNAL

Focus: matters of legal interest
Institutional affiliation: Emory University School of Law
Editor: Harold Yellin
Editorial address:
1722 North Decatur Road
Atlanta, GA 30322
Frequency: 4/year
Circulation: 1,850
Subscription rate(s): $12
Pages/issue: 350
Readership: legal community
Indexed/abstracted in: not given

Manuscripts
Query: no
Abstract: no
Style guide: HLRA
Preferred length: no preference
Number of copies: 1
Notes: bottom of page
Blind referee: no
Time to consider manuscript: 1 month
Proportion of manuscripts accepted: not given
Illustrations accepted: tables, graphs, charts, photos, drawings
Foreign languages: no

Reviews
Book review editor: Harold Yellin
Address: same as above
Seeking reviewers: yes
Unsolicited reviews accepted: yes
How to apply: letter of inquiry

Include in application: professional
degrees, institutional affiliation
Materials reviewed: anything of legal
interest
Length of review: 5–30 pages

Additional notes
Simultaneous submission is allowed.
Articles appear 3–5 months after
acceptance.

ENVIRONMENTAL REVIEW

Focus: interdisciplinary studies in an
environmental context
Institutional affiliation: Duquesne
University
Editor: John Opie
Editorial address:
Department of History
Duquesne University
Pittsburgh, PA 15219
Frequency: 3/year
Circulation: 300
Subscription rate(s): $16
Pages/issue: 64
Readership: academics, policy
specialists
Indexed/abstracted in: not given

Manuscripts
Query: no
Abstract: no
Style guide: depends on the discipline
Preferred length: 20 pages
Number of copies: 2
Notes: end of manuscript
Blind referee: no
Time to consider manuscript: 6
months
**Proportion of manuscripts
accepted:** 40 percent
Illustrations accepted: tables,
graphs, charts, photos
Foreign languages: no

Reviews
Book review editor: Kent Shifferd
Address: same as above
Seeking reviewers: yes
Unsolicited reviews accepted: yes
How to apply: letter of inquiry

Include in application: professional
degrees, institutional affiliation, areas
of expertise, current research
Materials reviewed: books
Length of review: 500–1,000 words

Additional notes
Simultaneous submission is not allowed.
Articles are published 6–12 months after
acceptance.

ETHICS: AN INTERNATIONAL JOURNAL OF SOCIAL, POLITICAL AND LEGAL PHILOSOPHY

Focus: the ideas and principles that
form the basis for individual and
collective action, with emphasis on a
variety of disciplinary and intellectual
perspectives
Institutional affiliation: University of
Chicago Press
Editor: Brian Barry
Editorial address:
Department of Political Science
Pick Hall
5828 South University Avenue
Chicago, IL 60637
Frequency: 4/year
Circulation: 4,300
Subscription rate(s): student $16,
individual $20, institutional $30
Pages/issue: 208
Readership: academics
Indexed/abstracted in: ABC POL SCI

Manuscripts
Query: no
Abstract: yes
Style guide: MOS
Preferred length: 15–20 pages
Number of copies: 4
Notes: end of manuscript
Blind referee: yes
Time to consider manuscript: 3
months
**Proportion of manuscripts
accepted:** 4 percent
Illustrations accepted: tables,
graphs, charts, drawings
Foreign languages: no

Reviews

Book review editor: Russell Hardin
Address: same as above
Seeking reviewers: no
Unsolicited reviews accepted: no
Materials reviewed: books
Length of review: book note, 200 words; review, 1,000 words; review essay 25 pages

ETHNIC AND RACIAL STUDIES

Focus: interdisciplinary studies of ethnic and racial groups worldwide
Editor: submit to the Editors
Editorial address:
Department of Urban Planning
Livingston College
Rutgers University
New Brunswick, NJ 08903
Frequency: 4/year
Circulation: 1,000
Subscription rate(s): $52
Pages/issue: 125
Readership: academics
Indexed/abstracted in: ABC POL SCI, Hist Abstr, Amer Hist and Life

Manuscripts

Query: no
Abstract: no
Style guide: see current issue or write for guidelines
Preferred length: no preference
Number of copies: 1
Notes: end of manuscript
Blind referee: no
Time to consider manuscript: not given
Proportion of manuscripts accepted: not given
Illustrations accepted: tables, charts
Foreign languages: no

Reviews

Book review editor: submit to the Editors
Address: same as above
Materials reviewed: books
Length of review: 2-3 pages

EUROPEAN JOURNAL OF POLITICAL RESEARCH

Focus: European comparative politics and international relations
Institutional affiliation: European Consortium for Political Research
Editor: Mogens N. Pedersen
Editorial address:
Institute of Social Sciences
Odense University
Campusvej 55
5230 Odense M
DENMARK
Frequency: 4/year
Circulation: 1,000
Subscription rate(s): individual $29.60, institutional $62.80; no extra postage is charged to subscribers in the U.S. and Canada
Pages/issue: 106
Readership: academics
Indexed/abstracted in: ABC POL SCI, Curr Cont, Int Polit Sci Abstr

Manuscripts

Query: no
Abstract: yes
Style guide: available on request
Preferred length: 5,000–10,000 words
Number of copies: 4
Notes: end of manuscript
Blind referee: no
Time to consider manuscript: 2–4 months
Proportion of manuscripts accepted: not given
Illustrations accepted: tables, graphs, charts, drawings
Foreign languages: no

Reviews

Book review editor: Mogens N. Pedersen
Address: same as above
Seeking reviewers: yes
Unsolicited reviews accepted: yes
How to apply: letter of inquiry
Include in application: professional degrees, institutional affiliation, areas of expertise, published works, current research
Materials reviewed: books
Length of review: 5–10 pages

Additional notes

The author will receive 50 free reprints of his/her paper. Simultaneous submission permitted. Articles are published 6–12 months after acceptance.

EUROPEAN STUDIES REVIEW

Focus: interdisciplinary study of European history and social and political thought from 1500 to 1950
Editor: submit to Rosemary Fenton, editorial assistant
Editorial address:
Department of History
University of Lancaster
Bailrigg, Lancaster
ENGLAND
Frequency: 4/year
Circulation: not given
Subscription rate(s): individual $22.50, institutional $50.40
Pages/issue: 110–120
Readership: academics
Indexed/abstracted in: Curr Cont, ABC POL SCI, SSCI

Manuscripts

Query: no
Abstract: no
Style guide: *Hart's Rules for Compositors and Readers*
Preferred length: no preference
Number of copies: 2
Notes: end of manuscript
Blind referee: no
Time to consider manuscript: not given
Proportion of manuscripts accepted: not given
Illustrations accepted: tables
Foreign languages: yes, any major European language

Reviews

Book review editors: Dick Geary, Ralph Gibson
Address: same as above
Materials reviewed: books
Length of review and review articles: 5–7 pages

EXPERIMENTAL STUDY OF POLITICS

Focus: the rapid dissemination of new ideas and developments in political research and theory
Editor: Marilyn K. Dantico
Editorial address:
Department of Political Science
Arizona State University
Tempe, AZ 85281
Frequency: 3/year
Circulation: not given
Subscription rate(s): $12
Pages/issue: 52
Readership: political scientists
Indexed/abstracted in: not given

Manuscripts

Query: no
Abstract: no
Style guide: write for guidelines
Preferred length: no preference
Number of copies: 4
Notes: bottom of page
Blind referee: no
Time to consider manuscript: not given
Proportion of manuscripts accepted: not given
Illustrations accepted: tables, graphs, figures
Foreign languages: no

Reviews

Book review editor: Marilyn K. Dantico
Address: same as above
Materials reviewed: books
Length of review: write for guidelines

Additional notes

Articles are reproduced by photo offset to ensure a rapid transition from manuscript to print. All manuscripts must be camera-ready; the author is responsible for all typographical errors. Write for typing guidelines.

EXPLORATIONS IN ETHNIC STUDIES

Focus: interdisciplinary study of ethnicity and the cultures and interrelations of ethnic groups and minorities
Institutional affiliation: National Association of Interdisciplinary Ethnic Studies
Editor: Charles Irby
Editorial address:
Ethnic Studies Department
Cal Poly University
3801 West Temple Avenue
Pomona, CA 91768
Frequency: 2/year
Circulation: 350
Subscription rate(s): student $10, individual $25, institutional $50
Pages/issue: not given
Readership: academics
Indexed/abstracted in: not given

Manuscripts
Query: no
Abstract: no
Style guide: MOS
Preferred length: 15 pages maximum
Number of copies: 4
Notes: not given
Blind referee: no
Time to consider manuscript: 2–3 months
Proportion of manuscripts accepted: not given
Illustrations accepted: not given
Foreign languages: no

Reviews
Book review editor: Charles Irby
Address: same as above
Materials reviewed: books

Additional notes
Simultaneous submission is not permitted. Articles appear 6 months to 1 year after acceptance.

FAR EASTERN ECONOMIC REVIEW

Focus: political and business affairs throughout Asia
Editor: Derek Davies
Editorial address:
Centre Point
181-185 Gloucester Road
HONG KONG
Frequency: 52/year
Circulation: 52,000
Subscription rate(s): $62
Pages/issue: 70
Readership: Asian specialists, academics, Asian business people, Asian politicians
Indexed/abstracted in: not given

Manuscripts
Query: no
Abstract: no
Style guide: see current issue
Preferred length: 1,000 words
Number of copies: 1
Notes: not given
Blind referee: no
Time to consider manuscript: varies
Proportion of manuscripts accepted: not given
Illustrations accepted: tables, graphs, photos, drawings
Foreign languages: no

Reviews
A review of books is a regular weekly feature. Write for information on how to become a reviewer.

Additional notes
Published authors receive $100–$150 per 1,000 words. Simultaneous submission is not allowed. Articles are published 2 weeks after acceptance.

FEMINIST STUDIES

Focus: women's studies and feminist theory
Institutional affiliation: University of Maryland
Editor: Claire Moses

Editorial address:
Women's Studies Program
University of Maryland
College Park, MD 20742
Frequency: 3/year
Circulation: 5,000
Subscription rate(s): not given
Pages/issue: 200
Readership: academics, general
public
Indexed/abstracted in: not given

Manuscripts
Query: no
Abstract: yes
Style guide: MOS
Preferred length: 15–25 pages
Number of copies: 2
Notes: end of manuscript
Blind referee: no
Time to consider manuscript: 3
months
**Proportion of manuscripts
accepted:** not given
Illustrations accepted: tables,
graphs, charts, photos
Foreign languages: no

Reviews
Book review editor: Claire Moses
Address: same as above
Seeking reviewers: yes
Unsolicited reviews accepted: yes
How to apply: letter of inquiry
Include in application: professional
degrees, institutional affiliation, areas
of expertise, published works,
foreign languages, current research
Materials reviewed: books
Length of review: 1,500–2,500 words

Additional notes
Simultaneous submission is allowed.
Publishing time after acceptance varies.

FIRST PRINCIPLES

Focus: civil liberties as effected by
national security issues
Institutional affiliation: Center for
National Security Studies (American
Civil Liberties Union project)

Editor: Ann Profozich
Editorial address:
Center for National Security Studies
122 Maryland Avenue NE
Washington, DC 20002
Frequency: 9/year
Circulation: 2,500
Subscription rate(s): $15
Pages/issue: 16
Readership: academics, members of
Congress and their staffs, lawyers,
civil libertarians, liberals

Manuscripts
Query: yes
Abstract: yes
Style guide: MOS
Preferred length: 12–20 pages
Number of copies: 1
Notes: end of manuscript
Blind referee: no
Time to consider manuscript: 2
months
**Proportion of manuscripts
accepted:** 50 percent
Illustrations accepted: tables,
graphs, charts, photos, drawings
Foreign languages: no

Reviews
Book review editor: Monica Andres
Address: same as above
Seeking reviewers: no
Unsolicited reviews accepted: yes
How to apply: letter of inquiry
Include in application: professional
degrees, institutional affiliation, areas
of expertise
Materials reviewed: books, films,
tapes, articles in other magazines or
newsletters
Length of review: 1 page, double-
spaced

Additional notes
Send all articles and reviews to Ann
Profozich, Managing Editor. Topics on
Freedom of Information Act, CIA, FBI,
National Security Agency, covert
operations and government spying on
Americans, as they affect civil liberties,
are most likely to be accepted.

THE FLETCHER FORUM

Focus: diplomacy, international law, international politics, security affairs, international finance, trade, and development

Institutional affiliation: The Fletcher School of Law and Diplomacy, Tufts University

Editor: Edward W. Desmond

Editorial address:
The Fletcher School of Law and Diplomacy
Tufts University
Medford, MA 02155

Frequency: 2/year

Circulation: 750

Subscription rate(s): $9

Pages/issue: 220

Readership: libraries, diplomatic missions, academics, other professional persons

Indexed/abstracted in: ABC POL SCI, CCLP, Stand Per Dir, Ulrich's Int Per Dir, Universal Ref Syst

Manuscripts

Query: no

Abstract: no

Style guide: MOS

Preferred length: 15–50 pages

Number of copies: 1

Notes: end of manuscript

Blind referee: no

Time to consider manuscript: decisions made in December and March

Proportion of manuscripts accepted: 25 percent

Illustrations accepted: tables, graphs, charts

Foreign languages: no

Reviews

Book review editor: Hugh Ralston

Address: same as above

Seeking reviewers: yes

Unsolicited reviews accepted: yes

How to apply: letter of inquiry

Include in application: professional degrees, institutional affiliation, areas of expertise, published works, foreign languages, current research

Materials reviewed: books

Length of review: 1,500–4,000 words

FOCUS

Focus: public policies and minorities

Institutional affiliation: Joint Center for Political Studies

Editor: Robert Anderson

Editorial address:
Suite 400
1301 Pennsylvania Avenue NW
Washington, DC 20004

Frequency: 11/year

Circulation: 8,500

Subscription rate(s): $12.50

Pages/issue: 8

Readership: Black elected officials, journalists, academics

Indexed/abstracted in: not given

Manuscripts

Query: not given

Abstract: no

Style guide: MOS

Preferred length: 1,000–2,000 words

Number of copies: 1

Notes: end of manuscript

Blind referee: no

Time to consider manuscript: 1 month

Proportion of manuscripts accepted: not given

Illustrations accepted: none

Foreign languages: no

Reviews

Seeking reviewers: no

Unsolicited reviews accepted: no

Additional notes

Focus publishes relatively brief analyses of public policy issues as they affect minorities, and of the political participation of Blacks and other minorities.

FOREIGN AFFAIRS

Focus: international relations
Institutional affiliation: Council on Foreign Relations
Editors: James Chace, William P. Bundy
Editorial address:
Council on Foreign Relations
58 East 68th Street
New York, NY 10021
Frequency: 5/year
Circulation: 88,000
Subscription rate(s): $22
Pages/issue: 20
Readership: general, with a large proportion political scientists and others interested in international affairs
Indexed/abstracted in: RG

Manuscripts
Query: no
Abstract: no
Style guide: none required
Preferred length: 5,000–7,000 words
Number of copies: 1
Notes: bottom of page
Blind referee: no
Time to consider manuscript: 1–2 months
Proportion of manuscripts accepted: not given
Illustrations accepted: tables, graphs, charts, photos, drawings
Foreign languages: occasionally

Reviews
Book review editor: Lucy Edwards Despard
Address: same as above
Seeking reviewers: no
Unsolicited reviews accepted: no
Materials reviewed: books

Additional notes
Publishing time after acceptance varies.

FOREIGN POLICY

Focus: American foreign policy and international affairs
Institutional affiliation: Carnegie Endowment for International Peace
Editor: Charles William Maynes
Editorial address:
11 Dupont Circle, NW
Washington, DC 20036
Frequency: 4/year
Circulation: 20,000
Subscription rate(s): $15
Pages/issue: 192
Readership: general public interested in foreign policy
Indexed/abstracted in: ABC POL SCI, Amer Hist and Life, Hist Abstr, RG, SSCI, Soc Sci Ind

Manuscripts
Query: no
Abstract: no
Style guide: MOS
Preferred length: 25–30 pages
Number of copies: 2
Notes: end of manuscript
Blind referee: no
Time to consider manuscript: 2 months
Proportion of manuscripts accepted: 10 percent
Illustrations accepted: tables, graphs, charts, drawings
Foreign languages: no

Reviews:
Book review editor: Charles William Maynes
Address: same as above
Materials reviewed: books

FOREIGN SERVICE JOURNAL

Focus: foreign affairs and professional issues in foreign affairs
Institutional affiliation: American Foreign Service Association
Editor: Stephen Dujack
Editorial address:
2101 E Street, NW
Washington, DC 20037

Frequency: 11/year
Circulation: 8,000
Subscription rate(s): $10
Pages/issue: 48
Readership: professionals in foreign affairs
Indexed/abstracted in: not given

Manuscripts
Query: yes
Abstract: no
Style guide: MOS
Preferred length: 1,000–3,500 words
Number of copies: 1
Notes: none
Blind referee: no
Time to consider manuscript: 6 weeks
Proportion of manuscripts accepted: 33 percent
Illustrations accepted: tables, graphs, charts, photos, drawings
Foreign languages: no

Reviews
Book review editor: Frances G. Burwell
Address: same as above
Seeking reviewers: yes
Unsolicited reviews accepted: no
How to apply: informal/please call
Include in application: professional degrees, institutional affiliation, areas of expertise, published works, current research
Materials reviewed: books
Length of review: 250–500 words

Additional notes
Always query before submitting anything for publication. Royalties are negotiable. Simultaneous submission is not permitted. Articles appear 1–6 months after acceptance.

FREE SPEECH YEARBOOK

Focus: scholarly articles on all aspects of free speech and the First Amendment
Institutional affiliation: Speech Communication Association

Editor: Henry Ewbank, Jr.
Editorial address:
Speech Communication Department
University of Arizona
Tucson, AZ 85721
Frequency: 1/year
Circulation: 500
Subscription rate(s): $6.50
Pages/issue: 128
Readership: academics (teachers, researchers, students)
Indexed/abstracted in: not given

Manuscripts
Query: no
Abstract: yes
Style guide: MLA
Preferred length: varies depending on specific topic and purpose
Number of copies: 2
Notes: end of manuscript
Blind referee: yes
Time to consider manuscript: 6 weeks
Proportion of manuscripts accepted: not given
Illustrations accepted: drawings
Foreign languages: no

Reviews
Seeking reviewers: no
Unsolicited reviews accepted: no

Additional notes
The *Yearbook* currently carries a review of Supreme Court/First Amendment decisions and a bibliography of freedom of speech articles in each annual volume. Volunteers or proposals for assuming the continuing responsibilities for these features, and/or the addition of significant and relevant other items, are welcome.

GENERAL SYSTEMS YEARBOOK

Focus: general systems, theories and models
Institutional affiliation: University of Louisville
Editor: Rammohan Ragade

Editorial address:
Systems Science Institute
University of Louisville
Louisville, KY 40292
Frequency: 1/year
Circulation: 2,000
Subscription rate(s): $28
Pages/issue: 250–300
Readership: academics
Indexed/abstracted in: ABC POL SCI

Manuscripts
Query: yes
Abstract: no
Style Guide: available on request
Preferred length: 10–30 pages
Number of copies: 2
Notes: end of manuscript
Blind referee: not given
Time to consider manuscript: 4–8 months
Proportion of manuscripts accepted: not given
Illustrations accepted: tables, graphs, charts, drawings
Foreign languages: no

Reviews
Book review editor: Dr. Robert Bosserman
Address: same as above
Seeking reviewers: no
Unsolicited reviews accepted: no

Additional notes
Simultaneous submission is allowed if editors are notified of such at the time of submission. Articles appear within 1 year of acceptance.

GEORGE WASHINGTON JOURNAL OF INTERNATIONAL LAW AND ECONOMICS

Focus: legal aspects of international business transactions; private international law
Institutional affiliation: George Washington University
Editor: Peter J. Plocki

Editorial address:
2000 H Street NW
Room B-01
George Washington University
Washington, DC 20037
Frequency: 3/year
Circulation: 700
Subscription rate(s): domestic $15, foreign $16
Pages/issue: 225
Readership: academics, lawyers, corporations, trade organizations
Indexed/abstracted in: Leg Per, CCLP

Manuscripts
Query: no
Abstract: no
Style guide: GPO, HLRA
Preferred length: 80 pages maximum
Number of copies: 1
Notes: no preference
Blind referee: no
Time to consider manuscript: 2–4 weeks
Proportion of manuscripts accepted: 10–20 percent
Illustrations accepted: tables, graphs, charts
Foreign languages: no

Reviews
Book review editor: Kevin O'Grady
Address: same as above
Seeking reviewers: yes
Unsolicited reviews accepted: yes
How to apply: letter of inquiry
Include in application: professional degrees, institutional affiliation, areas of expertise, published works, current research
Materials reviewed: books
Length of review: 7–10 pages maximum

Additional notes
Vol. 15:1 of the *Journal* (October 1981) is a bibliography of international law, accompanied by an explanatory article by John Williams. It is the first such bibliography of its kind to our knowledge and is an indispensable research tool. *Journal* readers rely on background

documentation (footnotes) to direct their research into the topics covered in the *Journal*. Authors should be especially diligent in documenting their articles.

GEORGE WASHINGTON LAW REVIEW

Focus: scholarly legal journal; national issues
Institutional affiliation: George Washington Law Center
Editor: Marjorie R. Freiman
Editorial address:
2000 H Street NW
Room 402C
Washington, DC 20002
Frequency: 5/year
Circulation: 2,000
Subscription rate(s): domestic $18, foreign $20
Pages/issue: 150–200
Readership: legal professionals, academics
Indexed/abstracted in: Curr Leg Per

Manuscripts
Query: no
Abstract: no
Style guide: none required
Preferred length: no preference
Number of copies: 1
Notes: end of manuscript
Blind referee: no
Time to consider manuscript: not given
Proportion of manuscripts accepted: less than 10 percent
Illustrations accepted: none
Foreign languages: no

Reviews
Book review editor: Carol Fortine
Address: same as above
Seeking reviewers: yes
Unsolicited reviews accepted: yes
How to apply: letter of inquiry

GERMAN STUDIES REVIEW

Focus: interdisciplinary study of German history, politics, society, and literature
Institutional affiliation: Western Association for German Studies
Editor: Gerald R. Kleinfeld
Editorial address:
Department of History
Arizona State University
Tempe, AZ 85281
Frequency: 3/year
Circulation: 1,050
Subscription rate(s): members $10, domestic $18, Canada $20, foreign $21
Pages/issue: 150
Readership: academics, students of German history and culture
Indexed/abstracted in: Hist Abstr, Curr Cont

Manuscripts
Query: yes
Abstract: no
Style guide: MLA or MOS
Preferred length: 25 pages
Number of copies: 2, double-spaced
Notes: end of manuscript
Blind referee: no
Time to consider manuscript: 3–6 months
Proportion of manuscripts accepted: not given
Illustrations accepted: not given
Foreign languages: German

Reviews
Book review editor: Wayne M. Senner
Address:
Arizona State University
Tempe, AZ 85281
Seeking reviewers: yes
Unsolicited reviews accepted: no
How to apply: letter of inquiry
Materials reviewed: books
Length of review: 2–3 pages

Additional notes
Simultaneous submission is not permitted. Articles are published within 1 year of acceptance. Book reviews are assigned; potential reviewers should contact the Book Review Editor.

GOVERNMENT AND OPPOSITION: A JOURNAL OF COMPARATIVE POLITICS

Focus: comparative studies of political developments in various countries
Institutional affiliation: London School of Economics and Political Science
Editor: submit to the Editors
Editorial address:
Houghton Street
London WC2 2AE
ENGLAND
Frequency: 4/year
Circulation: 1,500
Subscription rate(s): individual $50, institutional $60
Pages/issue: 120–130
Readership: academics, journalists, business people, government officials
Indexed/abstracted in: Hist Abstr, SSCI, Soc Sci Ind, ABC POL SCI, Amer Hist and Life, Int Polit Sci Abstr

Manuscripts
Query: no
Abstract: no
Style guide: see current issue or write for guidelines
Preferred length: 6,000 words
Number of copies: 2, double-spaced
Notes: bottom of page
Blind referee: no
Time to consider manuscript: 3–6 months
Proportion of manuscripts accepted: not given
Illustrations accepted: tables
Foreign languages: no

Reviews
Book review editor: submit to the Editors
Address: same as above
Seeking reviewers: yes
How to apply: letter of inquiry
Include in application: professional degrees, institutional affiliation, areas of expertise

Materials reviewed: books
Length of review: 2–5 pages, 10–15 pages for review articles

Additional notes
Authors receive £50 per article if published. Simultaneous submission is not permitted. Articles are published 6–18 months after acceptance.

GOVERNMENTAL FINANCE

Focus: governmental finance
Institutional affiliation: Municipal Finance Officers Association
Editor: Rebecca Russum
Editorial address:
180 North Michigan Avenue
Chicago, IL 60601
Frequency: 4/year
Circulation: 10,000
Subscription rate(s): $12
Pages/issue: 68
Readership: local, state, and federal finance officers
Indexed/abstracted in: ABC POL SCI, Acc Ind, PAIS

Manuscripts
Query: no
Abstract: no
Style guide: MOS
Preferred length: 20 pages
Number of copies: 1
Notes: end of manuscript
Blind referee: no
Time to consider manuscript: 6–8 weeks
Proportion of manuscripts accepted: 10 percent
Illustrations accepted: tables, graphs, charts, drawings
Foreign languages: no

Reviews
Book review editor: Rebecca Russum
Address: same as above
Seeking reviewers: yes
Unsolicited reviews accepted: yes
How to apply: letter of inquiry

Include in application: professional
degrees, institutional affiliation, areas
of expertise, current research
Materials reviewed: books, periodical
studies, published reports
Length of review: 4 pages maximum

GROWTH AND CHANGE: A JOURNAL OF REGIONAL DEVELOPMENT

Focus: policy-oriented articles on
aspects of regional development
from the fields of economics,
geography, political science,
sociology and anthropology
Institutional affiliation: University of
Kentucky, College of Business and
Economics
Editor: Hirofumi Shibata
Editorial address:
University of Kentucky
644 Maxwelton Court
Lexington, KY 40506
Frequency: 4/year
Circulation: 1,300
Subscription rate(s): individual $10,
institutional $12.50
Pages/issue: 64
Readership: academics, practitioners
in various fields which have a
bearing on regional development
Indexed/abstracted in: J of Econ Lit,
Curr Cont, Urb Aff Abstr, ABC POL
SCI, G Per Educ, USPSD, Human
Resour Abstr, Sage Urb Stud Abstr,
Sage Pub Admin Abstr

Manuscripts
Query: no
Abstract: no
Style guide: MOS
Preferred length: 3,500 words
Number of copies: 4
Notes: end of manuscript
Blind referee: yes
Time to consider manuscript: 6
months
**Proportion of manuscripts
accepted:** 27 percent

Illustrations accepted: tables,
graphs, charts
Foreign languages: no

Reviews
Book review editor: Karen F. Merris
Address: same as above
Seeking reviewers: yes (for books
and manuscripts)
Unsolicited reviews accepted: no
How to apply: letter of inquiry
Include in application: professional
degrees, institutional affiliation, areas
of expertise
Materials reviewed: books
Length of review: 500–700 words

Additional notes
Simultaneous submission is not
permitted. Articles appear 6–9 months
after acceptance.

HARVARD BUSINESS REVIEW

Focus: wide range of issues and
topics in business, government,
society, and management
Institutional affiliation: Harvard
Graduate School of Business
Administration
Editor: submit to the Editor
Editorial address:
Harvard Business Review
Harvard University
Boston, MA 02163
Frequency: 6/year
Circulation: 220,000
Subscription rate(s): $24
Pages/issue: 200
Readership: academics, business
people
Indexed/abstracted in: BPI, Comput
Rev, PAIS, Psychol Abstr, RG, SSCI,
Work Rel Abstr

Manuscripts
Query: no
Abstract: no
Style guide: available on request
Preferred length: 6–25 pages
Number of copies: 3
Notes: not given

Blind referee: no
Time to consider manuscript: 3–4 weeks
Proportion of manuscripts accepted: under 10 percent
Illustrations accepted: tables, graphs, charts, drawings
Foreign languages: no

Reviews

Write for information on how to become a reviewer for the *Harvard Business Review*.

Additional notes

Authors are paid $500 per accepted article. Simultaneous submission is not allowed. Articles are published 3–5 months after acceptance.

HARVARD CIVIL RIGHTS–CIVIL LIBERTIES LAW REVIEW

Focus: constitutional issues from civil liberties perspectives; development of doctrine and case law, statutory programs; jurisprudence
Institutional affiliation: Harvard Law School
Editors: Tiane Sommer, Richard C.P. de Bodo, Meryl S. Justin
Editorial address:
Harvard Law School
Cambridge, MA 02138
Frequency: 2/year
Circulation: 1,700
Subscription rate(s): $15
Pages/issue: 250–300
Readership: academics, litigators, judges
Indexed/abstracted in: Curr Law Ind, G Leg Per

Manuscripts

Query: no
Abstract: no
Style guide: HLRA
Preferred length: 50–200 pages
Number of copies: 1
Notes: bottom of page
Blind referee: no

Time to consider manuscript: 2 months
Proportion of manuscripts accepted: not given
Illustrations accepted: tables, graphs
Foreign languages: no

Reviews

Book review editor: Barbara S. Fischbein
Address: same as above
Seeking reviewers: yes
Unsolicited reviews accepted: yes
How to apply: letter of inquiry
Include in application: professional degrees, institutional affiliation, areas of expertise
Materials reviewed: books
Length of review: varies

Additional notes

Simultaneous submission is permitted if editors are notified at the time of submission. Articles appear 1–6 months after acceptance.

HARVARD INTERNATIONAL LAW JOURNAL

Focus: wide spectrum of topics dealing with (primarily private) international and transnational law
Institutional affiliation: Harvard Law School
Editor: Brian D. Kilb
Editorial address:
Hastings Hall, Harvard Law School
Cambridge, MA 02138
Frequency: 3/year
Circulation: 2,500
Subscription rate(s): $15/ volume (2–3 issues)
Pages/issue: 200
Readership: academics, professionals
Indexed/abstracted in: Leg Per

Manuscripts

Query: no
Abstract: no
Style guide: HLRA
Preferred length: 25–40 pages
Number of copies: 1

Notes: bottom of page
Blind referee: no
Time to consider manuscript: 1 month
Proportion of manuscripts accepted: 5–10 percent
Illustrations accepted: none
Foreign languages: no

Reviews
Book review editors: Gael Graham, Tania Matsuoka
Address: same as above
Seeking reviewers: no
Unsolicited reviews accepted: yes
Materials reviewed: books

Additional notes
Simultaneous submission is allowed. Articles are published 3–6 months after acceptance.

HARVARD JOURNAL ON LEGISLATION

Focus: legislation and the legislative process, with emphasis on legislative reform and on organizational and procedural factors that affect the efficiency and effectiveness of legislative decision-making
Institutional affiliation: Harvard Law School
Editor: submit to Articles Editor
Editorial address:
Harvard Law School
Cambridge, MA 02138
Frequency: 2/year
Circulation: 1,100
Subscription rate(s): $12.50
Pages/issue: 250
Readership: academics, lawyers, legislators
Indexed/abstracted in: PAIS, SSCI, CCLP

Manuscripts
Query: no
Abstract: not required, but preferred
Style guide: HLRA
Preferred length: 20–65 pages

Number of copies: 2
Notes: end of manuscript
Blind referee: no
Time to consider manuscript: 2–6 weeks
Proportion of manuscripts accepted: 5–10 percent
Illustrations accepted: tables, graphs, charts, photos, drawings
Foreign languages: no

Reviews
Seeking reviewers: yes
Unsolicited reviews accepted: yes
How to apply: letter of inquiry
Include in application: professional degrees, institutional affiliation, areas of expertise, published works
Materials reviewed: books
Length of review: 3–8 pages

Additional notes
Simultaneous submission is allowed, if editors are notified at the time of submission. Articles appear 3 months after acceptance.

HARVARD LAW REVIEW

Focus: general legal scholarship
Institutional affiliation: Harvard Law School
Editor: submit to Articles Editor
Editorial address:
Gannett House
Cambridge, MA 02138
Frequency: 8/year
Circulation: 10,000
Subscription rate(s): $28
Pages/issue: 250
Readership: academics, practicing attorneys and judges
Indexed/abstracted in: Ind Leg Per

Manuscripts
Query: no
Abstract: no
Style guide: GPO, HLRA
Preferred length: no preference
Number of copies: 1
Notes: no preference
Blind referee: yes

Time to consider manuscript: 2–3 months
Proportion of manuscripts accepted: 3 percent
Illustrations accepted: tables, graphs, charts
Foreign languages: no

Reviews
Book review editor: submit to Book Review Office
Address: same as above
Unsolicited reviews accepted: rarely
How to apply: letter of inquiry
Materials reviewed: books
Length of review: 10 printed pages

Additional notes
Simultaneous submission is allowed.

HASTINGS INTERNATIONAL AND COMPARATIVE LAW REVIEW

Focus: current issues in transnational and comparative law, including topics of practical and commercial significance
Institutional affiliation: Hastings College of the Law
Editor: Kevin K. Takeuchi
Editorial address:
Hastings College of the Law
200 McAllister Street
San Francisco, CA 94102
Frequency: 3/year
Circulation: 1,700
Subscription rate(s): $12
Pages/issue: 200–250
Readership: legal scholars, attorneys, academics
Indexed/abstracted in: Leg Per

Manuscripts
Query: yes
Abstract: yes
Style guide: HLRA
Preferred length: 60–80 pages
Number of copies: 1, double-spaced
Notes: end of manuscript
Blind referee: no

Time to consider manuscript: 2 weeks
Proportion of manuscripts accepted: 10 percent
Illustrations accepted: tables, graphs, charts, photos, drawings
Foreign languages: no

Reviews
Book review editor: Kevin K. Takeuchi
Address: same as above
Seeking reviewers: yes
Unsolicited reviews accepted: yes
How to apply: letter of inquiry
Include in application: professional degrees, institutional affiliation, areas of expertise, published works, foreign languages, current research
Materials reviewed: books
Length of review: 5–10 pages

HISTORY OF POLITICAL ECONOMY

Focus: economic thought and policy
Institutional affiliation: Duke University
Editor: Craufurd D. Goodwin
Editorial address:
Department of Economics
Duke University
Durham, NC 27706
Frequency: 4/year
Circulation: 1,500
Subscription rate(s): $20
Pages/issue: 135–140
Readership: academics, government officials
Indexed/abstracted in: Hist Abstr, SSCI, Soc Sci Ind, J of Econ Lit

Manuscripts
Query: no
Abstract: yes
Style guide: MOS
Preferred length: 20 pages maximum
Number of copies: 2
Notes: end of manuscript
Blind referee: no
Time to consider manuscript: 2–3 months

**Proportion of manuscripts
accepted:** 25 percent
Illustrations accepted: camera-ready
tables, graphs, charts, photos
Foreign languages: no

Reviews
Book review editor: S. Todd Lowry
Address: same as above
Seeking reviewers: yes
Unsolicited reviews accepted: no

Additional notes
Simultaneous submission is not
permitted. Articles are published 18
months after acceptance.

HISTORY OF POLITICAL THOUGHT

Focus: development of political theory
and belief
Editor: submit to the Editors
Editorial address:
Department of Politics
Amory Building
Rennes Drive
University of Exeter
Exeter EX4 4RJ
ENGLAND
Frequency: 3/year
Circulation: not given
Subscription rate(s): individual
£14.50, institutional £24
Pages/issue: 200
Readership: historians, political and
social scientists
Indexed/abstracted in: Hist Abstr,
Amer Hist and Life

Manuscripts
Query: no
Abstract: yes, 150 words
Style guide: Fowler, *Modern English
Usage*
Preferred length: no preference
Number of copies: 3
Notes: end of manuscript
Blind referee: no
Time to consider manuscript: not
given

**Proportion of manuscripts
accepted:** not given
Illustrations accepted: drawings
Foreign languages: no

Reviews
Book review editor: submit to the
Editors
Address: same as above
Materials reviewed: books
Length of review: 3–5 pages

THE HUMANIST

Focus: social issues and personal
concerns discussed in the light of
humanistic ideas and developments
in philosophy, psychology,
sociology, and science
Institutional affiliation: American
Humanistic Association
Editor: William J. Harnack
Editorial address:
7 Harwood Drive
Amherst, NY 14226
Frequency: 6/year
Circulation: 23,000
Subscription rate(s): $15
Pages/issue: 68
Readership: academics, general
public
Indexed/abstracted in: RG, Bk Rev
Ind, Curr Cont, SSCI

Manuscripts
Query: no
Abstract: no
Style guide: MOS
Preferred length: 6–12 pages
Number of copies: 3, double-spaced
Notes: not given
Blind referee: no
Time to consider manuscript: 2
months
**Proportion of manuscripts
accepted:** not given
Illustrations accepted: tables,
graphs, charts, photos, drawings
Foreign languages: no

Reviews

Book review editor: William J. Harnack
Address: same as above
Seeking reviewers: no
Unsolicited reviews accepted: no
Materials reviewed: books

Additional notes

A constructive tone, one which provides creative solutions and/or celebrates the human spirit is best. Simultaneous submission is not allowed. Articles appear 6 months after acceptance.

HUMAN RELATIONS

Focus: the application of a broad spectrum of problems and approaches toward the integration of the social sciences
Institutional affiliation: Tavistock Institute of Human Relations
Editors: Eric Trist, Michael Foster
Editorial address:
University of Pennsylvania
Wharton School
Management and Behavioral
Science Center
Philadelphia, PA 19104
Frequency: 12/year
Circulation: not given
Subscription rate(s): $95
Pages/issue: 74
Readership: social scientists
Indexed/abstracted in: Abstr Soc Work, Abstr Crim and Pen, Child Devel Abstr, Curr Cont, Educ Admin Abstr, Psychol Abstr, SSCI, Sociol Abstr, USPSD

Manuscripts

Query: no
Abstract: yes
Style guide: available on request
Preferred length: 3,000–4,000 words with a 5,000-word maximum
Number of copies: 3
Notes: bottom of page
Blind referee: no
Time to consider manuscript: 3–4 months

Proportion of manuscripts accepted: not given
Illustrations accepted: tables, graphs, charts, drawings
Foreign languages: no

Reviews
not applicable

Additional notes

Articles appear 4–8 months after acceptance.

HUMAN RIGHTS INTERNET REPORTER

Focus: international human rights
Editor: Laurie S. Wiseberg
Editorial address:
1502 Ogden Street, NW
Washington, DC 20010
Frequency: 5/year
Circulation: 1,300
Subscription rate(s): individual $35, institutional $50
Pages/issue: 150
Readership: academics, lawyers, journalists, officers of international nongovernmental organizations and intergovernmental organizations (U.N., etc), general public
Indexed/abstracted in: not given

Manuscripts

Query: no
Abstract: no
Style guide: none required
Preferred length: 750 words
Number of copies: 1
Notes: not given
Blind referee: no
Time to consider manuscript: 1 month
Proportion of manuscripts accepted: not given
Foreign languages: Spanish, French, German

Reviews

Book review editor: Laurie S. Wiseberg
Address: same as above

Seeking reviewers: yes
Unsolicited reviews accepted: yes
How to apply: letter of inquiry
Include in application: institutional affiliation, published works, current research
Materials reviewed: books, films, tapes, conferences, seminars
Length of review: 1 page

Additional notes

HRI Reporter is an information exchange, documenting the activities of human rights organizations and compiling current human rights bibliographies from general and scholarly publications, teaching materials, and other research. Simultaneous submission is allowed. Articles are published 2–3 months after acceptance.

HUMAN RIGHTS QUARTERLY

Focus: issues in international human rights
Institutional affiliation: Johns Hopkins University Press
Editor: Bert B. Lockwood, Jr.
Editorial address:
Urban Morgan Institute
for Human Rights
University of Cincinnati
College of Law
Cincinnati, OH 45221
Frequency: 4/year
Circulation: 1,000
Subscription rate(s): student $14, individual $16, institutional $30
Pages/issue: 130
Readership: academics, policymakers, and activists in the human rights field
Indexed/abstracted in: ABC POL SCI, Curr Cont, SSCI

Manuscripts
Query: no
Abstract: no
Style guide: MOS
Preferred length: 5,000–10,000 words
Number of copies: 3
Notes: end of manuscript

Blind referee: no
Time to consider manuscript: 5–8 weeks
Proportion of manuscripts accepted: 20 percent
Illustrations accepted: tables, graphs
Foreign languages: French, Spanish

Reviews
Book review editor: Bert B. Lockwood, Jr.
Address: same as above
Seeking reviewers: no
Unsolicited reviews accepted: no
How to apply: letter of inquiry
Include in application: professional degrees, institutional affiliation, areas of expertise, published works, current research
Materials reviewed: books
Length of review: 10–20 pages

Additional notes
All illustrations must be provided camera-ready.

HUMAN STUDIES

Focus: the intersection of philosophy and the social sciences
Institutional affiliation: Society for Phenomenology and the Human Sciences
Editor: George Psathas
Editorial address:
Boston University
Department of Sociology
100 Cummington Street
Boston, MA 02215
Frequency: 4/year
Circulation: not given
Subscription rate(s): individual $5, institutional $47.50
Pages/issue: 76
Readership: academics
Indexed/abstracted in: not given

Manuscripts
Query: no
Abstract: yes, 1 page
Style guide: available on request
Preferred length: 10–20 pages

Number of copies: 3
Notes: end of manuscript
Blind referee: yes
Time to consider manuscript: 3
months
**Proportion of manuscripts
accepted:** not given
Illustrations accepted: not given
Foreign languages: no

Reviews
Book review editor: Victor
Kestenbaum
Address:
Department of Humanistic and
Behavioral Studies
Boston University
232 Bay State Road
Boston, MA 02215
Unsolicited reviews accepted: yes
Materials reviewed: books
Length of review: 5–10 pages

Additional notes
Simultaneous submission is allowed.
Articles are published 1 year after
acceptance.

INDIAN JOURNAL OF POLITICAL SCIENCE

Focus: all aspects of political science
Institutional affiliation: Indian Political
Science Association
Editor: Madan Mohan Puri
Editorial address:
Department of Political Science
University Enclave
Panjab University
Chondigarh
160 014
INDIA
Frequency: 4/year
Circulation: not given
Subscription rate(s): $6
Pages/issue: 150
Readership: political and social
scientists
Indexed/abstracted in: ABC POL SCI

Manuscripts
Query: no
Abstract: yes, 300 words
Style guide: see current issue or write
for guidelines
Preferred length: 5,000–10,000 words
Number of copies: 2
Notes: bottom of page
Blind referee: yes
Time to consider manuscript: 3
months
**Proportion of manuscripts
accepted:** not given
Illustrations accepted: tables, charts
Foreign languages: no

Reviews
not applicable

Additional notes
Simultaneous submission or submission
of a previously published manuscript is
not permitted, and the manuscript must
come with a declaration that neither
condition exists. A brief biographical
sketch including recent institutional
affiliations, research interests, and
publications must accompany the
manuscript.

INDIAN JOURNAL OF POLITICS

Focus: all fields of political science
Editor: submit to the Editors
Editorial address:
Department of Political Science
Aligarh Muslim University
Aligarh-202001
INDIA
Frequency: 3/year
Circulation: 1,000
Subscription rate(s): $10
Pages/issue: 180–200
Readership: political and social
scientists
Indexed/abstracted in: Curr Cont,
Hist Abstr, Sociol Abstr, ABC POL
SCI, Int Polit Sci Abstr, SSCI

Manuscripts

Query: no
Abstract: yes, 100 words maximum
Style guide: see current issue or write for guidelines
Preferred length: 8,000 words
Number of copies: 1, double-spaced
Notes: end of manuscript
Blind referee: yes
Time to consider manuscript: 12 weeks
Proportion of manuscripts accepted: not given
Illustrations accepted: tables, charts
Foreign languages: no

Reviews

Book review editor: submit to the Editors
Address: same as above
Materials reviewed: books
Length of review: 1–3 pages

Additional notes

Simultaneous submission is not permitted.

INDIAN JOURNAL OF PUBLIC ADMINISTRATION

Focus: public administration
Institutional affiliation: The Indian Institute of Public Administration
Editor: submit to the Assistant Editor
Editorial address:
   The Indian Institute of Public Administration
   Indra prastha Estate
   Ring Road (East)
   New Delhi-110002
   INDIA
Frequency: 4/year
Circulation: not given
Subscription rate(s): $9.50
Pages/issue: 200–250
Readership: academics, public administrators
Indexed/abstracted in: ABC POL SCI

Manuscripts

Query: no
Abstract: no

Style guide: see current issue or write for guidelines
Preferred length: no preference
Number of copies: 2
Notes: bottom of page
Blind referee: no
Time to consider manuscript: not given
Proportion of manuscripts accepted: not given
Illustrations accepted: tables, graphs, charts
Foreign languages: no

Reviews

Book review editor: submit to the Assistant Editor
Address: same as above
Materials reviewed: books
Length of review: 5–10 pages

INDIAN JOURNAL OF SOCIAL RESEARCH

Focus: social science in general
Editor: G. C. Hallen
Editorial address:
   B-47, Shastri Nagar
   Tejgarhi, Meerut
   INDIA
Frequency: 3/year
Circulation: 800
Subscription rate(s): $15
Pages/issue: 150
Readership: social scientists
Indexed/abstracted in: Hist Abstr, SSCI, Sociol Abstr

Manuscripts

Query: no
Abstract: yes, 500 words, write for an abstract form
Style guide: see current issue
Preferred length: 3,000–5,000 words
Number of copies: 2
Notes: bottom of page
Blind referee: no
Time to consider manuscript: 2 months
Proportion of manuscripts accepted: not given

Illustrations accepted: tables, graphs, figures
Foreign languages: no

Reviews
not applicable

Additional notes
A personal vita and a $6 processing fee must accompany each submission.

INDIAN POLITICAL SCIENCE REVIEW

Focus: all aspects of political science
Editor: Harnam Singh
Editorial address:
Department of Political Science
University of Delhi
Delhi-110007
INDIA
Frequency: 2/year
Circulation: 4,000
Subscription rate(s): $12
Pages/issue: 110
Readership: political scientists
Indexed/abstracted in: Hist Abstr, SSCI, Amer Hist and Life, ABC POL SCI, Int Polit Sci Abstr

Manuscripts
Query: no
Abstract: no
Style guide: see current issue or write for guidelines
Preferred length: no preference
Number of copies: 1
Notes: bottom of page
Blind referee: no
Time to consider manuscript: not given
Proportion of manuscripts accepted: not given
Illustrations accepted: tables, graphs, figures
Foreign languages: no

Reviews
Book review editor: Harnam Singh
Address: same as above
Materials reviewed: books
Length of review: 2-3 pages

INDIA QUARTERLY: A JOURNAL OF INTERNATIONAL AFFAIRS

Focus: international studies
Institutional affiliation: Indian Council of World Affairs
Editor: submit to the Editor
Editorial address:
Indian Council of World Affairs
Sapru House
Barakhamba Road
New Delhi-110001
INDIA
Frequency: 4/year
Circulation: 4,400
Subscription rate(s): $16
Pages/issue: 150-200
Readership: political and social scientists
Indexed/abstracted in: PAIS, ABC POL SCI, Hist Abstr

Manuscripts
Query: no
Abstract: no
Style guide: see current issue or write for guidelines
Preferred length: no preference
Number of copies: 1
Notes: end of manuscript
Blind referee: no
Time to consider manuscript: not given
Proportion of manuscripts accepted: not given
Illustrations accepted: tables, charts
Foreign languages: no

Reviews
Book review editor: submit to the Editor
Address: same as above
Materials reviewed: books
Length of review: 3-4 pages

INDUSTRIAL AND LABOR RELATIONS REVIEW

Focus: furtherance of knowledge in all aspects of industrial and labor relations

Institutional affiliation: New York State School of Industrial and Labor Relations, Cornell University

Editor: Elaine F. Gruenfeld

Editorial address:
Cornell University
Ithaca, NY 14853

Frequency: 4/year

Circulation: 4,500

Subscription rate(s): student $7, individual $14, institutional $18

Pages/issue: 155

Readership: libraries, academics, professionals

Indexed/abstracted in: ABC POL SCI, Bk Rev Ind, PAIS, BPI, CIS Ind, Curr Cont, Curr Ind J Educ, Educ Admin Abstr, Human Resour Abstr, J of Econ Lit, Manage Abstr, Manage Cont, Pers Manage Abstr, SSCI, Sociol Abstr, USPSD, Wom Stud Abstr, Work Rel Abstr

Manuscripts

Query: no

Abstract: yes, when accepted

Style guide: available on request

Preferred length: 30 pages

Number of copies: 3

Notes: end of manuscript

Blind referee: yes

Time to consider manuscript: 3–6 months

Proportion of manuscripts accepted: 15 percent

Illustrations accepted: tables, graphs, charts, drawings

Foreign languages: no

Reviews

Book review editor: David B. Lipsky

Address: same as above

Seeking reviewers: yes

Unsolicited reviews accepted: rarely

How to apply: letter of inquiry

Include in application: professional degrees, institutional affiliation, areas of expertise

Materials reviewed: books

Length of review: 3 pages

Additional notes

Simultaneous submission is not permitted. Articles are published 6 months after acceptance.

INDUSTRIAL RELATIONS

Focus: all aspects of the employment relationship; new political, social, economic, and legal developments in the field of labor studies

Institutional affiliation: Institute of Industrial Relations, University of California, Berkeley

Editor: submit to the Managing Editor

Editorial address:
Institute of Industrial Relations
University of California
Berkeley, CA 94720

Frequency: 3/year

Circulation: 2,400

Subscription rate(s): individual $10, institutional $12

Pages/issue: 115

Readership: academics, professionals

Indexed/abstracted in: BPI, PAIS, J of Econ Abstr, Pers Manage Abstr, Work Rel Abstr

Manuscripts

Query: no

Abstract: no

Style guide: available on request

Preferred length: 5,000–7,000 words

Number of copies: 2

Notes: end of manuscript

Blind referee: no

Time to consider manuscript: 2 months

Proportion of manuscripts accepted: not given

Illustrations accepted: tables, charts, figures

Foreign languages: no

Reviews
not applicable

Additional notes
Simultaneous submission is not allowed.
Articles are published 6 months after
acceptance.

INDUSTRIAL RELATIONS/ RELATIONS INDUSTRIELLES

Focus: all fields of industrial and labor
relations with an emphasis, although
not exclusive, on Canada
Institutional affiliation: Canadian
Industrial Relations Research
Institute
Editor: Gérard Dion
Editorial address:
Department des relations
industrielles
Université Laval
Quebec G1K 7P4
CANADA
Frequency: 4/year
Circulation: 2,400
Subscription rate(s): $16 (Canadian)
Pages/issue: not given
Readership: academics, personnel
managers, union leaders
Indexed/abstracted in: SSCI, Can Ind

Manuscripts
Query: no, but preferable
Abstract: yes, 60 words
Style guide: available on request
Preferred length: 6,000 words
Number of copies: 4
Notes: not given
Blind referee: no
Time to consider manuscript: 1–3
months
**Proportion of manuscripts
accepted:** not given
Illustrations accepted: tables,
graphs, charts, diagrams
Foreign languages: French

Reviews
Book review editor: Gérard Dion
Address: same as above
Materials reviewed: books

Additional notes
Simultaneous submission is not allowed.
Articles are published 6–12 months after
acceptance.

INQUIRY: INTERDISCIPLINARY JOURNAL OF PHILOSOPHY AND THE SOCIAL SCIENCES

Focus: interdisciplinary studies of all
areas of philosophy; articulation of
philosophical inquiry with social
research
Editor: Alastair Hannay
Editorial address:
Institute of Philosophy
University of Oslo
P.O. Box 1024
Blindern, Oslo 3
NORWAY
Frequency: 4/year
Circulation: 1,500
Subscription rate(s): individual $16,
institutional $27
Pages/issue: 125
Readership: philosophers, social
scientists
Indexed/abstracted in: ABC POL SCI

Manuscripts
Query: no
Abstract: yes, 100–150 words
Style guide: see current issue or write
for guidelines
Preferred length: 10,000 words
Number of copies: 2
Notes: end of manuscript
Blind referee: no
Time to consider manuscript: 1–3
months
**Proportion of manuscripts
accepted:** not given
Illustrations accepted: tables, charts,
figures
Foreign languages: no

Reviews
Book review editor: Alastair Hannay
Address: same as above
Materials reviewed: books
Length of review: see additional
notes

Additional notes
Reviews are confined to extended discussions of books selected for their special interest. Simultaneous submission is not permitted. Articles are published 1 year after acceptance.

INTER-AMERICAN ECONOMIC AFFAIRS

Focus: political and economic relations between American nations
Editor: Simon G. Hanson
Editorial address:
P.O. Box 181
Washington, DC 20044
Frequency: 4/year
Circulation: not given
Subscription rate(s): domestic $25, foreign $27
Pages/issue: 96
Readership: academics, general public
Indexed/abstracted in: PAIS, Soc Sci Ind

Manuscripts
Query: no
Abstract: no
Style guide: MOS
Preferred length: 6,000 words
Number of copies: 2
Notes: bottom of page
Blind referee: no
Time to consider manuscript: 6 weeks
Proportion of manuscripts accepted: 15 percent
Illustrations accepted: tables
Foreign languages: no

Reviews
Book review editor: Simon G. Hanson
Address: same as above
Seeking reviewers: no
Unsolicited reviews accepted: no
Materials reviewed: books

INTERNATIONAL AFFAIRS

Focus: international political, economic, and monetary issues
Institutional affiliation: Royal Institute of International Affairs
Editor: David Stephen
Editorial address:
Chatham House
10 St. James' Square
London SW1Y 4LE
ENGLAND
Frequency: 4/year
Circulation: 7,750
Subscription rate(s): U.S. $30
Pages/issue: 200
Readership: academics, professionals, government officials, business people
Indexed/abstracted in: PAIS, SSCI, Soc Sci Ind

Manuscripts
Query: no, but advisable
Abstract: no
Style guide: available on request
Preferred length: 5,000–7,000 words
Number of copies: 1
Notes: bottom of page
Blind referee: no
Time to consider manuscript: 3 weeks
Proportion of manuscripts accepted: not given
Illustrations accepted: not given
Foreign languages: no

Reviews
Book review editor: Adeed I. Dawisha
Address: same as above
Materials reviewed: books
Length of review: 5–12 pages

Additional notes
Simultaneous submission is not allowed. Articles appear in 3–6 months. Authors receive £50–£70 per article.

THE INTERNATIONAL AND COMPARATIVE LAW QUARTERLY

Focus: public and private international law; comparative law; Commonwealth law; the law of international regional organizations
Institutional affiliation: British Institute of International and Comparative Law
Editor: submit to the General Editor
Editorial address:
British Institute of International and Comparataive Law
Charles Clore House
17 Russell Square
London WC1B 5DR
ENGLAND
Frequency: 4/year
Circulation: 3,000
Subscription rate(s): $45
Pages/issue: 200
Readership: legal scholars, academics, international lawyers
Indexed/abstracted in: Leg Per, Foreign Leg Per, ABC POL SCI

Manuscripts
Query: no
Abstract: no
Style guide: write for guidelines
Preferred length: no preference
Number of copies: 1
Notes: bottom of page
Blind referee: no
Time to consider manuscript: not given
Proportion of manuscripts accepted: not given
Illustrations accepted: not given
Foreign languages: no

Reviews
Book review editor: submit to the General Editor
Address: same as above
Materials reviewed: books
Length of review: 3–6 pages

INTERNATIONAL DEVELOPMENT REVIEW

Focus: practical and theoretical interdisciplinary articles on international social and economic development
Institutional affiliation: Society for International Development
Editor: submit to the Editor
Editorial address:
1346 Connecticut Avenue, NW
Washington, DC 20036
Frequency: 4/year
Circulation: 8,300
Subscription rate(s): institutional $12
Pages/issue: not given
Readership: academics, those interested or working in less developed countries
Indexed/abstracted in: Curr Cont, PAIS, SSCI, Soc Sci Ind, ABC POL SCI

Manuscripts
Query: no
Abstract: no
Style guide: available on request
Preferred length: 3,000–5,000 words
Number of copies: 2
Notes: not given
Blind referee: no
Time to consider manuscript: 1–2 months
Proportion of manuscripts accepted: not given
Illustrations accepted: not given
Foreign languages: French, Spanish

Reviews
Book review editor: submit to the Editor
Address: same as above
Materials reviewed: books, films

Additional notes
Simultaneous submission is not allowed. Articles are published 3–6 months after acceptance.

INTERNATIONAL INTERACTIONS

Focus: interdisciplinary understanding of ways to reduce hostility and promote peaceful interactions; included are forecasting theory and methodology, historical analysis, and crisis analysis
Institutional affiliation: Center for International Development
Editor: Edward E. Azar
Editorial address:
Department of Political Science
University of North Carolina
Chapel Hill, NC 27514
Frequency: 4/year
Circulation: 2,050
Subscription rate(s): individual $40, other $74
Pages/issue: 100
Readership: academics, institutions
Indexed/abstracted in: New Serial Titles 1971-75

Manuscripts
Query: no
Abstract: yes, 150 words
Style guide: MOS
Preferred length: 1,200 words
Number of copies: 3
Notes: end of manuscript
Blind referee: no
Time to consider manuscript: 3–8 weeks
Proportion of manuscripts accepted: 70 percent
Illustrations accepted: tables, graphs, charts, photos, drawings
Foreign languages: no

Reviews
Book review editor: Edward E. Azar
Address: same as above
Seeking reviewers: yes
Unsolicited reviews accepted: yes
How to apply: letter of inquiry
Include in application: professional degrees, institutional affiliation, areas of expertise, published works, current research, a full vita
Materials reviewed: books
Length of review: 150–300 words

Additional notes
Simultaneous submission is not allowed.

INTERNATIONAL JOURNAL

Focus: information and analysis about international affairs in the post-1914 period, with emphasis on current affairs and Canadian foreign policy
Institutional affiliation: Canadian Institute of International Affairs
Editors: James Eayrs, Robert Spencer
Editorial address:
15 King's College Circle
Toronto, Ontario M5S 2V9
CANADA
Frequency: 4/year
Circulation: 3,200
Subscription rate(s): subscriptions prepaid direct $18, others $21
Pages/issue: 200–225
Readership: academics, students, attentive public
Indexed/abstracted in: ABC POL SCI, Can Ind, Ind Can Leg Per Lit, SSCI, Universal Ref Syst, Int Polit Sci Abstr

Manuscripts
Query: not required, but preferred
Abstract: no
Style guide: MOS (except that British spelling is preferred)
Preferred length: 5,500 words
Number of copies: 2
Notes: end of manuscript
Blind referee: no
Time to consider manuscript: 3–5 weeks
Proportion of manuscripts accepted: not given
Illustrations accepted: tables, graphs, charts, drawings
Foreign languages: French

Reviews
Book review editors: James Eayrs, Robert Spencer
Address: same as above
Seeking reviewers: no
Unsolicited reviews accepted: rarely
How to apply: letter of inquiry

Include in application: professional degrees, institutional affiliation, areas of expertise
Materials reviewed: books
Length of review: 400 words

Additional notes

Each issue of *IJ* is centered on a specific theme which is announced at least 1 year in advance (listed on page ii of each issue). Potential authors should check for this before submitting manuscript or write and ask if a theme into which their piece might fit is projected. Because of our theme issues, many of our articles are solicited. We do not review text books except in rare instances; nor do we review books about the domestic affairs of foreign countries. Those submitting manuscripts should include a covering letter which includes their return address and a short current vita. Although acceptable, simultaneous submission is discouraged. Most articles appear 3–6 months after acceptance. Published authors are paid $125 (Canadian).

INTERNATIONAL JOURNAL OF MIDDLE EAST STUDIES

Focus: interdisciplinary studies of both the historical and contemporary Middle East
Editor: Afaf Lufti al-Sayyid-Marsot
Editorial address:
Center for Near Eastern Studies
University of California
Los Angeles, CA 90024
Frequency: 4/year
Circulation: 2,000
Subscription rate(s): $67.50
Pages/issue: 115
Readership: academics
Indexed/abstracted in: ABC POL SCI, Hist Abstr

Manuscripts
Query: no
Abstract: yes
Style guide: MOS

Preferred length: 12,000 words maximum
Number of copies: 2
Notes: end of manuscript
Blind referee: yes
Time to consider manuscript: 3 months
Proportion of manuscripts accepted: not given
Illustrations accepted: tables, graphs, charts, drawings
Foreign languages: no

Reviews
Book review editor: Michael W. Suleiman
Address:
Department of Political Science
Kansas State University
Manhattan, KS 66506
Seeking reviewers: yes
Unsolicited reviews accepted: yes
How to apply: letter of inquiry
Include in application: professional degrees, institutional affiliation, areas of expertise, published works, current research
Materials reviewed: books
Length of review: 3–4 pages

Additional notes

Authors receive 50 offprints of their article without charge; additional copies may be purchased if ordered at proof stage. Simultaneous submission is not allowed. Articles are published 1 year after acceptance.

INTERNATIONAL JOURNAL OF POLITICAL EDUCATION

Focus: studies on socialization theory and the development of political awareness
Editor: Willem Langeveld
Editorial address:
Department of Political Science
University of Amsterdam
Keizersgracht 73
1015 CE Amsterdam
THE NETHERLANDS
Frequency: 4/year

Circulation: 700
Subscription rate(s): $22.50
Pages/issue: not given
Readership: political scientists
Indexed/abstracted in: Curr Cont, ABC POL SCI

Manuscripts
Query: no
Abstract: yes, 300 words
Style guide: available on request
Preferred length: 5,000 words minimum
Number of copies: 3
Notes: not given
Blind referee: no
Time to consider manuscript: not given
Proportion of manuscripts accepted: not given
Illustrations accepted: not given
Foreign languages: no

Reviews
Book review editor: Willem Langeveld
Address: same as above
Materials reviewed: books

Additional notes
Send a brief biography with submitted manuscript. Simultaneous submission is not allowed. Articles are published 4–5 months after acceptance.

INTERNATIONAL JOURNAL OF URBAN AND REGIONAL RESEARCH

Focus: interdisciplinary urban studies
Editor: Michael Harloe
Editorial address:
Department of Sociology
University of Essex
Colchester, Essex
ENGLAND
Frequency: 4/year
Circulation: not given
Subscription rate(s): individual $39.50, institutional $59.50
Pages/issue: 135
Readership: academics
Indexed/abstracted in: not given

Manuscripts
Query: no
Abstract: yes, 250 words
Style guide: HLRA for references, write for guidelines
Preferred length: 8,000 words maximum
Number of copies: 3
Notes: not given
Blind referee: no
Time to consider manuscript: not given
Proportion of manuscripts accepted: not given
Illustrations accepted: tables, graphs, charts
Foreign languages: French, others may be considered for translation

Reviews
Book review editor: G. G. Pickvance
Address:
IJURR
Cornwalis Building
University of Kent
Canterbury, Kent
ENGLAND
Materials reviewed: books in any major language will be considered
Length of review: 1,000–3,000 words

INTERNATIONAL LABOR AND WORKING CLASS HISTORY

Focus: trade unionism, socialism, communism, and other workers' political movements; working class culture, immigration, women, and families
Institutional affiliation: Yale University
Editor: David Montgomery
Editorial address:
Department of History
Yale University
New Haven, CT 06520
Frequency: 2/year
Circulation: 450
Subscription rate(s): student $5, employed $8, institutional $13
Pages/issue: 100

Readership: academics, general public
Indexed/abstracted in: not given

Manuscripts
see additional notes

Reviews
Book review editor: David Moantgomery
Address: same as above
Seeking reviewers: yes
Unsolicited reviews accepted: yes
How to apply: letter of inquiry
Include in application: institutional affiliation, areas of expertise, current research
Materials reviewed: books, films, tapes
Length of review: 1,000–2,000 words

Additional notes
International Labor and Working Class History does not publish research articles. The majority of the journal is devoted to book reviews, with some attention paid to conferences, news, announcements, and listings of current research of people working in the field.

INTERNATIONAL LABOUR REVIEW

Focus: problems and issues confronting international labor and the formation of relevant social policy
Institutional affiliation: International Labour Office
Editor: submit to the Chief Editor
Editorial address:
International Labour Office
CH-1211
Geneva 22
SWITZERLAND
Frequency: 6/year
Circulation: 9,500
Subscription rate(s): $25.50
Pages/issue: 110
Readership: academics, professionals
Indexed/abstracted in: J of Econ Lit, PAIS, SSCI, Pers Manage Abstr, Work Rel Abstr

Manuscripts
Query: no, but advisable
Abstract: yes, 100 words
Style guide: see current issue
Preferred length: 6,250 words maximum
Number of copies: 1
Notes: end of manuscript
Blind referee: no
Time to consider manuscript: not given
Proportion of manuscripts accepted: not given
Illustrations accepted: tables, diagrams, drawings
Foreign languages: French, Spanish

Reviews
not applicable

Additional notes
Simultaneous submission is not permitted.

INTERNATIONAL MIGRATION REVIEW

Focus: interdisciplinary study of human migration and ethnic relations
Institutional affiliation: Center for Migration Studies
Editor: submit to the Editor
Editorial address:
Center for Migration Studies
209 Flagg Place
Staten Island, NY 10304
Frequency: 4/year
Circulation: 2,300
Subscription rate(s): individual $22.50, institutional $29.50
Pages/issue: 200
Readership: social scientists
Indexed/abstracted in: Sociol Abstr, Hist Abstr, Amer Hist and Life, Curr Cont, USPSD

Manuscripts
Query: no
Abstract: yes, 100 words maximum
Style guide: see current issue
Preferred length: no preference
Number of copies: 2

Notes: end of manuscript
Blind referee: yes
Time to consider manuscript: not given
Proportion of manuscripts accepted: not given
Illustrations accepted: tables, figures
Foreign languages: no

Reviews
Book review editor: submit to the Editor
Address: same as above
Materials reviewed: books
Length of review: 2–4 pages

INTERNATIONAL ORGANIZATION

Focus: international relations and international political economy
Editors: Peter Katzenstein, Roger Haydon
Editorial address:
130 Uris Hall
Cornell University
Ithaca, NY 14853
Frequency: 4/year
Circulation: 3,400
Subscription rate(s): individual $15, institutional $30
Pages/issue: 200
Readership: academics
Indexed/abstracted in: not given

Manuscripts
Query: no
Abstract: yes
Style guide: MOS
Preferred length of manuscript: no preference
Number of copies: 3
Notes: end of manuscript
Blind referee: yes
Time to consider manuscript: 2 months
Proportion of manuscripts accepted: 10 percent
Illustrations accepted: tables, graphs, charts
Foreign languages: no

Reviews
Book review editor: James A. Caporaso
Address: same as above
Seeking reviewers: no
Unsolicited reviews accepted: rarely
How to apply: letter of inquiry
Include in application: institutional affiliation, areas of expertise, published works, current research, books proposed for review
Materials reviewed: books
Length of review: varies

Additional notes
Address for all business inquiries: MIT Press Journals, 28 Carleton Street, Cambridge, MA 02142. Send all review copies to the editorial office. Reviews will be accepted in West European languages. Simultaneous submission is not permitted. Articles are published 6 months after acceptance.

INTERNATIONAL PERSPECTIVES

Focus: Canada and world affairs
Editor: Gordon Cullingham
Editorial address:
P.O. Box 949
Station "B"
Ottawa, Ontario, K1P 9Z9
CANADA
Frequency: 6/year
Circulation: 4,000
Subscription rate(s): $15
Pages/issue: 36
Readership: academics, diplomats, journalists, business people
Indexed/abstracted in: Can Ind

Manuscripts
Query: no
Abstract: no
Style guide: MOS
Preferred length: 2,500 words
Number of copies: 1
Notes: not used
Blind referee: no
Time to consider manuscript: 2 weeks

Proportion of manuscripts
    accepted: 50 percent
Illustrations accepted: tables, charts,
    photos
Foreign languages: French

Reviews
Book review editor: Gordon
    Cullingham
Address: same as above
Seeking reviewers: yes
Unsolicited reviews accepted: yes
How to apply: letter of inquiry
Include in application: institutional
    affiliation, areas of expertise,
    published works, current research
Materials reviewed: books
Length of review: 1,000 words

Additional notes
Authors receive $250 per article upon
publication.

INTERNATIONAL POLITICAL SCIENCE REVIEW/REVUE INTERNATIONALE DE SCIENCE POLITIQUE

Focus: central and currently
    controversial themes in political
    science; innovative concepts and
    methodologies of political analysis
Institutional affiliation: International
    Political Science Association
Editor: John Meisel
Editorial address:
    International Political Science
    Association
    University of Ottawa
    Ottawa, Ontario K1N 6N5
    CANADA
Frequency: 4/year
Circulation: 1,200
Subscription rate(s): individual $20,
    institutional $42
Pages/issue: 125
Readership: political and social
    scientists
Indexed/abstracted in: ABC POL SCI

Manuscripts
Query: no
Abstract: yes, 100–150 words
Style guide: available on request
Preferred length: 25–30 pages
Number of copies: 1
Notes: end of manuscript
Blind referee: yes
Time to consider manuscript: 1
    month
Proportion of manuscripts
    accepted: not given
Illustrations accepted: tables, charts
Foreign languages: French

Reviews
not applicable

Additional notes
Each issue has a different issue editor.
Prospective authors should examine a
recent copy of the journal for the names
and addresses of future issue editors
and subjects. Abstracts should state the
intellectual problem under consideration,
the method of argument addressed to
the problem, and the conclusions
reached by the author(s). A brief
biographic paragraph describing each
author's current affiliation, research
interests, and recent publications should
accompany the manuscript.

INTERNATIONAL PROBLEMS

Focus: studies of war, peace,
    international relations, the politics of
    developing nations, and the Middle
    East conflict
Institutional affiliation: Israeli Institute
    for the Study of International Affairs
Editor: Mushkat Marion
Editorial address:
    POB 17027
    Tel Aviv 61170
    ISRAEL
Frequency: 4/year
Circulation: 6,100
Subscription rate(s): $25
Pages/issue: not given

Readership: academics, students, politicians, journalists
Indexed/abstracted in: Hist Abstr, Peace Res Abstr

Manuscripts
Query: no
Abstract: yes
Style guide: none required
Preferred length: 6,000–9,000 words
Number of copies: 2
Notes: not given
Blind referee: no
Time to consider manuscript: 6–8 weeks
Proportion of manuscripts accepted: not given
Illustrations accepted: not given
Foreign languages: no

Reviews
Book review editor: Mushkat Marion
Address: same as above
Materials reviewed: books

Additional notes
Simultaneous submission not allowed. Articles appear 6–9 months after acceptance.

INTERNATIONAL REGIONAL SCIENCE REVIEW

Focus: interdisciplinary approach to the theoretical and empirical study of regional science and spatial analysis
Institutional affiliation: Regional Science Association
Editor: Andrew M. Isserman
Editorial address:
    347 Jessup Hall
    University of Iowa
    Iowa City, IA 52242
Frequency: 3/year
Circulation: 3,000
Subscription rate(s): student $8, individual $16, institutional $30
Pages/issue: 95

Readership: social scientists
Indexed/abstracted in: ABC POL SCI, Curr Cont, Geo Abstr, J of Econ Lit, Popul Ind, SSCI, Sage Pub Admin Abstr, Sage Urb Stud Abstr

Manuscripts
Query: no
Abstract: yes, 100 words maximum
Style guide: available on request
Preferred length: 15–25 pages
Number of copies: 4
Notes: bottom of page
Blind referee: no
Time to consider manuscript: 3–4 months
Proportion of manuscripts accepted: not given
Illustrations accepted: tables, graphs, charts, maps
Foreign languages: no

Reviews
not applicable

INTERNATIONAL REVIEW OF HISTORY AND POLITICAL SCIENCE

Focus: international historical and political studies
Editor: D. P. Rastogi
Editorial address:
    Review Publications
    Rastogi Street
    Subhash Bazar
    Meerut 2
    INDIA
Frequency: 4/year
Circulation: 1,500
Subscription rate(s): $10 (in India)
Pages/issue: 75
Readership: academics
Indexed/abstracted in: CRIS, Int Polit Sci Abstr, SSCI, Sociol Abstr, Hist Abstr

Manuscripts
Query: no
Abstract: no
Style guide: see current issue or write for guidelines
Preferred length: 10–30 pages

Number of copies: 1
Notes: bottom of page
Blind referee: no
Time to consider manuscript: not given
Proportion of manuscripts accepted: not given
Illustrations accepted: tables, graphs, charts, drawings
Foreign languages: no

Reviews
Book review editor: submit to the Editor
Address: same as above
Materials reviewed: books
Length of review: 5–10 pages

INTERNATIONAL SECURITY

Focus: all aspects of national and international security policy, including political instability, resource scarcity, foreign policy, military strategy, and strategic and conventional arms control
Institutional affiliation: Center for Science and International Affairs, Harvard University
Editor: Steven E. Miller
Editorial address:
Center for Science and International Affairs
Kennedy School of Government
79 Boylston Street
Cambridge, MA 02138
Frequency: 4/year
Circulation: 7,000
Subscription rate(s): individual $18, institutional $40
Pages/issue: 200
Readership: academics in the fields of international relations, defense and foreign policy; national security policymakers and practitioners; military officials; journalists; industrialists
Indexed/abstracted in: ABC POL SCI, SSCI, Curr Cont, RG

Manuscripts
Query: no
Abstract: no
Style guide: MOS
Preferred length: 20–30 pages
Number of copies: 3, double-spaced
Notes: end of manuscript
Blind referee: yes
Time to consider manuscript: 2–3 months
Proportion of manuscripts accepted: 6 percent
Illustrations accepted: tables, graphs
Foreign languages: no

Reviews
Book review editor: Steven E. Miller
Address: Same as above
Seeking reviewers: yes
Unsolicited reviews accepted: yes
How to apply: letter of inquiry
Include in application: institutional affiliation, areas of expertise, current research.
Materials reviewed: books
Length of review: 10–20 pages, double-spaced

Additional notes
Substantively, articles must deal with defense and/or foreign policy as it bears upon the use or threat of force in international affairs. The essay is the primary vehicle for such discussions; research notes (usually on newly-surfaced historical documents) and book review essays, as well as debates and Point/Counterpoint pieces, usually complement a roster of 7–8 essays at a rate of about two per issue. Articles must be policy-relevant as well as scholarly and analytical. The editors consider a submitted essay's timeliness and originality, as well as its fit into editorial priorities, the balance and diversity of an issue's contents, and scheduling. *International Security* has a production lead-time of 3½ months, and an editorial decision-making time of at least 2 months. Articles must, therefore, be able to stand up against the vicissitudes of official decisions and the course of world events, while remaining

timely. Since review essays take the form of an extended critique of one, two, or three books, permitting the author to air his/her own views, the author should be a recognized expert in the areas covered in the books reviewed.

INTERNATIONAL SECURITY REVIEW

Focus: national security of the United States
Institutional affiliation: The Center for International Security Studies of the American Security Council Foundation
Editor: Debra H. Lewin
Editorial address:
The Center for International Security Studies
Boston, VA 22713
Frequency: 4/year
Circulation: 4,000
Subscription rate(s): domestic $14, foreign $20
Pages/issue: 125
Readership: members of Congress and staff, academics, professionals

Manuscripts
Query: no
Abstract: not required, but preferred
Style guide: available on request
Preferred length: 15–30 pages
Number of copies: 1–2, double-spaced
Notes: end of manuscript
Blind referee: no
Time to consider manuscript: 6–8 weeks
Proportion of manuscripts accepted: 25 percent
Illustrations accepted: tables, graphs, charts
Foreign languages: no

Reviews
not applicable

Additional notes
Biographic information on author required with manuscript.

INTERNATIONAL SOCIAL SCIENCE JOURNAL

Focus: social science
Editor: Peter Lengyel
Editorial address:
Unesco
7 Place de Fontenay
75700 Paris
FRANCE
Frequency: 4/year
Circulation: 4,500
Subscription rate(s): $23
Pages/issue: 120–150
Readership: social scientists
Indexed/abstracted in: PAIS, Psychol Abstr, SSCI, Soc Sci Ind, ABC POL SCI

Manuscripts
Query: no, but advisable
Abstract: no
Style guide: write for guidelines
Preferred length: no preference
Number of copies: 2
Notes: end of manuscript
Blind referee: no
Time to consider manuscript: not given
Proportion of manuscripts accepted: not given
Illustrations accepted: tables, charts, photos, diagrams
Foreign languages: French, Spanish, and Arabic editions are published

Reviews
not applicable

INTERNATIONAL SOCIAL SCIENCE REVIEW

Focus: all social sciences
Institutional affiliation: Pi Gamma Mu
Editor: Panos D. Bardis
Editorial address:
Toledo University
Toledo, OH 43606
Frequency: 4/year
Circulation: 12,000
Subscription rate(s): $10
Pages/issue: 64

Readership: academics
Indexed/abstracted in: not given

Manuscripts
Query: no
Abstract: yes
Style guide: MOS
Preferred length: 15–20 pages
Number of copies: 2
Notes: end of manuscript
Blind referee: yes
Time to consider manuscript: 6 weeks
Proportion of manuscripts accepted: 25 percent
Illustrations accepted: tables, graphs, charts, drawings
Foreign languages: no

Reviews
Book review editor: Panos D. Bardis
Address: same as above
Seeking reviewers: yes
Unsolicited reviews accepted: yes
How to apply: letter of inquiry
Include in application: professional degrees, institutional affiliation, areas of expertise, published works, foreign languages, current research
Materials reviewed: books
Length of review: 1–3 pages

Additional notes
The *Review* is an interdisciplinary, international publication interested in useful, scholarly studies, not pretentious jargon.

INTERNATIONAL STUDIES NOTES

Focus: innovative research and curricular and program reports on international affairs
Institutional affiliation: International Studies Association
Editor: Joan K. Wadlow
Editorial address:
College of Arts and Sciences
University of Wyoming
Laramie, WY 82071
Frequency: 4/year

Circulation: 2,000
Subscription rate(s): $20
Pages/issue: 20
Readership: academics, practitioners, and others concerned with the international arena
Indexed/abstracted in: ABC POL SCI, Amer Hist and Life, Hist Abstr

Manuscripts
Query: no
Abstract: no
Style guide: MOS
Preferred length: 15 pages
Number of copies: 4
Notes: end of manuscript
Blind referee: yes
Time to consider manuscript: 6–12 weeks
Proportion of manuscripts accepted: 33 percent
Illustrations accepted: tables, graphs, charts
Foreign languages: no

Reviews
not applicable

Additional notes
The editors are extremely anxious to help those trying to break into the publishing field. International studies explored from an interdisciplinary perspective are especially welcome. Bibliographical essays are also encouraged.

INTERNATIONAL STUDIES QUARTERLY

Focus: promotion of interdisciplinary, problem-oriented, scholarly research in international studies, including international relations and comparative studies, utilizing cross-cultural, legal, economic, historical, and behavioral modes of analysis
Institutional affiliation: International Studies Association
Editors: P. Terrence Hopmann, Raymond D. Duvall, Brian L. Job, Robert T. Kudrle

Editorial address:
Harold Scott Quigley Center of
International Studies
1246 Social Sciences Building
267 19th Avenue South
University of Minnesota
Minneapolis, MN 55455
Frequency: 4/year
Circulation: 3,350
Subscription rate(s): student $10, ISA
member $20–$35 (depending on
income)
Pages/issue: 160
Readership: scholars, policymakers
Indexed/abstracted in: not given

Manuscripts
Query: no
Abstract: yes
Style guide: SAGE
Preferred length: 20–40 pages
Number of copies: 4
Notes: end of manuscript
Blind referee: yes
Time to consider manuscript: 3
months
**Proportion of manuscripts
accepted:** 15 percent
Illustrations accepted: tables,
graphs, charts, drawings
Foreign languages: no

Reviews
not applicable

Additional notes
Simultaneous submission is not allowed.
Articles appear 6–12 months after
acceptance.

INTERPRETATION: A JOURNAL OF POLITICAL PHILOSOPHY

Focus: political philosophy
Editor: submit to the Editor-in-Chief
Editorial address:
Building G 101
Queens College
Flushing, NY 11367
Frequency: 3/year
Circulation: 700

Subscription rate(s): $10
Pages/issue: 225
Readership: political and social
scientists
Indexed/abstracted in: Phil Ind

Manuscripts
Query: no
Abstract: no
Style guide: MLA
Preferred length: no preference
Number of copies: 1, ribbon copy
Notes: end of manuscript
Blind referee: no
Time to consider manuscript: not
given
**Proportion of manuscripts
accepted:** not given
Illustrations accepted: tables, charts,
maps
Foreign languages: no

Reviews
Book review editor: submit to the
Editor-in-Chief
Address: same as above
Materials reviewed: books
Length of review: 5–10 pages

ISSUE: A QUARTERLY JOURNAL OF AFRICANIST OPINION

Focus: political, social, economic, and
cultural development in Africa
Institutional affiliation: African
Studies Association
Editor: submit to the Editor
Editorial address:
African Studies Association
255 Kinsey Hall
405 Hilgard Avenue
Los Angeles, CA 90024
Frequency: 4/year
Circulation: 2,200
Subscription rate(s): included in ASA
membership dues
Pages/issue: 80
Readership: academics
Indexed/abstracted in: Hist Abstr

Manuscripts

Query: no
Abstract: no
Style guide: MOS
Preferred length: no preference
Number of copies: 2
Notes: end of article
Blind referee: no
Time to consider manuscript: not given
Proportion of manuscripts accepted: not given
Illustrations accepted: tables, graphs, charts
Foreign languages: no

Reviews

Book review editor: submit to the Editor
Address: same as above
Materials reviewed: books
Length of review: 10–15 pages

ISSUES AND STUDIES: A JOURNAL OF CHINA STUDIES AND INTERNATIONAL AFFAIRS

Focus: problems of Chinese Communism and other Communist systems; general international affairs; international affairs of Communist systems
Institutional affiliation: Institute of International Relations, National Chengchi University
Editor: submit to the Managing Editor
Editorial address:
Institute of International Relations
64 Wan Shou Road
Mucha, Taipei
REPUBLIC OF CHINA
Frequency: not given
Circulation: not given
Subscription rate(s): $22
Pages/issue: 125
Readership: specialists in China studies, other academics
Indexed/abstracted in: Curr Cont, ABC POL SCI, Int Polit Sci Abstr, Hist Abstr, Amer Hist and Life

Manuscripts

Query: no
Abstract: no
Style guide: see current issue or write for guidelines
Preferred length: no preference
Number of copies: 2
Notes: end of manuscript
Blind referee: no
Time to consider manuscript: not given
Proportion of manuscripts accepted: not given
Illustrations accepted: tables
Foreign languages: no

Reviews

Book review editor: submit to the Managing Editor
Address: same as above
Materials reviewed: books

THE JAPAN INTERPRETER: A JOURNAL OF SOCIAL AND POLITICAL IDEAS

Focus: current Japanese thinking on political, social, and economic issues, both domestic and international
Institutional affiliation: Center for Japanese Social and Political Studies
Editor: submit to the Publisher
Editorial address:
Center for Japanese Social and Political Studies
2-8-8 Nishinogawa
Komae-shi
Tokyo 201
JAPAN
Frequency: 2/year
Circulation: 3,000
Subscription rate(s): $15
Pages/issue: 150–160
Readership: academics
Indexed/abstracted in: Hist Abstr, SSCI, ABC POL SCI

Manuscripts

Query: no
Abstract: no

Style guide: write for guidelines
Preferred length: no preference
Number of copies: 1
Notes: end of manuscript
Blind referee: no
Time to consider manuscript: not given
Proportion of manuscripts accepted: not given
Illustrations accepted: tables
Foreign languages: Japanese

Reviews
Book review editor: submit to the Publisher
Address: same as above
Materials reviewed: books
Length of review: 4-6 pages

JERUSALEM JOURNAL OF INTERNATIONAL RELATIONS

Focus: interdisciplinary approach to all areas of international politics
Institutional affiliation: The Leonard Davis Institute for International Relations, The Hebrew University of Jerusalem
Editor: Gabriel Sheffer
Editorial address:
The Leonard Davis Institute for International Relations
The Hebrew University
Mount Scopus
91905 Jerusalem
ISRAEL
Frequency: 4/year
Circulation: not given
Subscription rate(s): $25
Pages/issue: 100
Readership: academics
Indexed/abstracted in: ABC POL SCI, Hist Abstr

Manuscripts
Query: no
Abstract: no
Style guide: see current issue or write for guidelines
Preferred length: 6,000-7,500 words
Number of copies: 2
Notes: end of manuscript

Blind referee: yes
Time to consider manuscript: not given
Proportion of manuscripts accepted: not given
Illustrations accepted: tables
Foreign languages: no

Reviews
Book review editor: Uri Bialer
Address: same as above
Materials reviewed: books
Length of review: 1-3 pages

Additional notes
Simultaneous submission is not permitted.

JOURNAL OF AFRICAN STUDIES

Focus: African studies
Institutional affiliation: African Studies Center, UCLA
Editor: Lorraine Gardner
Editorial address:
African Studies Center
University of California
Los Angeles, CA 90024
Frequency: 4/year
Circulation: 600
Subscription rate(s): $12
Pages/issue: 64
Readership: African specialists, academics, general public
Indexed/abstracted in: not given

Manuscripts
Query: no
Abstract: no
Style guide: MOS
Preferred length: 30 pages
Number of copies: 1
Notes: end of manuscript
Blind referee: no
Time to consider manuscript: 6-12 months
Proportion of manuscripts accepted: 66 percent
Illustrations accepted: camera-ready tables, graphs, charts, photos
Foreign languages: no

Reviews

Book review editor: Lorraine Gardner
Address: same as above
Seeking reviewers: yes
Unsolicited reviews accepted: yes
How to apply: letter of inquiry
Include in application: institutional
affiliation
Materials reviewed: books

Additional notes

Simultaneous submission is allowed.
Articles are published 1–2 years after
acceptance.

JOURNAL OF AMERICAN CULTURE

Focus: American culture and society
Institutional affiliation: Bowling Green
State University
Editor: Ray B. Browne
Editorial address:
Popular Culture Center
Bowling Green State University
Bowling Green, OH 43403
Frequency: 4/year
Circulation: 1,000
Subscription rate(s): $15
Pages/issue: 200
Readership: academics
Indexed/abstracted in: not given

Manuscripts

Query: no
Abstract: no
Style guide: MLA
Preferred length: 12–18 pages
Number of copies: 1
Notes: end of manuscript
Blind referee: no
Time to consider manuscript: 1
month
**Proportion of manuscripts
accepted:** 20 percent
Illustrations accepted: tables,
graphs, charts, photos
Foreign languages: no

Reviews

Book review editor: Pat Browne
Address: same as above

Seeking reviewers: yes
Unsolicited reviews accepted: yes
How to apply: letter of inquiry
Include in application: professional
degrees, institutional affiliation, areas
of expertise, current research
Materials reviewed: trade books
Length of review: 150–250 words

JOURNAL OF AMERICAN STUDIES

Focus: the politics, history, society,
economics, government, and arts of
the United States
Institutional affiliation: British
Association for American Studies
Editor: submit to the Editor
Editorial address:
School of English and American
Studies
University of East Anglia
Norwich NR4 7TJ
ENGLAND
Frequency: 3/year
Circulation: 1,500
Subscription rate(s): $65
Pages/issue: 150
Readership: academics
Indexed/abstracted in: Hist Abstr

Manuscripts

Query: no
Abstract: no
Style guide: MLA or write for
guidelines
Preferred length: 5,000 words
Number of copies: 1
Notes: end of manuscript
Blind referee: no
Time to consider manuscript: 3
months
**Proportion of manuscripts
accepted:** not given
Illustrations accepted: not given
Foreign languages: no

Reviews

Book review editor: submit to the
Editor
Address: same as above

Materials reviewed: books
Length of review: 3-5 pages

Additional notes

Simultaneous submission is not allowed. Articles appear 6-7 months after acceptance.

THE JOURNAL OF APPLIED BEHAVIORAL SCIENCE

Focus: theories of planned change applicable to individuals and systems; strategies of social intervention or innovation; the interplay among theory, practice, and values in the domain of planned change
Institutional affiliation: NTL Institute for Applied Behavioral Science
Editor: Susan Sherman
Editorial address:
NTL Institute
P.O. Box 9155 Rosslyn Station
Arlington, VA 22209
Frequency: 4/year
Circulation: 4,177
Subscription rate(s): individual $33, institutional $40
Pages/issue: 140-190
Readership: academics, particularly in the field of applied behavioral science
Indexed/abstracted in: Educ Admin Abstr, Pers Manage Abstr, Soc Work Res and Abstr

Manuscripts

Query: no
Abstract: yes
Style guide: APA
Preferred length: 10-20 pages
Number of copies: 5, double-spaced
Notes: end of manuscript
Blind referee: yes
Time to consider manuscript: 6 weeks
Proportion of manuscripts accepted: 6-10 percent
Illustrations accepted: tables, graphs, charts
Foreign languages: no

Reviews

Book review editor: Meyer Michael Cahn
Address: same as above
Seeking reviewers: yes
Unsolicited reviews accepted: no
How to apply: letter of inquiry
Include in application: professional degrees, institutional affiliation, areas of expertise, published works, current research
Materials reviewed: books
Length of review: 5-10 pages, double-spaced

Additional notes

Simultaneous submission is not permitted. Articles appear 1 year after acceptance.

JOURNAL OF ARAB AFFAIRS

Focus: current Arab affairs
Institutional affiliation: Middle East Research Group
Editor: Tawfic Farah
Editorial address:
2611 North Fresno Street
Fresno, CA 93703
Frequency: 2/year
Circulation: 1,300
Subscription rate(s): individual $15, institutional $25
Pages/issue: 150
Readership: academics, business people, government officials
Indexed/abstracted in: ABC POL SCI, Curr Cont, Int Polit Sci Abstr, PAIS, Mid East Abstr Ind, SSCI, Sociol Abstr, USPSD

Manuscripts

Query: no
Abstract: yes, 150 words
Style guide: none required
Preferred length: 25 pages
Number of copies: 3
Notes: end of manuscript
Blind referee: yes
Time to consider manuscript: 3 months
Proportion of manuscripts accepted: 20 percent

Illustrations accepted: tables, graphs, charts, drawings
Foreign languages: no

Reviews
Book review editor: Tawfic Farah
Address: same as above
Seeking reviewers: yes
Unsolicited reviews accepted: no
How to apply: letter of inquiry
Include in application: professional degrees, institutional affiliation, areas of expertise, published works, foreign languages, current research
Materials reviewed: books
Length of review: 900 words

JOURNAL OF AREA STUDIES

Focus: theoretical and methodological discussion of area studies as a field of study
Editor: submit to the Editors
Editorial address:
Portsmouth Polytechnic School of Languages and Area Studies
Hampshire Terrace
Portsmouth P01 2B6
ENGLAND
Frequency: 2/year
Circulation: not given
Subscription rate(s): £4
Pages/issue: 40
Readership: specialists in area studies, social scientists
Indexed/abstracted in: ABC POL SCI, Hist Abstr, Amer Hist and Life

Manuscripts
Query: no
Abstract: no
Style guide: see current issue or write for guidelines
Preferred length: 5,000 words maximum
Number of copies: 1
Notes: end of manuscript
Blind referee: no
Time to consider manuscript: not given
Proportion of manuscripts accepted: not given

Illustrations accepted: camera-ready tables, graphs, diagrams, maps
Foreign languages: yes, other languages will be considered for translation

Reviews
Book review editor: submit to the Editors
Address: same as above
Materials reviewed: books
Length of review: 2–3 pages

JOURNAL OF ASIAN AND AFRICAN STUDIES

Focus: studies of man and society in the developing nations of Asia and Africa
Editor: K. Ishwaran
Editorial address:
Department of Sociology
York University
Downsview, Ontario M3J 1P3
CANADA
Frequency: 4/year
Circulation: not given
Subscription rate(s): 84 Dutch guilders
Pages/issue: 80
Readership: academics
Indexed/abstracted in: SSCI, ABC POL SCI, Hist Abstr

Manuscripts
Query: no
Abstract: no
Style guide: see current issue or write for guidelines
Preferred length: no preference
Number of copies: 1
Notes: end of manuscript
Blind referee: no
Time to consider manuscript: not given
Proportion of manuscripts accepted: not given
Illustrations accepted: tables
Foreign languages: no

Reviews
not applicable

THE JOURNAL OF ASIAN STUDIES

Focus: southern and eastern Asia
Institutional affiliation: Association for Asian Studies
Editor: Joyce K. Kallgren
Editorial address:
12 Barrows Hall
University of California
Berkeley, CA 94720
Frequency: 4/year
Circulation: 7,000
Subscription rate(s): student and retired $12.50, individual $25, institutional $60
Pages/issue: 220
Readership: scholars
Indexed/abstracted in: ABC POL SCI, Hist Abstr

Manuscripts
Query: no
Abstract: yes
Style guide: MOS
Preferred length: 50 pages maximum
Number of copies: 3
Notes: end of manuscript
Blind referee: yes
Time to consider manuscript: 2-3 months
Proportion of manuscripts accepted: 15 percent
Illustrations accepted: tables, graphs, charts, photos
Foreign languages: no

Reviews
Book review editor: see additional notes below
Seeking reviewers: yes
Unsolicited reviews accepted: yes
How to apply: letter of inquiry
Include in application: professional degrees, institutional affiliation, areas of expertise, published works, foreign languages, current research
Materials reviewed: books, films
Length of review: 600-1,000 words

Additional notes
Book review editors deal with six Asian geographical regions:
Asia General:
Joyce K. Kallgren
12 Barrows Hall
University of California
Berkeley, CA 94720
China and Inner Asia:
Guy S. Alitto
Department of History
University of Chicago
Chicago, IL 60637
Japan:
Susan Matisoff
Asian Languages Department
Stanford University
Stanford, CA 94305
Korea:
Karl Moskowitz
Department of East Asian Languages and Civilization
Harvard University
2 Divinity Avenue
Cambridge, MA 02138
South Asia:
Barbara Metcalf
c/o *Journal of Asian Studies*
12 Barrows Hall
University of California
Berkeley, CA 94720
Southeast Asia:
Charles Keyes or E. Jane Keyes
Department of Anthropology
University of Washington
Seattle, WA 98195

JOURNAL OF BLACK STUDIES

Focus: interdisciplinary African and African-American studies
Editor: Molefi Kete Asante
Editorial address:
Department of African/African-American Studies
State University of New York-Buffalo
Buffalo, NY 14214
Frequency: 4/year
Circulation: 3,500
Subscription rate(s): individual $15, institutional $28

Pages/issue: 120
Readership: academics
Indexed/abstracted in: Curr Cont, Hist Abstr, PAIS, SSCI, Amer Hist and Life, Soc Sci Ind, Sociol Abstr

Manuscripts
Query: no
Abstract: no
Style guide: SAGE
Preferred length: 25 pages maximum
Number of copies: 2
Notes: end of manuscript
Blind referee: yes
Time to consider manuscript: 2 months
Proportion of manuscripts accepted: not given
Illustrations accepted: tables, graphs, charts, photos
Foreign languages: no

Reviews
Book review editor: James Pitts
Address: same as above
Unsolicited reviews accepted: yes
How to apply: letter of inquiry
Include in application: professional degrees, institutional affiliation, areas of expertise, foreign languages
Materials reviewed: books, films, tapes
Length of review: 3 pages

Additional notes
Simultaneous submission is permitted, but discouraged. Articles are published 6–9 months after acceptance.

JOURNAL OF CANADIAN STUDIES/REVUE D'ETUDES CANADIENNES

Focus: Canada
Institutional affiliation: Trent University
Editor: Arlene David
Editorial address:
Champlain College
Trent University
Peterborough, Ontario K9J 7B8
CANADA

Frequency: 4/year
Circulation: 1,650
Subscription rate(s): individual $10 (Canadian), institutional $20 (Canadian)
Pages/issue: 128
Readership: academics, academic libraries
Indexed/abstracted in: Hist Abstr, Hum Ind, SSCI, Can Ind

Manuscripts
Query: no
Abstract: no
Style guide: none required
Preferred length: 2,000–10,000 words
Number of copies: 2
Notes: end of manuscript
Blind referee: no
Time to consider manuscript: 6 months
Proportion of manuscripts accepted: not given
Illustrations accepted: tables, graphs, charts, photos
Foreign languages: French

Reviews
Book review editor: John Wadland
Address: same as above
Seeking reviewers: no

Additional notes
Simultaneous submission is permitted, but discouraged.

JOURNAL OF COMMON MARKET STUDIES

Focus: interdisciplinary studies on the integration process throughout the international system, but especially in Western Europe
Institutional affiliation: University Association for Contemporary European Studies
Editor: Loukas Tsoukalis
Editorial address:
UACES Secretariat
c/o King's College
The Stroud
London WC2R 2LS
ENGLAND

Frequency: 4/year
Circulation: 1,350
Subscription rate(s): individual $42.50, institutional $56
Pages/issue: 100
Readership: political and social scientists
Indexed/abstracted in: PAIS, SSCI, Soc Sci Ind, ABC POL SCI

Manuscripts
Query: no
Abstract: no
Style guide: available on request
Preferred length: no preference
Number of copies: 2
Notes: end of manuscript
Blind referee: no
Time to consider manuscript: not given
Proportion of manuscripts accepted: not given
Illustrations accepted: tables
Foreign languages: no

Reviews
Book review editor: Geoffrey Edwards
Address: same as above
Materials reviewed: books
Length of review: 1-2 pages

THE JOURNAL OF COMMONWEALTH AND COMPARATIVE POLITICS

Focus: comparative political studies of Commonwealth and other nations
Institutional affiliation: Institute of Commonwealth Studies, University of London
Editor: W. H. Morris-Jones
Editorial address:
Administrative Editor
Institute of Commonwealth Studies
27 Russell Square
London WC1B 5DS
ENGLAND
Frequency: 3/year
Circulation: 800
Subscription rate(s): individual £16, institutional £22.50

Pages/issue: 100-120
Readership: political and social scientists
Indexed/abstracted in: PAIS, ABC POL SCI

Manuscripts
Query: no
Abstract: no
Style guide: write for guidelines
Preferred length: 5,000-8,000 words
Number of copies: 1
Notes: end of manuscript
Blind referee: no
Time to consider manuscript: not given
Proportion of manuscripts accepted: not given
Illustrations accepted: tables
Foreign languages: no

Reviews
Book review editor: submit to the Administrative Editor
Address: same as above
Materials reviewed: books
Length of review: 1-3 pages

JOURNAL OF CONFLICT RESOLUTION

Focus: theory and research on peace and war within and between nations
Institutional affiliation: Yale University
Editor: submit to the Editor
Editorial address:
Political Science Department
Box 3532
Yale Station
New Haven, CT 06520
Frequency: 4/year
Circulation: 2,500
Subscription rate(s): individual $25, institutional $52.00
Pages/issue: 185
Readership: academics
Indexed/abstracted in: not given

Manuscripts
Query: no
Abstract: yes
Style guide: SAGE

Preferred length: 35 pages
Number of copies: 3
Notes: end of manuscript
Blind referee: yes
Time to consider manuscript: 3 months
Proportion of manuscripts accepted: 20 percent
Illustrations accepted: tables, graphs, charts, drawings
Foreign languages: no

Reviews
Seeking reviewers: no
Unsolicited reviews accepted: no
Materials reviewed: books

Additional notes
Simultaneous submission is not permitted. Articles are published 6–9 months after acceptance.

JOURNAL OF CONTEMPORARY HISTORY

Focus: current affairs
Editor: Walter Laqueur
Editorial address:
4 Devonshire Street
London W1N 2BH
ENGLAND
Frequency: 4/year
Circulation: not given
Subscription rate(s): individual $22.50, institutional $50.40
Pages/issue: 200
Readership: academics, students
Indexed/abstracted in: ABC POL SCI, Abstr Pop Cult, Curr Cont, Hist Abstr, Sage Pub Admin Abstr, Sage Urb Stud Abstr

Manuscripts
Query: no
Abstract: no
Style guide: available on request
Preferred length: 7,000 words maximum
Number of copies: 2
Notes: end of manuscript
Blind referee: no

Time to consider manuscript: 6–8 weeks
Proportion of manuscripts accepted: not given
Illustrations accepted: tables
Foreign languages: no

Reviews
not applicable

Additional notes
Simultaneous submission is allowed, but discouraged. Articles appear 15 months after acceptance.

JOURNAL OF CONTEMPORARY STUDIES

Focus: public policy, foreign and domestic
Institutional affiliation: Institute for Contemporary Studies
Editor: Walter J. Lammi
Editorial address:
260 California Street
Suite 811
San Francisco, CA 94111
Frequency: 4/year
Circulation: 2,500
Subscription rate(s): $15
Pages/issue: 104
Readership: policymakers, academics, educated general public
Indexed/abstracted in: not given

Manuscripts
Query: no
Abstract: no
Style guide: MOS
Preferred length: 20–25 pages
Number of copies: 1
Notes: end of manuscript
Blind referee: no
Time to consider manuscript: 4–6 weeks
Proportion of manuscripts accepted: varies
Illustrations accepted: tables, graphs, charts
Foreign languages: no

Reviews

Book review editor: Robert Kiernan
Address: same as above
Seeking reviewers: yes
Unsolicited reviews accepted: yes
How to apply: letter of inquiry
Include in application: institutional affiliation, areas of expertise, published works, current research
Materials reviewed: books (university press or nonprofit institution public policy books only)
Length of review: 5 pages

Additional notes

Articles may be data-backed and fairly technical, but must be written so as to be accessible to the nonspecialist general reader. Simultaneous submission is not allowed. Articles appear 2 months after acceptance.

JOURNAL OF DEVELOPING AREAS

Focus: interdisciplinary focus on the Third World and lesser developed regions of developed countries
Institutional affiliation: Western Illinois University
Editor: Nicholas C. Pano
Editorial address:
Western Illinois University
Macomb, IL 61455
Frequency: 4/year
Circulation: 1,500
Subscription rate(s): not given
Pages/issue: 150–160
Readership: academics, development specialists
Indexed/abstracted in: Amer Hist and Life, Econ Abstr, Hist Abstr, Sociol Abstr, USPSD, IBR, IBZ

Manuscripts

Query: no
Abstract: no
Style guide: MOS
Preferred length: 25–35 pages
Number of copies: 3
Notes: end of manuscript
Blind referee: yes

Time to consider manuscript: 4 months
Proportion of manuscripts accepted: 9–10 percent
Illustrations accepted: tables, graphs, charts
Foreign languages: no

Reviews

Book review editor: Richard T. Schaefer
Address: same as above
Seeking reviewers: yes
Unsolicited reviews accepted: no
How to apply: letter of inquiry
Include in application: professional degrees, institutional affiliation, areas of expertise, published works, current research
Materials reviewed: books
Length of review: 500–1,200 words

Additional notes

Simultaneous submission is allowed if editors are notified of such at the time of submission. Articles are published 1 year after acceptance.

THE JOURNAL OF DEVELOPMENT STUDIES

Focus: all aspects of development studies
Editor: submit to the Administrative Editor
Editorial address:
Journal of Development Studies
Frank Cass & Co. Ltd.
11 Gainsborough Road
London E11 1RS
ENGLAND
Frequency: 4/year
Circulation: 2,000
Subscription rate(s): individual £24, institutional £44
Pages/issue: 140
Readership: academics
Indexed/abstracted in: PAIS, SSCI, Soc Sci Ind, ABC POL SCI, J of Econ Lit, Work Rel Abstr

Manuscripts

Query: no
Abstract: yes, 100 words maximum
Style guide: see current issue or write for guidelines
Preferred length: 5,000–6,000 words
Number of copies: 2
Notes: end of manuscript
Blind referee: no
Time to consider manuscript: not given
Proportion of manuscripts accepted: not given
Illustrations accepted: camera-ready tables, graphs, charts
Foreign languages: no

Reviews

Book review editor: submit to the Administrative Editor
Address: same as above
Materials reviewed: books
Length of review: brief notes on books received by the *Journal*

Additional notes

Simultaneous submission is not permitted.

JOURNAL OF ECONOMIC HISTORY

Focus: demography, econometrics, history of economic thought
Institutional affiliation: North Carolina State University
Editor: Richard Sylla
Editorial address:
Department of Business and Economics
North Carolina State University
Raleigh, NC 27650
Frequency: 4/year
Circulation: 2,500
Subscription rate(s): student $5, individual $15, institutional $25
Pages/issue: 250
Readership: academics
Indexed/abstracted in: not given

Manuscripts

Query: no
Abstract: yes, after acceptance
Style guide: MOS
Preferred length: 30 pages maximum
Number of copies: 3
Notes: end of manuscript
Blind referee: yes
Time to consider manuscript: 3 months
Proportion of manuscripts accepted: 8–10 percent
Illustrations accepted: professionally drawn tables, graphs, charts, drawings
Foreign languages: French (rarely)

Reviews

Book review editor: Richard Sylla
Address: same as above
Seeking reviewers: yes
Unsolicited reviews accepted: no
How to apply: either a special form or a letter of inquiry
Include in application: professional degrees, institutional affiliation, areas of expertise, published works, foreign languages, current research
Materials reviewed: books
Length of review: 500 words maximum

Additional notes

Articles submitted by authors who are not members of the Economic History Association should be accompanied by a $15 submission fee. Simultaneous submission is not allowed. Articles are published 6 months after acceptance.

JOURNAL OF ENERGY AND DEVELOPMENT

Focus: multidisciplinary approach with emphasis on economic and policy aspects of energy and development; deals with domestic U.S. and international subjects
Institutional affiliation: International Research Center for Energy and Economic Development
Editor: Ragaei El Mallakh

Editorial address:
216 Economics Building
Box 256
University of Colorado
Boulder, CO 80309
Frequency: 2/year
Circulation: 2,200
Subscription rate(s): academic
(faculty/student) $14, university/
public libraries $24, institutional/
general $32
Pages/issue: 175–185
Readership: academics, industry,
business and finance, policymakers
in national and international areas
Indexed/abstracted in: ABC POL
SCI; Curr Cont, J of Econ Lit, SSCI,
Environ Per Bibl

Manuscripts
Query: no
Abstract: no
Style guide: MOS, MFW
Preferred length: 18–28 pages
Number of copies: 2, double-spaced
Notes: end of manuscript
Blind referee: no
Time to consider manuscript: 3
months
**Proportion of manuscripts
accepted:** 10 percent
Illustrations accepted: tables,
graphs, charts, drawings
Foreign languages: no

Reviews
Book review editor: Carl McGuire
Address:
same as above, or 770 18th Street
Boulder, CO 80302
Seeking reviewers: yes
Unsolicited reviews accepted:
occasionally
How to apply: letter of inquiry
Include in application: professional
degrees, institutional affiliation, areas
of expertise, foreign languages,
current research
Materials reviewed: books
Length of review: varies

Additional notes
Authors can contact the editors by
telephone to receive guidance or
suggestions on manuscripts and
reviews—303/492-7667 or 442-4014. Try
to keep technical material as
understandable to a general social
science readership as possible and,
where it fits in, attempt to draw policy
implications.

THE JOURNAL OF ETHNIC STUDIES

Focus: interdisciplinary scholarship,
opinion, and creative expression
Institutional affiliation: Western
Washington University
Editor: Jesse Hiraoka
Editorial address:
College of Ethnic Studies
Western Washington University
Bellingham, WA 98225
Frequency: 4/year
Circulation: 800
Subscription rate(s): $12
Pages/issue: 128
Readership: academics, government
officials, general public, social
scientists
Indexed/abstracted in: Amer Hist
and Life, Geo Abstr

Manuscripts
Query: no
Abstract: no
Style guide: MLA
Preferred length: no preference
Number of copies: 2
Notes: end of manuscript
Blind referee: no
Time to consider manuscript: 3
months
**Proportion of manuscripts
accepted:** 5–10 percent
Illustrations accepted: tables,
graphs, charts, photos
Foreign languages: no

Reviews
Book review editor: Jesse Hiraoka
Address: same as above

Seeking reviewers: yes
Unsolicited reviews accepted: yes
How to apply: letter of inquiry
Include in application: institutional affiliation, areas of expertise
Materials reviewed: books, fiction
Length of review: varies

Additional notes

Simultaneous submission is not permitted. Articles are published 4–6 months after acceptance.

JOURNAL OF HUMAN RESOURCES

Focus: policy formulation and implementation in education, manpower allocation, and welfare
Institutional affiliation: The Industrial Relations Research Institute and the Institute for Research on Poverty
Editor: W. Lee Hansen
Editorial address:
Social Science Building
1180 Observatory Drive
Madison, WI 53706
Frequency: 4/year
Circulation: 2,400
Subscription rate(s): individual $15, institutional $30
Pages/issue: 150
Readership: academics
Indexed/abstracted in: Pers Manage Abstr, Soc Sci Ind, SSCI, Work Rel Abstr

Manuscripts

Query: no
Abstract: yes, 100 words maximum
Style guide: write for guidelines
Preferred length: 20 pages maximum
Number of copies: 3
Notes: end of manuscript
Blind referee: no
Time to consider manuscript: not given
Proportion of manuscripts accepted: not given
Illustrations accepted: tables, figures
Foreign languages: no

Reviews

not applicable

JOURNAL OF INTERAMERICAN STUDIES AND WORLD AFFAIRS

Focus: interdisciplinary social science journal concerned with Latin America and the Caribbean and their relations with the rest of the world
Institutional affiliation: University of Miami, Sage Publications
Editor: John P. Harrison
Editorial address:
University of Miami
P.O. Box 248134
Coral Gables, FL 33124
Frequency: 4/year
Subscription rate(s): individual $20, institutional $42, foreign add $4.00
Readership: academics, professionals, businesses concerned with Latin America, general public
Indexed/abstracted in: Hist Abstr, Human Resour Abstr, Sage Urb Stud Abstr, Int Polit Sci Abstr, PAIS, Curr Cont, SSCI, Soc Sci Ind, ABC POL SCI, USPSD

Manuscripts

Query: no
Abstract: no
Style guide: SAGE
Preferred length: 25–30 pages
Number of copies: 2, double-spaced
Notes: end of manuscript
Blind referee: yes
Time to consider manuscript: 3 months
Proportion of manuscripts accepted: 20 percent
Illustrations accepted: tables, graphs, charts, maps
Foreign languages: yes, languages which referees competent on topic can read; the *Journal* pays for translation if accepted

Reviews

Review essays only. Recent books or monographs on a topic are combined to provide an expert forum for his/her own thoughts as generated by the books reviewed. Review essays are arranged for in communication with the editor. Unsolicited review essays are not encouraged.

Additional notes

Substantive and problem-oriented articles are preferred to those purely descriptive or exploring a methodologica approach. Simultaneous submission is allowed, but discouraged. Articles are published 6–9 months after acceptance.

THE JOURNAL OF INTERDISCIPLINARY HISTORY

Focus: methodological and substantive articles devoted to the application of other disciplines to research in history without geographical or chronological boundaries
Institutional affiliation: Massachusetts Institute of Technology School of Humanities and Social Science
Editor: T. K. Rabb
Editorial address: History Department Princeton University Princeton, NJ 08544
Frequency: 4/year
Circulation: 1,825
Subscription rate(s): student or retired $20, individual $25, institutional $50
Pages/issue: 190
Readership: historians, social scientists
Indexed/abstracted in: ABC POL SCI, Amer Hist and Life, Curr Cont, Hist Abstr

Manuscripts

Query: no
Abstract: no

Style guide: available on request
Preferred length: 30 pages maximum
Number of copies: 2, see additional notes
Notes: end of manuscript
Blind referee: no
Time to consider manuscript: 1 month
Proportion of manuscripts accepted: 10 percent
Illustrations accepted: tables, graphs, charts
Foreign languages: no

Reviews

Book review editor: T. K. Rabb
Address: same as above
Seeking reviewers: yes
Unsolicited reviews accepted: rarely
How to apply: letter of inquiry
Include in application: professional degrees, institutional affiliation, areas of expertise, published works, current research
Materials reviewed: books
Length of review: 2–3 pages

Additional notes

A ribbon copy should be sent to the editorial office of the *Journal*, 14N-323, M.I.T., Cambridge, MA 02139. The second copy should go to Professor T. K. Rabb at Princeton University. The ribbon copy should be accompanied by a self-addressed, stamped postcard for purposes of acknowledgment and postage to cover the return of the manuscript if it is not accepted. Simultaneous submission is not allowed. Articles are published 1 year after acceptance.

JOURNAL OF INTERNATIONAL AFFAIRS

Focus: international affairs
Institutional affiliation: Columbia University
Editor: Gordon Gray

Editorial address:
  Box 4
  International Affairs Building
  Columbia University
  New York, NY 10027
Frequency: 2/year
Circulation: 2,000
Subscription rate(s): individual $10,
  institutional $20
Pages/issue: 200–225
Readership: academics,professionals
Indexed/abstracted in: Soc Sci and
  Human Ind, ABC POL SCI, Int Polit
  Sci Abstr

Manuscripts
Query: yes
Abstract: yes
Style guide: MOS
Preferred length: not given
Number of copies: 3
Notes: end of manuscript
Blind referee: no
Time to consider manuscript: not
  given
**Proportion of manuscripts
  accepted:** not given
Illustrations accepted: tables,
  graphs, charts
Foreign languages: French

Reviews
Book review editors: Carlta Vitzthum,
  Christine Thomson
Address: same as above
Seeking reviewers: yes
Unsolicited reviews accepted: yes
How to apply: letter of inquiry
Include in application: professional
  degrees, institutional affiliation, areas
  of expertise, published works,
  current research
Materials reviewed: books
Length of review: 1,000 words

Additional notes
Contact editor-in-chief before submitting
manuscripts.

JOURNAL OF JAPANESE STUDIES

Focus: Japanese area studies
Institutional affiliation: Society for
  Japanese Studies
Editor: Susan B. Hanley
Editorial address:
  Thomson Hall
  DR-05
  University of Washington
  Seattle, WA 98195
Frequency: 2/year
Circulation: 1,500
Subscription rate(s): individual $12,
  institutional $14
Pages/issue: 235
Readership: academics, general
  public
Indexed/abstracted in: not given

Manuscripts
Query: no
Abstract: no
Style guide: MOS
Preferred length: 35–40 pages
Number of copies: 3
Notes: end of manuscript
Blind referee: yes
Time to consider manuscript: 2–3
  months
**Proportion of manuscripts
  accepted:** 15 percent
Illustrations accepted: tables,
  graphs, charts, photos
Foreign languages: Japanese, major
  European languages

Reviews
Book review editor: Roy Andrew
  Miller
Address: same as above
Seeking reviewers: no
Unsolicited reviews accepted: no
Materials reviewed: books

Additional notes
Papers on Japan in any discipline are
accepted, but jargon should be avoided
and specialized terms explained in the
text or a footnote. Stress is put on
interpretation and analysis. Simultaneous
submission is not permitted. Articles
appear within 1 year of acceptance.

JOURNAL OF LABOR RESEARCH

Focus: all aspects of labor studies
Editor: James T. Bennett
Editorial address:
Department of Economics
George Mason University
Fairfax, VA 22030
Frequency: 2/year
Circulation: not given
Subscription rate(s): individual $25, institutional $47
Pages/issue: not given
Readership: academics
Indexed/abstracted in: not given

Manuscripts

Query: no
Abstract: yes, 100 words
Style guide: available on request
Preferred length: no preference
Number of copies: 3
Notes: not given
Blind referee: no
Time to consider manuscript: not given
Proportion of manuscripts accepted: not given
Illustrations accepted: tables, graphs, charts
Foreign languages: no

Reviews

Book review editor: James T. Bennett
Address: same as above
Materials reviewed: books

Additional notes

A submission fee of $20 for nonsubscribers must accompany each manuscript.

JOURNAL OF LATIN AMERICAN STUDIES

Focus: the interdisciplinary study of Latin America
Institutional affiliation: Institutes of Latin American Studies at the Universities of Cambridge, Essex, Glasgow, Liverpool, London, and Oxford

Editor: Harold Blakemore
Editorial address:
Institute of Latin American Studies
31 Tavistock Square
London WC1H 9HA
ENGLAND
Frequency: 2/year
Circulation: not given
Subscription rate(s): individual $29.50, institutional $58.50
Pages/issue: 223
Readership: social scientists, Latin American specialists
Indexed/abstracted in: ABC POL SCI, Hist Abstr

Manuscripts

Query: no
Abstract: no
Style guide: available on request
Preferred length: 8,000 words maximum
Number of copies: 2
Notes: not given
Blind referee: no
Time to consider manuscript: not given
Proportion of manuscripts accepted: not given
Illustrations accepted: tables, graphs, charts, maps by arrangement only
Foreign languages: yes, for all other languages arrangements will be made as required for translation into English

Reviews

Book review editor: Harold Blakemore
Address: same as above
Seeking reviewers: yes
How to apply: letter of inquiry
Materials reviewed: books
Length of review: 2–3 pages

Additional notes

Contributors should keep one copy of the typescript for use in correcting proofs. Each contributor will receive, free of charge, 25 offprints of his or her article and a copy of the issue of the *Journal* in which it appears. Simultaneous submission is not allowed.

THE JOURNAL OF LAW AND ECONOMICS

Focus: economic problems as they relate to the law; effects of economic regulation, laws, and legal institutions on economic behavior
Institutional affiliation: University of Chicago Law School
Editors: William M. Landes, Dennis W. Carlton, Frank Easterbrook
Editorial address:
University of Chicago Law School
1111 East 60th Street
Chicago, IL 60637
Frequency: 2/year
Circulation: 3,400
Subscription rate(s): student $12, individual $18, institutional $25
Pages/issue: 200
Readership: academics, professional economists, legal scholars and students
Indexed/abstracted in: ABC POL SCI, Amer Hist and Life, Hist Abstr

Manuscripts
Query: no
Abstract: no
Style guide: MOS
Preferred length: 30–60 pages
Number of copies: 2
Notes: end of manuscript
Blind referee: no
Time to consider manuscript: 1–6 months
Proportion of manuscripts accepted: 10 percent
Illustrations accepted: tables, graphs, charts
Foreign languages: no

Reviews
not applicable

JOURNAL OF LEGAL STUDIES

Focus: theoretical and empirical research on law and legal institutions
Institutional affiliation: University of Chicago Law School

Editor: Richard A. Epstein
Editorial address:
University of Chicago Law School
1111 East 60th Street
Chicago, IL 60637
Frequency: 2/year
Circulation: 1,400
Subscription rate(s): individual $15, institutional $20
Pages/issue: 200
Readership: academics
Indexed/abstracted in: Leg Per, Curr Law Ind

Manuscripts
Query: no
Abstract: no
Style guide: MOS, HLRA
Preferred length: no preference
Number of copies: 3
Notes: end of manuscript
Blind referee: no
Time to consider manuscript: varies
Proportion of manuscripts accepted: not given
Illustrations accepted: tables, graphs, charts, photos, drawings
Foreign languages: no

Reviews
not applicable

JOURNAL OF LEGISLATION

Focus: law articles dealing with legislation, regulatory affairs, and public policy.
Institutional affiliation: Notre Dame Law School
Editor: Mary G. Persyn
Editorial address:
Notre Dame Law School
Notre Dame, IN 46556
Frequency: 2/year
Circulation: 1,500
Subscription rate(s): $12
Pages/issue: 200
Readership: lawyers, academics
Indexed/abstracted in: Curr Law Ind, CCLP, ABC POL SCI, Energy Abstr, Sage Human Resour Abstr, Ulrich's Int Per Dir

Manuscripts

Query: no
Abstract: no
Style guide: HLRA
Preferred length: 50 pages
Number of copies: 1
Notes: bottom of page
Blind referee: no
Time to consider manuscript: 2 months
Proportion of manuscripts accepted: not given
Illustrations accepted: tables, graphs, charts
Foreign languages: no

Reviews

Book review editor: Jane Harris Conley
Address: same as above
Seeking reviewers: yes
Unsolicited reviews accepted: yes
How to apply: letter of inquiry
Materials reviewed: books
Length of review: 10 pages

JOURNAL OF LIBERTARIAN STUDIES—AN INTERDISCIPLINARY REVIEW

Focus: an interdisciplinary exploration of all aspects of human liberty, and an understanding of human action and the institutions and ethical foundation of a free society.
Institutional affiliation: Center for Libertarian Studies
Editors: Alyson J. Tufts, Murray N. Rothbard
Editorial address:
200 Park Avenue South
New York, NY 10003
Frequency: 4/year
Circulation: 700
Subscription rate(s): individuals $14, institutional $22
Pages/issue: 120
Readership: university libraries, academics, general public
Indexed/abstracted in: Universal Ref Syst, Phil Ind, Amer Hist and Life

Manuscripts

Query: no
Abstract: no
Style guide: MOS
Preferred length: 25–50 pages
Number of copies: 1
Notes: end of manuscript
Blind referee: no
Time to consider manuscript: 2 months
Proportion of manuscripts accepted: 40 percent
Illustrations accepted: tables, graphs, charts
Foreign languages: no

Reviews

not applicable

Additional notes

A brief biographical note describing the author's affiliation and research interests should accompany the manuscript. Only papers not previously published will be accepted. Free reprints will be supplied to each author.

THE JOURNAL OF MODERN AFRICAN STUDIES

Focus: the politics, economics, and societies of contemporary Africa
Institutional affiliation: Cambraidge University Press
Editor: David Kimble
Editorial address:
University of Malawi
P.O. Box 278
Zomba, Malawi
Frequency: 4/year
Circulation: 2,010
Subscription rate(s): individual $39.50, institutional $79.50
Pages/issue: 180
Readership: academics, political scientists, politicians, administrators, economists, business people
Indexed/abstracted in: ABC POL SCI, Hist Abstr

Manuscripts

Query: not necessary, but preferable
Abstract: no
Style guide: available on request
Preferred length: 4,000–6,000 words
Number of copies: 1
Notes: bottom of page
Blind referee: no
Time to consider manuscript: not given
Proportion of manuscripts accepted: not given
Illustrations accepted: tables, graphs, charts
Foreign languages: yes

Reviews

Book review editor: David Kimble
Address: same as above
Seeking reviewers: yes
Unsolicited reviews accepted: yes
How to apply: letter of inquiry
Include in application: professional degrees, institutional affiliation, areas of expertise, published works, current research
Materials reviewed: books
Length of review: 1–2 pages

Additional notes

Each contributor will receive 25 offprints of his/her article free of charge. Simultaneous submission is not allowed.

JOURNAL OF PALESTINE STUDIES

Focus: Palestinian affairs (political, economic, sociological, and historical analyses); U.S. and European policy toward the Palestine problem; Arab-Israeli conflict
Institutional affiliation: Institute for Palestine Studies, Kuwait University
Editor: Hisham Sharabi
Editorial address:
P.O. Box 11-7164
Beirut, Lebanon
or
P.O. Box 19449
Washington, DC 20036

Frequency: 4/year
Circulation: 5,000
Subscription rate(s): $18, additional airmail charge ($5)
Pages/issue: 200
Readership: general public; specialists in Middle East affairs, international relations, and U.S. policy
Indexed/abstracted in: Hist Abstr, Sociol Abstr, Curr Cont, SSCI, Universal Ref Syst

Manuscripts

Query: no
Abstract: no
Style guide: none required
Preferred length: 4,000–5,000 words
Number of copies: 2
Notes: bottom of page
Blind referee: no
Time to consider manuscript: varies
Proportion of manuscripts accepted: 15 percent
Illustrations accepted: tables, graphs, charts
Foreign languages: French, Arabic

Reviews

Book review editor: Hisham Sharabi
Address: same as above
Seeking reviewers: yes
Unsolicited reviews accepted: yes
How to apply: letter of inquiry
Include in application: professional degrees, institutional affiliation, areas of expertise, published works
Materials reviewed: books
Length of review: 800–1,000 words

Additional notes

Simultaneous submission is allowed, but discouraged. Articles are published 6–12 months after acceptance.

JOURNAL OF PEACE RESEARCH

Focus: interdisciplinary and international journal of scientific reports in peace research
Institutional affiliation: International Peace Research Institute

Editor: submit to the Editor
Editorial address:
Journal of Peace Research
Radhusgt. 4
Oslo 1
NORWAY
Frequency: 4/year
Circulation: 1,300
Subscription rate(s): individual $24,
institutional $28
Pages/issue: 100
Readership: social scientists, peace
movement activists
Indexed/abstracted in: Soc Sci Ind,
SSCI, ABC POL SCI, Hist Abstr

Manuscripts
Query: no
Abstract: yes, 250 words
Style guide: see current issue
Preferred length: no preference
Number of copies: 3
Notes: end of manuscript
Blind referee: yes
Time to consider manuscript: not
given
**Proportion of manuscripts
accepted:** not given
Illustrations accepted: tables
Foreign languages: no

Reviews
The *Journal* publishes brief book notes;
write for information.

Additional notes
All submissions should include a brief
biographical sketch.

JOURNAL OF POLICY ANALYSIS AND MANAGEMENT

Focus: formulation of public policy
Institutional affiliation: Association for
Public Policy Analysis and
Management
Editor: Raymond Vernon

Editorial address:
John F. Kennedy School of
Government
79 Boylston Street
Cambridge, MA 02138
Frequency: 4/year
Circulation: 2,500
Subscription rate(s): individual $32,
institutional $40
Pages/issue: 145
Readership: academics
Indexed/abstracted in: ABC POL
SCI, Amer Hist and Life

Manuscripts
Query: no
Abstract: yes, 125 words
Style guide: MOS
Preferred length: 5,000–7,000 words
Number of copies: 3
Notes: end of manuscript
Blind referee: yes
Time to consider manuscript: 1
month
**Proportion of manuscripts
accepted:** 20 percent
Illustrations accepted: tables, graphs
Foreign languages: no

Reviews
Book review editor: Derek Leebaert
Address: same as above
Seeking reviewers: yes
Unsolicited reviews accepted: no
How to apply: letter of inquiry
Include in application: institutional
affiliation, areas of expertise, current
research
Materials reviewed: books, reports
Length of review: 100 words
maximum

JOURNAL OF POLICY MODELING

Focus: modeling and formalized
approaches to socio-economic
processes that provide policymakers
with scientific foundations to
decision-making
Institutional affiliation: Society for
Policy Modeling

Editor: Antonio M. Costa
Editorial address:
P.O. Box 3299
Grand Central Station
New York NY 10017
Frequency: 3/year
Circulation: 1,800
Subscription rate(s): individuals $15, institutional $45
Pages/issue: 150
Readership: academics in all social sciences; policymakers; corporate, national, international organizations
Indexed/abstracted in: not given

Manuscripts
Query: no
Abstract: yes
Style guide: available on request
Preferred length: 20–25 pages
Number of copies: 3
Notes: bottom of page
Blind referee: no
Time to consider manuscript: 2 months
Proportion of manuscripts accepted: 5 percent
Illustrations accepted: tables, graphs, charts, photos, drawings
Foreign languages: no

Reviews
Book review editor: Douglas Walker
Address: same as above
Seeking reviewers: yes
Unsolicited reviews accepted: yes
How to apply: letter of inquiry
Materials reviewed: books
Length of review: 2–5 pages

JOURNAL OF POLITICAL AND MILITARY SOCIOLOGY

Focus: advancement of sociological knowledge in the fields of political and military sociology through interdisciplinary and comparative approaches
Editors: George A. Kourvetaris, Betty A. Dobratz

Editorial address:
c/o New Life Center
Department of Sociology
Northern Illinois University
DeKalb, IL 60115
Frequency: 2/year
Circulation: 1,500
Subscription rate(s): individuals $12, institutional $16.50, foreign add $2
Pages/issue: 168
Readership: sociologists, political scientists, social scientists, military personnel
Indexed/abstracted in: Sociol Abstr, PAIS, Int Polit Sci Abstr, SSCI, Hist Abstr, Amer Hist and Life, Universal Ref Syst, ABC POL SCI

Manuscripts
Query: no
Abstract: yes
Style guide: available on request
Preferred length: 25 pages
Number of copies: 4
Notes: end of manuscript
Blind referee: yes
Time to consider manuscript: 12–16 weeks
Proportion of manuscripts accepted: 15–20 percent
Illustrations accepted: tables, graphs, charts
Foreign languages: no

Reviews
Book review editor: Dr. Richard Braungart
Address:
Department of Sociology
Syracuse University
Syracuse, NY 13210
Seeking reviewers: yes
Unsolicited reviews accepted: occasionally
How to apply: letter of inquiry
Include in application: current vita, professional degrees, institutional affiliation, area of expertise, published works, foreign languages, current research
Materials reviewed: books
Length of review: 2–3 pages

Additional notes

The *JPMS* occasionally has guest editors for issues. There is a section of mini-reviews of books as well as book reviews. Policy papers are welcome, as are rejoinders and debates about current issues. Simultaneous submission is not permitted. Most articles appear 4 months after acceptance.

JOURNAL OF POLITICAL ECONOMY

Focus: all fields of economics
Institutional affiliation: University of Chicago
Editors: George J. Stigler, Jacob A. Frenkel, Sam Peltzman, James J. Heckman
Editorial address:
1126 East 59th Street
Chicago, IL 60637
Frequency: 6/year
Circulation: 7,200
Subscription rate(s): individual $27, institutional $45
Pages/issue: 224
Readership: economists, both academic and nonacademic
Indexed/abstracted in: J. Econ. Lit

Manuscripts

Query: no
Abstract: yes
Style guide: MOS
Preferred length: no preference
Number of copies: 3
Notes: end of manuscript
Blind referee: no
Time to consider manuscript: 3–6 months
Proportion of manuscripts accepted: 14 percent
Illustrations accepted: tables, graphs, charts
Foreign languages: no

Reviews

Seeking reviewers: no
Unsolicited reviews accepted: no
How to apply: editors choose reviewers

Materials reviewed: books
Length of review: 8 pages

Additional notes

Simultaneous submission is not permitted. Articles appear 10–12 months after acceptance.

JOURNAL OF POLITICAL SCIENCE

Focus: political science, all fields
Institutional affiliation: Clemson University
Editor: Martin Slann
Editorial address:
Department of Political Science
Clemson University
Clemson, SC 29631
Frequency: 2/year
Circulation: 300
Subscription rate(s): $4
Pages/issue: 72
Readership: academics, libraries
Indexed/abstracted in: ABC POL SCI

Manuscripts

Query: no
Abstract: no
Style guide: MFW
Preferred length: 15–25 pages
Number of copies: 2
Notes: end of manuscript
Blind referee: yes
Time to consider manuscript: 3 months
Proportion of manuscripts accepted: 33 percent
Illustrations accepted: tables, graphs, charts
Foreign languages: no

Reviews

Book review editor: Melford A. Wilson
Address:
Department of Political Science
Winthrop College
Rock Hill, SC 29730
Seeking reviewers: yes
Unsolicited reviews accepted: no
How to apply: letter of inquiry

Include in application: professional degrees, institutional affiliation, areas of expertise
Materials reviewed: books
Length of review: 400 words

Additional notes

Author should submit tightly organized manuscripts with only necessary jargon and without excessive wordage. Authors should expect a lag time of about 2 years between acceptance of the manuscript and publication. Reviewers should be prompt in their reviews.

THE JOURNAL OF POLITICS

Focus: ongoing research of an empirical or quantitative nature on various aspects of contemporary politics; normative theoretical essays
Institutional affiliation: University of Florida
Editor: Allan Kornberg
Editorial address:
Department of Political Science
Duke University
Durham, NC 27706
Frequency: 4/year
Circulation: 3,600
Subscription rate(s): student and retired $8, individual $15, institutional $23
Pages/issue: 300
Readership: political and social scientists
Indexed/abstracted in: ABC POL SCI, Amer Hist and Life, Bk Rev Ind, Curr Cont, Hist Abstr, Int Polit Sci Abstr, PAIS, Soc Sci Ind, USPSD

Manuscripts

Query: no
Abstract: yes, 100 words
Style guide: available on request
Preferred length: 20–25 pages
Number of copies: 4
Notes: end of manuscript
Blind referee: yes
Time to consider manuscript: 3 months

Proportion of manuscripts accepted: 10 percent
Illustrations accepted: tables, graphs, charts
Foreign languages: no

Reviews

Book review editor: Murray Clark Havens
Address:
Department of Government
Texas Tech University
Lubbock, TX 79409
Seeking reviewers: yes
Unsolicited reviews accepted: no
How to apply: letter of inquiry
Include in application: professional degrees, institutional affiliation, areas of expertise, current research
Materials reviewed: books
Length of review: 1,000–1,500 words

Additional notes

Articles appear 6–8 months after acceptance.

JOURNAL OF POPULAR CULTURE

Focus: popular culture
Institutional affiliation: Bowling Green State University
Editor: Ray P. Browne
Editorial address:
Popular Culture Center
Bowling Green State University
Bowling Green, OH 43403
Frequency: 4/year
Circulation: 2,500
Subscription rate(s): $15
Pages/issue: 200
Readership: academics, general public
Indexed/abstracted in: not given

Manuscripts

Query: no
Abstract: no
Style guide: MLA
Preferred length: 12–18 pages
Number of copies: 1
Notes: end of manuscript

Blind referee: no
Time to consider manuscript: 1 month
Proportion of manuscripts accepted: 20 percent
Illustrations accepted: tables, graphs, charts, photos
Foreign languages: no

Reviews
Book review editor: Pat Browne
Address: same as above
Seeking reviewers: yes
Unsolicited reviews accepted: yes
How to apply: letter of inquiry
Include in application: professional degrees, institutional affiliation, areas of expertise, current research
Materials reviewed: trade books
Length of review: 150–250 words

Additional notes
Simultaneous submission is permitted. Articles are published 1–2 years after acceptance.

JOURNAL OF PUBLIC AND INTERNATIONAL AFFAIRS

Focus: public policy research and analysis; international affairs; administration and management
Institutional affiliation: Graduate School of Public and International Affairs
Editor: Richard J. Picardi
Editorial address:
University of Pittsburgh
3R03 Forbes Quadrangle
Pittsburgh, PA 15260
Frequency: 2/year
Circulation: 500
Subscription rate(s): student $8, individual $11, foreign/institutional $15
Pages/issue: 110
Readership: related practitioners, academics, students, general public
Indexed/abstracted in: not given

Manuscripts
Query: no
Abstract: no
Style guide: MOS
Preferred length: 10–20 pages
Number of copies: 2
Notes: end of manuscript
Blind referee: yes
Time to consider manuscript: 6–8 weeks
Proportion of manuscripts accepted: 20 percent
Illustrations accepted: tables, graphs, charts
Foreign languages: no

Reviews
Book review editor: Ned Ruhe
Address: same as above
Seeking reviewers: no
Unsolicited reviews accepted: no
Materials reviewed: books, conferences

JOURNAL OF PUBLIC ECONOMICS

Focus: the problems of public sector economics, with emphasis on the application of modern economic theory and the methods of quantitative analysis
Editor: A. B. Atkinson
Editorial address:
London School of Economics
Houghton Street
London WC2A 2AE
ENGLAND
Frequency: 9/year
Circulation: not given
Subscription rate(s): $104.50 for 3 volumes of 3 issues each
Pages/issue: 135
Readership: public officials, economists, other social scientists
Indexed/abstracted in: Curr Cont, J of Econ Lit

Manuscripts
Query: no
Abstract: yes, 100 words maximum
Style guide: available on request

Preferred length: no preference
Number of copies: 3
Notes: end of manuscript
Blind referee: yes
Time to consider manuscript: 3 months
Proportion of manuscripts
accepted: not given
Illustrations accepted: tables, figures
Foreign languages: no

Reviews
Book review editor: A. B. Atkinson
Address: same as above
Materials reviewed: books

Additional notes
Simultaneous submission is not allowed.

JOURNAL OF REGIONAL SCIENCE

Focus: structure, function, and operation of regions from an economic, social, and political standpoint
Institutional affiliation: Regional Science Research Institute, Department of Regional Science, University of Pennsylvania
Editor: Ronald E. Miller
Editorial address:
Regional Science Department
University of Pennsylvania
3718 Locust Walk
Philadelphia, PA 19104
Frequency: 4/year
Circulation: 2,700
Subscription rate(s): domestic $35, foreign $40
Pages/issue: 136
Readership: academics
Indexed/abstracted in: J of Econ Lit, Curr Cont, Curr Manage Lit

Manuscripts
Query: no
Abstract: no
Style guide: MOS
Preferred length: 25 pages maximum
Number of copies: 2
Notes: end of manuscript

Blind referee: no
Time to consider manuscript: 3–4 months
Proportion of manuscripts
accepted: 20–25 percent
Illustrations accepted: tables, figures
Foreign languages: not given

Reviews
Book review editor: William B. Beyers
Address:
Department of Geography
University of Washington
Seattle, WA 98195
Seeking reviewers: no
Unsolicited reviews accepted: no
Materials reviewed: books
Length of review: 800 words maximum

Additional notes
Simultaneous submission is not permitted. Articles appear 10 months after acceptance. There is a voluntary page charge of $30 per page.

THE JOURNAL OF SOCIAL ISSUES

Focus: psychological applications to social issues
Institutional affiliation: The Society for the Psychological Study of Social Issues
Editor: Carolyn W. Sherif
Editorial address:
Department of Psychology
Pennsylvania State University
University Park, PA 16802
Frequency: 4/year
Circulation: 7,000
Subscription rate(s): individual $22.50, institutional $45
Pages/issue: 180
Readership: psychologists, social scientists, academics
Indexed/abstracted in: ABC POL SCI, Amer Hist and Life

Manuscripts
Query: yes
Abstract: yes

Style guide: APA
Preferred length: 20–25 pages
Number of copies: 4
Notes: end of manuscript
Blind referee: no
Time to consider manuscript: see additional notes
Proportion of manuscripts accepted: see additional notes
Illustrations accepted: tables, graphs
Foreign languages: no

Reviews
not applicable

Additional notes
Unsolicited manuscripts are rarely accepted. In order to be published, an author must write in and either propose an issue on a certain topic or inquire if a *Journal* issue covering his/her topic will be coming out.

JOURNAL OF SOCIAL POLICY

Focus: historical and theoretical analysis of international social policy
Institutional affiliation: Cambridge University Press
Editor: Ken Judge
Editorial address:
Personal Social Services Research Unit,
Cornwallis Building
The University
Canterbury, Kent CT2 7NF
ENGLAND
Frequency: 4/year
Circulation: 1,300
Subscription rate(s): $88
Pages/issue: 144
Readership: academics
Indexed/abstracted in: ABC POL SCI, SSCI

Manuscripts
Query: no
Abstract: yes, 100–200 words
Style guide: see current issue or write for guidelines
Preferred length: 5,000–10,000 words
Number of copies: 2

Notes: end of article
Blind referee: no
Time to consider manuscript: not given
Proportion of manuscripts accepted: not given
Illustrations accepted: tables
Foreign languages: no

Reviews
Book review editor: A. M. Rees
Address:
Department of Sociology and Social Administration
University of Southampton
Highfield, Southampton SO9 5NH
ENGLAND
Materials reviewed: books
Length of review: 1–2 pages

Additional notes
Include a title page providing information about the position(s) held by the author(s) and giving full details of any acknowledgments. Authors of articles and review articles (but not book reviews) receive 25 free offprints.

JOURNAL OF SOCIAL, POLITICAL AND ECONOMIC STUDIES

Focus: current economic, social, and political issues
Institutional affiliation: Council for Social and Economic Studies
Editor: Roger Pearson
Editorial address:
Suite 520, 1629 K Street, NW
Washington, DC 20006
Frequency: 4/year
Subscription rate(s): individual $20, institutional $40
Pages/issue: 112
Readership: academics
Indexed/abstracted in: not given

Manuscripts
Query: yes
Abstract: no
Style guide: available on request
Preferred length: 2,000 words

Number of copies: 1
Notes: end of manuscript
Blind referee: no
Time to consider manuscript: varies
Proportion of manuscripts accepted: 10 percent
Illustrations accepted: tables, graphs, charts, photos, drawings
Foreign languages: no

Reviews

Book review editor: Roger Pearson
Address: same as above
Seeking reviewers: no
Unsolicited reviews accepted: occasionally
How to apply: letter of inquiry (with sample review and self-addressed, stamped envelope)
Include in application: professional degrees, institutional affiliation, published works
Materials reviewed: books

Additional notes

Write before submitting a manuscript. Always enclose a self-addressed, stamped envelope.

JOURNAL OF SOUTH ASIAN AND MIDDLE EASTERN STUDIES

Focus: political, economic, and social developments in the nations of North Africa, the Middle East, and South Asia
Institutional affiliation: Pakistan American Foundation
Editor: Hafeez Malik
Editorial address:
138 Tolentine Hall
Villanova University
Villanova, PA 19085
Frequency: 4/year
Circulation: 7,500
Subscription rate(s): domestic $10, foreign $15
Pages/issue: not given
Readership: academics, libraries, policymakers, general public
Indexed/abstracted in: not given

Manuscripts

Query: no
Abstract: no
Style guide: MOS
Preferred length: 20–25 pages
Number of copies: 3
Notes: not given
Blind referee: no
Time to consider manuscript: 3 months
Proportion of manuscripts accepted: not given
Illustrations accepted: not given
Foreign languages: no

Reviews

Book review editor: Hafeez Malik
Address: same as above
Materials reviewed: books

Additional notes

Include biographical data with submitted manuscript. Simultaneous submission is not permitted. Articles are published 6 months after acceptance.

JOURNAL OF SOUTHEAST ASIAN STUDIES

Focus: interdisciplinary studies of Southeast Asian societies
Editor: submit to the Editor
Editorial address:
Department of History
National University of Singapore
1025
SINGAPORE
Frequency: 2/year
Circulation: 1,500
Subscription rate(s): $17.50 per issue
Pages/issue: 275
Readership: academics
Indexed/abstracted in: ABC POL SCI, Amer Hist and Life, Hist Abstr, Hum Ind, SSCI

Manuscripts

Query: no
Abstract: no
Style guide: see current issue or write for guidelines
Preferred length: 4,000–8,000 words

Number of copies: 2
Notes: bottom of page
Blind referee: no
Time to consider manuscript: not given
Proportion of manuscripts accepted: not given
Illustrations accepted: tables, graphs, charts, drawings, maps
Foreign languages: no

Reviews

Book review editor: submit to the Editor
Address: same as above
Materials reviewed: books
Length of review: 1–3 pages

Additional notes

Contributors receive 30 offprints of their article and a copy of the *Journal.*

JOURNAL OF SOUTHERN AFRICAN AFFAIRS

Focus: interdisciplinary studies of the peoples and cultures of Southern Africa
Institutional affiliation: Southern African Research Association
Editor: Mariyawanda Nzuwah
Editorial address:
2021 K Street, NW, Suite 312
Washington, DC 20036
Frequency: 4/year
Circulation: 1,500
Subscription rate(s): individual, $20, institutional, $30
Pages/issue: 128
Readership: academics
Indexed/abstracted in: ABC POL SCI, Hist Abstr

Manuscripts

Query: no
Abstract: no
Style guide: MOS
Preferred length: 15–25 pages
Number of copies: 3
Notes: end of manuscript
Blind referee: yes

Time to consider manuscript: not given
Proportion of manuscripts accepted: not given
Illustrations accepted: tables
Foreign languages: Portuguese

Reviews

Book review editor: Mariyawanda Nzuwah
Address: same as above
Materials reviewed: books
Length of review: 500–1,500 words

Additional notes

Include a cover page giving title, authorship, affiliation, and address. Especially welcome are manuscripts on strategies for development in Southern Africa, regional integration in Southern Africa, and transfer and development of technology in Southern Africa.

JOURNAL OF SOUTHERN AFRICAN STUDIES

Focus: interdisciplinary approach to the study of Southern African nations and societies
Institutional affiliation: Institute of Commonwealth Studies
Editor: submit to the Editors
Editorial address:
Queen Elizabeth House
21 St. Giles
Oxford OX1 3LA
ENGLAND
Frequency: 2/year
Circulation: not given
Subscription rate(s): $29
Pages/issue: 150
Readership: social scientists, African specialists
Indexed/abstracted in: ABC POL SCI

Manuscripts

Query: no
Abstract: no
Style guide: none required
Preferred length: no preference
Number of copies: 3
Notes: bottom of page

Blind referee: no
Time to consider manuscript: not given
Proportion of manuscripts accepted: not given
Illustrations accepted: tables, graphs, charts, maps
Foreign languages: no

Reviews
Book review editor: submit to the Editors
Address: same as above
Materials reviewed: books

THE JOURNAL OF STRATEGIC STUDIES

Focus: foreign policy; international and strategic studies
Editors: Amos Perlmutter, John Gooch
Editorial address:
Amos Perlmutter
School of Government
The American University
Washington, DC 20016
or
John Gooch
Department of History
University of Lancaster
Lancaster LA1 4YG
ENGLAND
Frequency: 4/year
Circulation: not given
Subscription rate(s): individual £18, institutional £30
Pages/issue: 110
Readership: academics
Indexed/abstracted in: not given

Manuscripts
Query: no
Abstract: yes, 100 word maximum
Style guide: available on request
Preferred length: 7,000–10,000 words
Number of copies: 2
Notes: end of manuscript
Blind referee: no
Time to consider manuscript: not given
Proportion of manuscripts accepted: not given

Illustrations accepted: camera-ready tables, graphs, charts
Foreign languages: no

Reviews
Book review editor: Amos Perlmutter, John Gooch
Address: same as above
Materials reviewed: books
Length of review: approximately 4–5 pages

Additional notes
Simultaneous submission is not permitted unless the editors are notified of such at the time of submission.

JOURNAL OF THE AMERICAN PLANNING ASSOCIATION

Focus: physical, economic, and social planning at the local, regional, state, and national levels
Institutional affiliation: American Planning Association
Editor: Submit to the Editors
Editorial address:
Department of City and Regional Planning
Ohio State University
248 Brown Hall
190 West 17th Avenue
Columbus, OH 43210
Frequency: 4/year
Circulation: 16,000
Subscription rate(s): $22
Pages/issue: 144
Readership: local, regional, and state planners
Indexed/abstracted in: ABC POL SCI, Amer Hist and Life, Art Ind, Curr Cont, CIJE, Environ Per Bibl, Hist Abstr, PAIS, Soc Sci Ind, USPSD, Urb Aff Abstr

Manuscripts
Query: no
Abstract: yes, 100 words
Style guide: MOS
Preferred length: 20 pages maximum
Number of copies: 4
Notes: end of manuscript

Blind referee: yes
Time to consider manuscript: 12 weeks
Proportion of manuscripts accepted: 15 percent
Illustrations accepted: tables, graphs, charts, photos, drawings, maps
Foreign languages: no

Reviews
Book review editor: submit to the Editors
Address: same as above
Seeking reviewers: yes
Unsolicited reviews accepted: yes
How to apply: special form
Include in application: professional degrees, institutional affiliation, areas of expertise, current research
Materials reviewed: books
Length of review: 750–900 words

Additional notes
Include a biographical sketch of about 50 words. Simultaneous submission is not allowed. Articles appear 4 months after acceptance.

JOURNAL OF THE HISTORY OF THE BEHAVIORAL SCIENCES

Focus: interdisciplinary and international history of the behavioral and social sciences
Institutional affiliation: University of Massachusetts, Boston
Editor: submit to the Editor
Editorial address:
  Department of Psychology
  University of Massachusetts
  Boston, MA 02125
Frequency: 4/year
Circulation: 1,050
Subscription rate(s): APA members $20, others $30, institutional $50
Pages/issue: 100
Readership: social scientists
Indexed/abstracted in: Curr Cont, Psychol Abstr, SSCI, Sociol Abstr

Manuscripts
Query: no
Abstract: yes
Style guide: MOS
Preferred length: 6–10 pages
Number of copies: 3
Notes: end of manuscript
Blind referee: yes
Time to consider manuscript: 3 months
Proportion of manuscripts accepted: not given
Illustrations accepted: occasionally
Foreign languages: no

Reviews
Book review editor: submit to the Editor
Address: same as above
Seeking reviewers: no
Unsolicited reviews accepted: no
How to apply: letter of inquiry
Include in application: institutional affiliation, areas of expertise
Materials reviewed: books

Additional notes
Simultaneous submission is not allowed. Articles appear 9–12 months after acceptance.

THE JOURNAL OF THE POLYNESIAN SOCIETY

Focus: the study of Polynesian societies and cultures
Institutional affiliation: The Polynesian Society
Editor: submit to the Editor
Editorial address:
  Anthropology Department
  University of Auckland
  Private Bag, Auckland
  NEW ZEALAND
Frequency: 4/year
Circulation: not given
Subscription rate(s): $28 (New Zealand)
Pages/issue: 150
Readership: anthropologists, social scientists
Indexed/abstracted in: Curr Cont

Manuscripts

Query: no, but advisable
Abstract: no
Style guide: see current issue or write for guidelines
Preferred length: no preference
Number of copies: 1
Notes: end of manuscript
Blind referee: no
Time to consider manuscript: not given
Proportion of manuscripts accepted: not given
Illustrations accepted: photos, drawings, maps
Foreign languages: no

Reviews

Book review editor: submit to the Editor
Address: same as above
Materials reviewed: books
Length of review: 2–4 pages

JOURNAL OF URBAN HISTORY

Focus: cities and urban societies in all periods of human history and in all geographical areas of the world
Editor: Blaine A. Brownell
Editorial address:
Center for Urban Affairs
University of Alabama
University Station
Birmingham, AL 35294
Frequency: 4/year
Circulation: 1,000
Subscription rate(s): individual $20, institutional $42
Pages/issue: 125
Readership: academics
Indexed/abstracted in: ABC POL SCI, Amer Hist and Life, Curr Cont, Hist Abstr, Comm Devel Abstr, Hum Resour Abstr, Sage Urb Stud Abstr, SSCI, Sociol Abstr

Manuscripts

Query: no
Abstract: no
Style guide: MOS

Preferred length: 30 pages maximum
Number of copies: 3
Notes: end of manuscript
Blind referee: yes
Time to consider manuscript: 3 months
Proportion of manuscripts accepted: 50 percent
Illustrations accepted: tables, graphs, drawings
Foreign languages: no

Reviews

Book review editor: Raymond A. Mohl
Address:
Department of History
Florida Atlantic University
Boca Raton, FL 33432
Seeking reviewers: yes
Unsolicited reviews accepted: no
How to apply: letter of inquiry
Include in application: professional degrees, institutional affiliation, areas of expertise, published works, current research
Materials reviewed: books
Length of review: 5–10 pages

Additional notes

A brief biographical paragraph describing each author's current affiliation, research interests, and recent publications should accompany the manuscript. Simultaneous submission is not permitted. Articles appear 2 years after acceptance.

THE KOREAN JOURNAL OF INTERNATIONAL STUDIES

Focus: all aspects of contemporary international affairs
Institutional affiliation: The Korean Institute of International Studies
Editor: Chong-Ki Choi
Editorial address:
The Korean Institute of International Studies
K.P.O. Box 426
Seoul
KOREA

Frequency: 4/year
Circulation: 2,000
Subscription rate(s): $30
Pages/issue: not given
Readership: academics
Indexed/abstracted in: not given

Manuscripts
Query: no
Abstract: no
Style guide: see current issue or write for guidelines
Preferred length: no preference
Number of copies: 1
Notes: not given
Blind referee: no
Time to consider manuscript: not given
Proportion of manuscripts accepted: not given
Illustrations accepted: tables, graphs, charts, maps
Foreign languages: no

Reviews
Book review editor: Chong-Ki Choi
Address: same as above
Materials reviewed: books

LABOR STUDIES JOURNAL

Focus: professional journal for academic faculty in labor studies, labor education, and related fields
Institutional affiliation: University and College Labor Education Association
Editor: Jacqueline Brophy
Editorial address:
George Meany Center for Labor Studies
10,000 New Hampshire Avenue
Silver Spring, MD 20903
Frequency: 3/year
Circulation: not given
Subscription rate(s): individual and institutional $12
Pages/issue: not given
Readership: specialists in labor studies, other academics, union professionals
Indexed/abstracted in: not given

Manuscripts
Query: no
Abstract: no
Style guide: available on request
Preferred length: 30 pages maximum
Number of copies: 2
Notes: not given
Blind referee: no
Time to consider manuscript: 1–4 months
Proportion of manuscripts accepted: not given
Illustrations accepted: tables, figures
Foreign languages: no

Reviews
not applicable

Additional notes
Simultaneous submission is not permitted. Publication time after acceptance varies.

LABOUR, CAPITAL AND SOCIETY

Focus: socio-economic studies of labor problems and developments in Third World nations
Institutional affiliation: Centre for Developing Areas Studies, McGill University
Editor: Rosalind E. Boyd
Editorial address:
Centre for Developing Areas Studies
McGill University
815 Sherbrooke Street West
Montreal H3A 2K6
CANADA
Frequency: 6/year
Circulation: 1,100
Subscription rate(s): $7.50
Pages/issue: not given
Readership: labor union professionals, academics
Indexed/abstracted in: PAIS, Soc Sci Ind, Human Resour Abstr

Manuscripts
Query: no
Abstract: no

Style guide: see current issue or write for guidelines
Preferred length: 500–2,000 words
Number of copies: 2
Notes: end of manuscript
Blind referee: no
Time to consider manuscript: 2 months
Proportion of manuscripts accepted: not given
Illustrations accepted: not given
Foreign languages: French, Spanish

Reviews
Book review editor: Rosalind E. Boyd
Address: same as above
Material reviewed: books
Length of review: not given

Additional notes
Simultaneous submission is permitted. Articles are published 6 weeks after acceptance.

LATIN AMERICAN PERSPECTIVES: A JOURNAL ON CAPITALISM AND SOCIALISM

Focus: Latin American political economy and theory
Institutional affiliation: Latin American Perspectives, Inc.
Editor: Ronald H. Chilcote
Editorial address:
P.O. Box 5703
Riverside, CA 92517
Frequency: 4/year
Circulation: 2,000
Subscription rate(s): student, $13, individual $16
Pages/issue: 128
Readership: academics, students, general public, study groups
Indexed/abstracted in: ABC POL SCI, Alt Press Ind, Bibl Ind, Hist Abstr, IBR, IBZ, Peace Res Abstr, Universal Ref Syst

Manuscripts
Query: no
Abstract: no

Style guide: MOS
Preferred length: 25 pages
Number of copies: 5, double-spaced
Notes: bottom of page
Blind referee: no
Time to consider manuscript: 6 months
Proportion of manuscripts accepted: 20 percent
Illustrations accepted: tables, graphs, charts, photos, drawings
Foreign languages: Spanish, Portuguese, French, German

Reviews
Book review editor: James Dietz
Address: same as above
Seeking reviewers: no
Unsolicited reviews accepted: yes
How to apply: letter of inquiry
Include in application: areas of expertise, published works, foreign languages, current research (must be working on Latin America)
Materials reviewed: books
Length of review: 1,000 words

Additional notes
Write for additional style guidelines. Simultaneous submission is not allowed. Articles are published 1 year after acceptance.

LATIN AMERICAN RESEARCH REVIEW

Focus: scholarly studies of Latin American politics and culture
Institutional affiliation: Latin American Studies Association
Editor: Gilbert W. Merkx
Editorial address:
Latin American Institute
801 Yale NE
University of New Mexico
Albuquerque, NM 87131
Frequency: 3/year
Circulation: 3,800
Subscription rate(s): student $10, individual $15, institutional $30
Pages/issue: 280

Manuscripts
Query: no
Abstract: no
Style guide: MOS
Preferred length: 50 pages maximum
Number of copies: 3
Notes: end of manuscript
Blind referee: yes
Time to consider manuscript: 3
months
Proportion of manuscripts
accepted: 15 percent
Illustrations accepted: tables,
graphs, charts, photos, drawings
Foreign languages: Spanish,
Portuguese

Reviews
Book review editor: Gilbert W. Merkx
Address: same as above
Seeking reviewers: yes
Unsolicited reviews accepted:
occasionally
How to apply: letter of inquiry
Include in application: professional
degrees, institutional affiliation, areas
of expertise, published works,
foreign languages, current research
Materials reviewed: books
Length of review: varies

Additional notes
Reviews of single books are rarely
published. Simultaneous submission is
not permitted. Articles are published 1
year after acceptance.

LAW AND HUMAN BEHAVIOR

Focus: multidisciplinary perspectives
on law-related issues concerning
human behavior
Editor: Bruce Dennis Sales
Editorial address:
Department of Psychology
University of Arizona
Tucson, AZ 85721
Frequency: 4/year

Circulation: not given
Subscription rate(s): $22.50
Pages/issue: 100
Readership: academics
Indexed/abstracted in: Abstr Crim
and Pen, Biol Abstr, Community
Ment Health Rev, CCLP, Curr Law
Ind, Leg Resour Ind, Psychol Abstr,
Ref ZH, Sociol Abstr

Manuscripts
Query: no
Abstract: yes
Style guide: APA
Number of copies: 3
Notes: end of manuscript
Blind referee: yes
Time to consider manuscript: 3
months maximum
Proportion of manuscripts
accepted: 15 percent
Illustrations accepted: tables,
graphs, charts, photos, drawings
Foreign languages: no

Reviews
Book review editors: John Carroll,
Stephen Morse
Address:
U.S.C. Law Center
University Park
Los Angeles, CA 90007
Seeking reviewers: no
Unsolicited reviews accepted: yes
Materials reviewed: books

Additional notes
Simultaneous submission is not allowed.
Articles are published 3 months after
acceptance.

LAW AND POLICY QUARTERLY

Focus: the impact and effect of law
upon issues of policy, particularly
regulation
Institutional affiliation: Baldy Center,
State University of New York at
Buffalo
Editor: Wendy Katkin

Editorial address:
Baldy Center for Law and Social
Policy
SUNY at Buffalo
511 O'Brian Hall
Amherst Campus
Amherst, NY 14260
Frequency: 4/year
Circulation: 650
Subscription rate(s): individual $18,
institutional $36
Pages/issue: 150
Readership: academics, government
officials, lawyers, policymakers
Indexed/abstracted in: not given

Manuscripts
Query: no
Abstract: yes
Style guide: available on request
Preferred length: 30 pages
Number of copies: 4, double-spaced
Notes: end of manuscript
Blind referee: yes (name should be on
cover sheet)
Time to consider manuscript: 6
weeks
**Proportion of manuscripts
accepted:** not given
Illustrations accepted: tables, graphs
Foreign languages: no

Reviews
Seeking reviewers: no
Unsolicited reviews accepted: no,
only if they are tied into articles

Additional notes
Simultaneous submission not permitted.
Articles published 6 months after
acceptance.

LAW AND SOCIETY REVIEW

Focus: articles by lawyers, social
scientists, and scholars that bear on
the relationship between society and
the legal process
Institutional affiliation: Law and
Society Association
Editor: Joel B. Grossman

Editorial address:
Social Science Building
University of Wisconsin
Madison, WI 53706
Frequency: 4/year
Circulation: 2,400
Subscription rate(s): $35
Pages/issue: 640
Readership: academics
Indexed/abstracted in: ABC POL
SCI, Abstr Crim and Pen, Hist Abstr,
Amer Hist and Life, Leg Per, Int Bibl
Soc Sci, Soc Sci Ind, Sociol Abstr

Manuscripts
Query: no
Abstract: yes
Style guide: HLRA
Number of copies: 1
Notes: bottom of page
Blind referee: no
Time to consider manuscript: 2
months
**Proportion of manuscripts
accepted:** 10 percent
Illustrations accepted: tables,
graphs, charts, photos, drawings
Foreign languages: no

Additional notes
Especially welcome are brief, well-
written, easily read articles showing
substantial work in the fields of law and
society. Royalties are equally divided
between the author and the Law and
Society Association. Simultaneous
submission is not permitted. Articles are
published 6 months after acceptance.

LEGISLATIVE STUDIES
QUARTERLY

Focus: devoted to legislative research
throughout the world, comparative
perspective preferred
Institutional affiliation: Comparative
Legislative Research Center,
University of Iowa
Editor: Gerhard Loewenberg
Editorial address:
304 Schaeffer Hall
University of Iowa
Iowa City, IA 52242

Frequency: 4/year
Circulation: 1,000
Subscription rate(s): individual $16.50, institutional $33
Pages/issue: 150
Readership: those interested in legislative research, including legislative scholars and members of legislative staffs
Indexed/abstracted in: ABC POI SCI, Int Polit Sci Abstr, USPSD

Manuscripts
Query: no
Abstract: yes
Style guide: available on request
Preferred length: 30 pages maximum
Number of copies: 3
Notes: end of manuscript
Blind referee: yes
Time to consider manuscript: 2 months
Proportion of manuscripts accepted: 20 percent
Illustrations accepted: tables, graphs, charts, drawings
Foreign languages: no

Reviews
Seeking reviewers: no
Unsolicited reviews accepted: no

Additional notes
Any figures, graphs, etc. for inclusion in articles are prepared by the Comparative Legislative Research Center at author's expense. Simultaneous submission is not permitted. Articles appear 3–6 months after acceptance.

LIBERTARIAN FORUM

Focus: addresses a variety of issues from a libertarian ideological viewpoint; interested in economics, political theory, philosophy of history, and the arts
Editor: Murray N. Rothbard
Editorial address:
Box 341
Madison Square Station
New York, NY 10010

Frequency: 12/year
Circulation: 700
Subscription rate(s): $15
Pages/issue: 8
Readership: academics, general public, philosophical anarchists
Indexed/abstracted in: not given

Manuscripts
Query: no
Abstract: no
Style guide: MOS
Preferred length: 1,500 words maximum
Number of copies: 1
Notes: end of manuscript
Blind referee: no
Time to consider manuscript: 2 months
Proportion of manuscripts accepted: 50 percent
Illustrations accepted: none
Foreign languages: no

Reviews
Book review editor: Joseph R. Peden
Address: same as above
Seeking reviewers: no
Unsolicited reviews accepted: yes
How to apply: letter of inquiry
Include in application: areas of expertise, current research
Materials reviewed: books
Length of review: 1,000 words maximum

Additional notes
The *Forum's* readers are of a libertarian philosophic viewpoint and articles or reviews should reflect this fact. Simultaneous submission is permitted. Articles appear 3 months after acceptance.

MANAGEMENT INTERNATIONAL REVIEW

Focus: the advancement and dissemination of international applied research in the fields of management and business
Editor: Klaus Macharzina

Editorial address:
Universität Hohenheim (510)
Schloss-Postfach 700 562
D-7000 Stuttgart 70
FEDERAL REPUBLIC OF GERMANY
Frequency: 4/year
Circulation: 3,000
Subscription rate(s): $42
Pages/issue: 90–100
Readership: professionals in
international management and
business, academics
Indexed/abstracted in: BPI, SSCI

Manuscripts
Query: no
Abstract: yes, 100 words maximum
Style guide: see current issue
Preferred length: 5,000 words
maximum
Number of copies: 3
Notes: end of manuscript
Blind referee: yes
Time to consider manuscript: not
given
**Proportion of manuscripts
accepted:** not given
Illustrations accepted: tables, figures
Foreign languages: yes, there are
French and German editions

Reviews
not applicable

MANAGEMENT REVIEW

Focus: techniques, practices, and
trends in the field of management
Institutional affiliation: American
Management Association
Editor: James H. Chiarkos
Editorial address:
American Management Association
135 West 50th Street
New York, NY 10020
Frequency: 12/year
Circulation: 85,000
Subscription rate(s): $24
Pages/issue: not given

Readership: professional managers,
academics
Indexed/abstracted in: BPI, Pers
Manage Abstr, Psychol Abstr, Work
Rel Abstr

Manuscripts
Query: no
Abstract: no
Style guide: MOS
Preferred length: 1,500–3,500 words
Number of copies: 2
Notes: not given
Blind referee: no
Time to consider manuscript: 4
weeks
**Proportion of manuscripts
accepted:** not given
Illustrations accepted: tables,
graphs, charts, diagrams
Foreign languages: no

Reviews
Book review editor: James H.
Chiarkos
Address: same as above
Materials reviewed: books

Additional notes
Simultaneous submission is not
permitted. Articles appear 3–6 months
after acceptance.

MANAGEMENT SCIENCE

Focus: theory and methods of
managerial procedure and decision
making
Institutional affiliation: The Institute of
Management Sciences
Editor: Martin K. Starr
Editorial address:
The Institute of Management
Sciences
146 Westminster Street
Providence, RI 02903
Frequency: 12/year
Circulation: 11,000
Subscription rate(s): individual $45,
institutional $65
Pages/issue: 110

Readership: managers, management scientists
Indexed/abstracted in: not given

Manuscripts
Query: no
Abstract: no
Style guide: available on request
Preferred length: 10–20 pages
Number of copies: 4
Notes: bottom of page
Blind referee: no
Time to consider manuscript: 6 months
Proportion of manuscripts accepted: not given
Illustrations accepted: tables, graphs, charts, drawings
Foreign languages: no

Reviews
not applicable

Additional notes
Simultaneous submission is not permitted. Articles are published 1 year after acceptance.

MATHEMATICAL SOCIAL SCIENCES

Focus: international, interdisciplinary research in the mathematical social sciences
Editor: Ki Hang Kim
Editorial address:
Mathematics Research Group
Box 69
Alabama State University
Montgomery, AL 36101
Frequency: 6/year
Circulation: not given
Subscription rate(s): $148 for 2 annual volumes
Pages/issue: 100
Readership: mathematicians, social scientists
Indexed/abstracted in: not given

Manuscripts
Query: no
Abstract: yes, 200 words maximum

Style guide: see current issue or write for guidelines
Preferred length: no preference
Number of copies: 3
Notes: not given
Blind referee: yes
Time to consider manuscript: not given
Proportion of manuscripts accepted: not given
Illustrations accepted: tables, figures
Foreign languages: no

Reviews
Book review editor: Ki Hang Kim
Address: same as above
Materials reviewed: books
Length of review: 2–3 pages

MERIP REPORTS

Focus: political and economic developments in the Middle East, North Africa, and the Horn of Africa; United States policy in the region
Institutional affiliation: Middle East Research and Information Project
Editor: Joe Stork
Editorial address:
P.O. Box 3122
Columbia Heights Station
Washington, DC 20010
Frequency: 10/year
Circulation: 3,000
Subscription rate(s): individual $11, institutional $30
Pages/issue: 28
Readership: academic libraries, scholars, activists
Indexed/abstracted in: Alt Press Ind

Manuscripts
Query: no
Abstract: no
Style guide: available on request
Preferred length: see additional notes
Number of copies: 2
Notes: end of manuscript
Blind referee: no
Time to consider manuscript: 1 month

Proportion of manuscripts
   accepted: not given
Illustrations accepted: tables,
   graphs, charts, photos
Foreign languages: French, Arabic,
   German, Spanish

Reviews
Book review editor: Philip Khoury
Address:
   P.O. Box 48
   Cambridge, MA 02138
Seeking reviewers: yes
Unsolicited reviews accepted: yes
How to apply: letter of inquiry
Include in application: areas of
   expertise, current research
Materials reviewed: books, films

Additional notes
Articles should analyze in depth a
theoretical question, an institution, a
social class, a particular struggle, or a
cultural or ideological production.
"Country studies" are less desirable.
Length of articles and reviews: analytical
article (4,000–6,000 words), review article
(2,000–4,000), interview (1,500–3,000),
regular review (1,000–2,000), review
notes (50–1,000), special reports (500–
2,000), current events articles (400–
1,000).

MICHIGAN LAW REVIEW

Focus: all areas of the law
Institutional affiliation: Michigan Law
   Review Association
Editor: submit to the Editor
Editorial address:
   Michigan Law Review
   Hutchins Hall
   University of Michigan
   Ann Arbor, MI 48109
Frequency: 8/year
Circulation: 3,000
Subscription rate(s): domestic $25,
   foreign $27
Pages/issue: 220
Readership: legal scholars and
   students, academics
Indexed/abstracted in: Leg Per,
   PAIS, SSCI

Manuscripts
Query: no
Abstract: no
Style guide: write for guidelines
Preferred length: no preference
Number of copies: 1
Notes: not given
Blind referee: no
Time to consider manuscript: not
   given
**Proportion of manuscripts
   accepted:** not given
Illustrations accepted: tables, figures
Foreign languages: no

Reviews
not applicable

MICROPOLITICS

Focus: individual and group level
   political behavior, encompassing the
   disciplines of political science,
   psychology, sociology, and
   economics
Institutional affiliation: Center for the
   Study of Business and Government,
   Baruch College
Editor: Samuel Long
Editorial address:
   Center for the Study of Business
   and Government
   Baruch College
   City University of New York
   17 Lexington Avenue
   New York, NY 10010
Frequency: 4/year
Circulation: not given
Subscription rate(s): $44
Pages/issue: 105
Readership: social scientists
Indexed/abstracted in: ABC POL
   SCI, Sage Pub Admin Abstr

Manuscripts
Query: no
Abstract: yes, 150 words
Style guide: MOS
Preferred length: 20–35 pages
Number of copies: 3
Notes: end of manuscript

Blind referee: no
Time to consider manuscript: not given
Proportion of manuscripts accepted: not given
Illustrations accepted: tables, graphs, charts, drawings
Foreign languages: no

Reviews
Seeking reviewers: no
Unsolicited reviews accepted: no

Additional notes
See "Information for Authors " page in journal for additional guidelines. Illustrations should be provided camera-ready.

MIDDLE EASTERN STUDIES

Focus: contemporary Middle East
Editor: Elie Kedourie
Editorial address:
London School of Economics
Houghton Street
Aldwych, London WC2 2AE
ENGLAND
Frequency: 4/year
Circulation: 1,000
Subscription rate(s): individual £22.50, institutional £36
Pages/issue: 100
Readership: political scientists, historians
Indexed/abstracted in: Soc Sci Ind, SSCI

Manuscripts
Query: no
Abstract: no
Style guide: none required
Preferred length: no preference
Number of copies: 2
Notes: end of manuscript
Blind referee: no
Time to consider manuscript: 1 month
Proportion of manuscripts accepted: not given

Illustrations accepted: tables, graphs, charts, drawings
Foreign languages: no

Reviews
Book review editor: Elie Kedourie
Address: same as above
Materials reviewed: books
Length of review: 1–2 pages

Additional notes
Simultaneous submission is not permitted. Publishing time after acceptance varies.

MIDDLE EAST JOURNAL

Focus: contemporary Middle East, from North Africa through Afghanistan and Pakistan
Institutional affiliation: Middle East Institute
Editor: Richard B. Parker
Editorial address:
1761 N Street, NW
Washington, DC 20036
Frequency: 4/year
Circulation: 4,400
Subscription rate(s): $15
Pages/issue: 160
Readership: government, business, academic audiences
Indexed/abstracted in: Soc Sci and Human Ind, PAIS, Curr Cont, Bk Rev Ind, Int Polit Sci Abstr

Manuscripts
Query: yes
Abstract: no
Style guide: available on request
Preferred length: 5,000 words
Number of copies: 2
Notes: end of manuscript
Blind referee: no
Time to consider manuscript: 6 weeks– 6 months
Proportion of manuscripts accepted: 10 percent
Illustrations accepted: tables, graphs, charts
Foreign languages: no

Reviews
Book review editor: C. Darald Thomas
Address: same as above
Seeking reviewers: yes
Unsolicited reviews accepted: no
How to apply: letter of inquiry
Include in application: professional degrees, institutional affiliation, areas of expertise, published works, foreign languages, current research
Materials reviewed: books
Length of review: 750 words

Additional notes
Simultaneous submission is not permitted. Articles are published 6 months after acceptance.

MIDDLE EAST PERSPECTIVE

Focus: anti-Zionist, supporting Arab position in the Middle East; analyzes little noticed news items on the area and exposes inaccuracies and misinformation in the media; explores cult of anti-anti-Semitism, the deliberate analogizing of everyday happenings to Jews, Israelis, and Israel with Hitlerian anti-Semitism
Editor: Alfred M. Lilienthal
Editorial address:
850 Seventh Avenue
New York, NY 10102
Frequency: 11/year
Circulation: 5,500
Subscription rate(s): student $6, domestic $20, foreign $23
Pages/issue: 6–8
Readership: academics, government officials, general public with an interest in Middle Eastern affairs
Indexed/abstracted in: not given

Manuscripts
Query: no
Abstract: no
Style guide: none required
Preferred length: 5 pages
Number of copies: 2
Notes: end of manuscript

Blind referee: not given
Time to consider manuscript: 3 weeks
Proportion of manuscripts accepted: not given
Illustrations accepted: none
Foreign languages: no

Reviews
Book review editor: Margaret Howell
Address: same as above
Seeking reviewers: no
Unsolicited reviews accepted: no
Materials reviewed: books
Length of review: 5 pages

Additional notes
Royalties of $75 per article are paid to the author. Simultaneous submission permitted. Articles published 1–3 months after acceptance.

MIDDLE EAST REVIEW

Focus: all aspects of the Middle East
Institutional affiliation: The American Academic Association for Peace in the Middle East
Editor: Anne Sinai
Editorial address:
Suite 606
330 Seventh Avenue
New York, NY 10001
Frequency: 4/year
Circulation: 11,500
Subscription rate(s): student $10, individual $12
Pages/issue: 70
Readership: academics
Indexed/abstracted in: Sociol Abstr

Manuscripts
Query: no
Abstract: no
Style guide: see current issue or write for guidelines
Preferred length: no preference
Number of copies: 1
Notes: end of manuscript
Blind referee: no
Time to consider manuscript: not given

Proportion of manuscripts
accepted: not given
Illustrations accepted: tables, maps
Foreign languages: no

Reviews
Book review editor: Anne Sinai
Address: same as above
Materials reviewed: books
Length of review: 3–4 pages

MIDDLE EAST STUDIES ASSOCIATION BULLETIN

Focus: information on research activities in all areas of Middle East studies
Institutional affiliation: Middle East Studies Association
Editor: Jere Bacharach
Editorial address:
Department of History
University of Washington
Seattle, WA 98195
Frequency: 2/year
Circulation: 1,500
Subscription rate(s): student and institutional $15, members $40
Pages/issue: not given
Readership: academics
Indexed/abstracted in: not given

Manuscripts
Query: no, but preferable
Abstract: no
Style guide: see latest issue or write for guidelines
Preferred length: 30 pages
Number of copies: 1
Notes: not given
Blind referee: no
Time to consider manuscript: 2 weeks
Proportion of manuscripts accepted: not given
Illustrations accepted: not given
Foreign languages: no

Reviews
Book review editor: Jere Bacharach
Address: same as above
Materials reviewed: books

Additional notes
Simultaneous submission is not allowed. Articles are published 2–3 months after acceptance.

MILITARY LAW REVIEW

Focus: military law, especially criminal, international, and administrative law, and government contract law in a military setting; military legal history; foreign military law
Institutional affiliation: U.S. Army Judge Advocate General's School
Editor: Major Percival D. Park
Editorial address:
Judge Advocate General's School
Charlottesville, VA 22901
Frequency: 4/year
Circulation: 5,500
Subscription rate(s): $11
Pages/issue: 220
Readership: military attorneys on active duty, attorneys in Army Reserve and National Guard, other government attorneys
Indexed/abstracted in: Leg Per, ABC POL SCI, CCLP, Monthly Catalog of U.S. Government Publications, Law Review Digest, Ind U.S. Gov Per, Leg Resour Ind

Manuscripts
Query: no
Abstract: no
Style guide: none required
Preferred length: 30–100 pages
Number of copies: 2
Notes: end of manuscript
Blind referee: no
Time to consider manuscript: 1–2 months
Proportion of manuscripts accepted: 50 percent
Illustrations accepted: tables, graphs, charts, photos, drawings
Foreign languages: no

Reviews
Book review editor: Major Percival D. Park
Address: same as above

Seeking reviewers: no
Unsolicited reviews accepted: yes
How to apply: letter of inquiry, telephone call
Include in application: professional degrees, institutional affiliation, published works, information about any past or current military service
Materials reviewed: books, films, tapes
Length of review: 2–10 pages

Additional notes

We have a companion publication, *The Army Lawyer*, a magazine published monthly, which takes short articles on topics of military law of current interest. Articles should deal with military law, or law from military perspective, especially Army perspective. Simultaneous submission is not permitted. Articles appear 3 months after acceptance.

MILLENNIUM: JOURNAL OF INTERNATIONAL STUDIES

Focus: all areas of international studies
Institutional affiliation: London School of Economics
Editor: submit to the Editors
Editorial address:
    London School of Economics
    Houghton Street
    London WC2A 2AE
    ENGLAND
Frequency: 3/year
Circulation: 1,500
Subscription rate(s): individual $20, institutional $40
Pages/issue: 80–100
Readership: academics, students
Indexed/abstracted in: ABC POL SCI, Br Hum Ind, Hist Abstr, Amer Hist and Life, Int Polit Sci Abstr

Manuscripts

Query: no
Abstract: yes, 60–70 words
Style guide: none required
Preferred length: 6,000–8,000 words
Number of copies: 3
Notes: end of manuscript

Blind referee: no
Time to consider manuscript: 2–3 months
Proportion of manuscripts accepted: not given
Illustrations accepted: not given
Foreign languages: no

Reviews

Book review editor: submit to Book Review Editors
Address: same as above
Materials reviewed: books
Length of review: 2–3 pages

Additional notes

Simultaneous submission is not allowed. Articles are published 3 months after acceptance.

MINNESOTA LAW REVIEW

Focus: developments in the law or legal system
Institutional affiliation: University of Minnesota Law School
Editor: submit to Articles Editor
Editorial address:
    229 19th Avenue South
    Minneapolis, MN 55455
Frequency: 6/year
Circulation: 1,950
Subscription rate(s): $15
Pages/issue: 200
Readership: lawyers, law professors
Indexed/abstracted in: Leg Per

Manuscripts

Query: no
Abstract: no
Style guide: MOS, HLRA
Preferred length: no preference
Number of copies: 1
Notes: end of manuscript
Blind referee: no
Time to consider manuscript: 1 month minimum
Proportion of manuscripts accepted: 5 percent
Illustrations accepted: tables, graphs, charts
Foreign languages: no

Reviews

Book review editor: submit to Book Review Editor
Address: same as above
Seeking reviewers: yes
Unsolicited reviews accepted: yes
How to apply: letter of inquiry
Include in application: professional degrees, institutional affiliation, areas of expertise, published works
Materials reviewed: books
Length of review: 5–10 pages

MODERN ASIAN STUDIES

Focus: history, geography, politics, sociology, and economics of southern and eastern Asia, China, and Japan
Institutional affiliation: Cambridge University Press
Editor: Gordon Johnson
Editorial address:
Selwyn College
Cambridge CB3 9DQ
ENGLAND
Frequency: 4/year
Circulation: not given
Subscription rate(s): individual $49, institutional $98
Pages/issue: 176
Readership: academics
Indexed/abstracted in: ABC POL SCI, Hist Abstr

Manuscripts

Query: no
Abstract: no
Style guide: available on request
Preferred length: 2,000–8,000 words
Number of copies: 2
Notes: bottom of page
Blind referee: no
Time to consider manuscript: not given
Proportion of manuscripts accepted: not given
Illustrations accepted: tables
Foreign languages: no

Reviews

Book review editor: Gordon Johnson
Address: same as above
Materials reviewed: books
Length of review: 2–20 pages

Additional notes

Each author will receive 25 free offprints of his/her article and a copy of the issue in which it appears. Contributions should be based on original research or field-work. Simultaneous submission is not permitted.

MODERN CHINA: AN INTERNATIONAL QUARTERLY OF HISTORY AND SOCIAL SCIENCE

Focus: China, 1800 to the present
Editor: Philip C. C. Huang
Editorial address:
Department of History
University of California
Los Angeles, CA 90024
Frequency: 4/year
Circulation: 1,000
Subscription rate(s): individual $20, institutional $42
Pages/issue: 125
Readership: academics, others interested in modern China
Indexed/abstracted in: ABC POL SCI, Curr Cont, Hist Abstr, Human Resour Abstr, SSCI, USPSD

Manuscripts

Query: no
Abstract: no
Style guide: available on request
Preferred length: 40 pages maximum
Number of copies: 3
Notes: end of manuscript
Blind referee: yes
Time to consider manuscript: 2 months
Proportion of manuscripts accepted: 20 percent
Illustrations accepted: tables, graphs, charts, photos
Foreign languages: no

Reviews
Seeking reviewers: no
Unsolicited reviews accepted: no

Additional notes
Special emphasis is placed on society, economy, and popular movements. The editors welcome articles based on original research; articles devoted to new interpretations, new questions, or new answers to old questions; substantial review articles on particular areas of scholarship, and shorter reviews of books in Asian languages.

MONOGRAPH SERIES IN WORLD AFFAIRS

Focus: theoretic developments and research results dealing with contemporary problems of international relations since 1963
Institutional affiliation: Graduate School of International Studies, University of Denver
Editor: Millie Van Wyke
Editorial address:
Graduate School of International Studies
University of Denver
Denver, CO 80208
Frequency: 4/year
Circulation: 350
Subscription rate(s): $18
Pages/issue: 100
Readership: academics, social science professionals
Indexed/abstracted in: not given

Manuscripts
Query: no
Abstract: yes
Style guide: MOS
Preferred length: 100–200 pages
Number of copies: 3
Notes: end of manuscript
Blind referee: no
Time to consider manuscript: 4–6 months
Proportion of manuscripts accepted: varies

Illustrations accepted: tables, graphs, charts, photos, drawings
Foreign languages: no

Reviews
not applicable

Additional notes
Author's name, title, publications, research interest, academic or other professional affiliations should be on a separate page accompanying the manuscript. Authors receive an honorarium of $100 upon sale of 1,000 copies.

MONTHLY REVIEW

Focus: social science articles with a socialist focus
Editor: Submit to the Editors
Editorial address:
62 West 14th Street
New York, NY 10011
Frequency: 11/year
Circulation: 13,000
Subscription rate(s): $18
Pages/issue: 64
Readership: academics, political activists
Indexed/abstracted in: not given

Manuscripts
Query: yes
Abstract: no
Style guide: MOS
Preferred length: 5,000 words maximum
Number of copies: 2
Notes: not given
Blind referee: no
Time to consider manuscript: 2 months
Proportion of manuscripts accepted: 10 percent
Illustrations accepted: tables, graphs, charts
Foreign languages: French, Spanish

Reviews

Book review editor: Bobby Ortiz
Address:
  same as above
Seeking reviewers: no
Unsolicited reviews accepted: yes
How to apply: letter of inquiry
Include in application: areas of
  expertise
Materials reviewed: books
Length of review: 3,000 words

Additional notes

Simultaneous submission is not allowed.
Articles are published 3 months after
acceptance.

NACLA REPORT ON THE AMERICAS

Focus: political, social, and economic
  events in Latin America; U.S-Latin
  American relations
Institutional affiliation: North
  American Congress on Latin
  America
Editor: Judy Butler
Editorial address:
  151 West 19th Street, 9th Floor
  New York, NY 10011
Frequency: 6/year
Circulation: 5,000
Subscription rate(s): individual $15,
  institutional $29
Pages/issue: 52
Readership: academics, journalists,
  political activists, students,
  specialists and nonspecialists
Indexed/abstracted in: Alt Press Ind,
  Hisp Amer Per Ind

Manuscripts

Query: no
Abstract: no
Style guide: none required
Preferred length: 40–80 pages
Number of copies: 2
Notes: end of manuscript
Blind referee: no
Time to consider manuscript: 2
  months

**Proportion of manuscripts
  accepted:** less than 10 percent
Illustrations accepted: tables,
  graphs, charts, photos, drawings
Foreign languages: Spanish, French

Reviews

Book review editor: Martha Doggett
Address: same as above
Seeking reviewers: yes
Unsolicited reviews accepted: yes
How to apply: letter of inquiry
Include in application: institutional
  affiliation, areas of expertise,
  published works, foreign languages
Materials reviewed: books
Length of review: 1,200–1,800 words

THE NATION

Focus: American foreign policy and
  domestic politics; civil liberties;
  social issues and ideas
Institutional affiliation: Nation
  Institute, Spectrum Advertising
  Network
Editor: Victor Navasky
Editorial address:
  72 Fifth Avenue
  New York, NY 10011
Frequency: 47/year
Circulation: 49,000
Subscription rate(s): $30
Pages/issue: 32
Readership: educated general public
Indexed/abstracted in: Alt Press Ind,
  Nation Index, RG

Manuscripts

Query no
Abstract: no
Style guide: NYT
Preferred length: 300–2,500 words
Number of copies: 1
Notes: none
Blind referee: no
Time to consider manuscript: 2
  weeks
**Proportion of manuscripts
  accepted:** not given
Illustrations accepted: none
Foreign languages: none

Reviews

Book review editor: Elizabeth Pochoda
Address: same as above
Seeking reviewers: yes
Unsolicited reviews accepted: yes
How to apply: letter of inquiry
Include in application: brief description of background, nature of proposed review
Materials reviewed: books
Length of review: 700 words

Additional notes

An average one-third of each issue is devoted to reviews of literature and the arts. Special single topic issues include a spring and a fall book issue. Royalties depend upon the length and nature of the article. Simultaneous submission is not allowed. Articles are published 1 week–2 months after acceptance.

NATIONAL CIVIC REVIEW

Focus: state, local, and regional government; intergovernmental relations; citizen action and organization
Institutional affiliation: Citizens Forum on Self-Government, National Municipal League
Editor: Joan A. Casey
Editorial address:
47 East 68th Street
New York, NY 10021
Frequency: 11/year
Circulation: 5,500
Subscription rate(s): libraries $10, individual $25 (with membership)
Pages/issue: 56–60
Readership: citizens, students, business executives, government officials, academics
Indexed/abstracted in: PAIS, ABC POL SCI, Bk Rev Ind

Manuscripts
Query: no
Abstract: no
Style guide: MOS
Preferred length: 2,800–3,000 words

Number of copies: 2
Notes: end of manuscript
Blind referee: no
Time to consider manuscript: 6 weeks
Proportion of manuscripts accepted: 60 percent
Illustrations accepted: tables, graphs, charts
Foreign languages: no

Reviews
Book review editor: Jewel Bellush
Address: same as above
Seeking reviewers: yes
Unsolicited reviews accepted: yes
Materials reviewed: books
Length of review: 800–1,000 words

NATIONAL REVIEW

Focus: conservative journal of opinion; focus on politics, foreign and domestic
Editor: Priscilla L. Buckley
Editorial address:
150 East 35th Street
New York, NY 10016
Frequency: 26/year
Circulation: 110,000
Subscription rate(s): $26
Pages/issue: 56
Indexed/abstracted in: RG

Manuscripts
Query: no
Abstract: no
Style guide: none required
Preferred length: 900–2,500 words
Number of copies: 1
Notes: not given
Blind referee: no
Time to consider manuscript: 1 month
Proportion of manuscripts accepted: 2–3 percent
Illustrations accepted: tables, graphs, charts, photos, drawings
Foreign languages: no

Reviews
Book review editor: Chilton Williamson, Jr
Address: same as above
Unsolicited reviews accepted: yes
How to apply: letter of inquiry
Materials reviewed: books, films
Length of review: 800 words

Additional notes
In submitting articles, authors should try to make them as factual as possible. Editorializing should be kept to a minimum. Simultaneous submission is not permitted. Publishing time after acceptance varies.

NATURAL RESOURCES JOURNAL

Focus: resource law and economics; policy-oriented, interdisciplinary journal covering water, minerals and mining, energy, solar applications, pollution, air quality, weather control, land use, forestry, and taxation
Institutional affiliation: University of New Mexico School of Law
Editor: Albert E. Utton
Editorial address:
University of New Mexico School of Law
1117 Stanford NE
Albuquerque, NM 87131
Frequency: 4/year
Circulation: 2,000
Subscription rate(s): domestic $17, foreign $18
Pages/issue: 250
Readership: academics, attorneys, government officials, economists, political scientists, administrators
Indexed/abstracted in: Leg Per, J of Econ Abstr

Manuscripts
Query: no
Abstract: yes
Style guide: MOS, HLRA
Preferred length: 6,000 words maximum
Number of copies: 3

Notes: end of manuscript
Blind referee: no
Time to consider manuscript: depends upon time of year submitted
Proportion of manuscripts accepted: 25–50 percent
Illustrations accepted: tables, graphs, charts, drawings
Foreign languages: no

Reviews
Book review editor: Helen Rucker
Address: same as above
Seeking reviewers: yes
Unsolicited reviews accepted: yes
How to apply: letter of inquiry, send review
Materials reviewed: books
Length of review: 775 words maximum

Additional notes
Simultaneous submission is not permitted. Articles are published 3–15 months after acceptance.

THE NEW INTERNATIONAL REVIEW

Focus: a forum for social democratic theory and discussion
Institutional affiliation: Fist and Rose Publications
Editor: Eric Lee
Editorial address:
c/o Nitzberg 190-05 Hillside Avenue #6R
Holliswood, NY 11423
or
Box 126
Afula, Israel
Frequency: 4/year
Circulation: 2,000
Subscription rate(s): $14/8 issues
Pages/issue: 64
Readership: socialists, trade unionists, political analysts
Indexed/abstracted in: Alt Press Ind

Manuscripts

Query: no
Abstract: no
Style guide: none required
Preferred length: 5–50 pages
Number of copies: 3, double-spaced
Notes: end of manuscript
Blind referee: no
Time to consider manuscript: 3 months
Proportion of manuscripts accepted: not given
Illustrations accepted: tables, graphs, charts, photos, drawings
Foreign languages: no

Reviews

Book review editor: Eric Lee
Address: same as above
Seeking reviewers: yes
Unsolicited reviews accepted: yes
How to apply: letter of inquiry
Include in application: professional degrees, institutional affiliation, areas of expertise, published works, current research, political affiliations
Materials reviewed: books
Length of review: 200–1,000 words

THE NEW REPUBLIC

Focus: weekly journal of politics and opinion
Editor: Dorothy Wickenden
Editorial address:
1220 19th Street, NW
Washington, DC 20036
Frequency: 48/year
Circulation: 100,000
Subscription rate(s): $32
Pages/issue: 44
Readership: general public, academics
Indexed/abstracted in: RG

Manuscripts

Query: no
Abstract: no
Style guide: available on request
Preferred length: 100–3,000 words
Number of copies: 1
Notes: not given

Blind referee: no
Time to consider manuscript: 3 weeks
Proportion of manuscripts accepted: not given
Illustrations accepted: tables, graphs, charts, photos, drawings
Foreign languages: French

Reviews

Book review editor: Jack Beatty
Address: same as above
Seeking reviewers: yes
Unsolicited reviews accepted: yes
How to apply: letter of inquiry
Include in application: professional degrees, institutional affiliation, areas of expertise, published works, foreign languages, current research
Materials reviewed: books
Length of review: 2,500 words maximum

Additional notes

Simultaneous submission is permitted.

NEW YORK UNIVERSITY JOURNAL OF INTERNATIONAL LAW AND POLITICS

Focus: theoretical and practical aspects of international/comparative law and politics
Institutional affiliation: New York University
Editor: submit to Editor-in-Chief
Editorial address:
137 MacDougal Street
Room 2Y
New York, NY 10012
Frequency: 4/year
Circulation: 1,200
Subscription rate(s): domestic $15, foreign $17
Pages/issue: 325
Readership: academics, legal scholars and practitioners, political scientists
Indexed/abstracted in: CCLP, Leg Per, Ind For Leg Per

Manuscripts

Query: no
Abstract: yes, 200 words
Style guide: available on request, HLRA for citations
Number of copies: 2
Notes: end of manuscript
Blind referee: no
Time to consider manuscript: 3–4 weeks
Proportion of manuscripts accepted: not given
Illustrations accepted: tables, graphs, charts
Foreign languages: no

Reviews

Book review editor: submit to Book Review Editor
Address: same as above
Seeking reviewers: yes
Unsolicited reviews accepted: no
How to apply: letter of inquiry
Include in application: professional degrees, institutional affiliation, areas of expertise, published works, current research
Materials reviewed: books
Length of review: 2,000–3,000 words

Additional notes

Write for guidelines for authors and book reviewers. Simultaneous submission is permitted if the editors are notified of such at the time of submission. Articles appear 3–6 months after acceptance.

NEW YORK UNIVERSITY LAW REVIEW

Focus: law and jurisprudence
Institutional affiliation: New York University School of Law
Editor: Jane Lee Vris
Editorial address:
New York University Law Review
249 Sullivan Street
New York, NY 10012
Frequency: 6/year
Circulation: 3,450
Subscription rate(s): domestic $18, foreign $19.50

Pages/issue: 225
Readership: lawyers, judges, professors, law students
Indexed/abstracted in: CCLP, Leg Per

Manuscripts

Query: no
Abstract: no
Style guide: HLRA
Preferred length: no preference
Number of copies: 1
Notes: end of manuscript
Blind referee: no
Time to consider manuscript: 1 week–3 months
Proportion of manuscripts accepted: 3 percent
Illustrations accepted: tables, graphs, charts, photos, drawings
Foreign languages: no

Reviews

Book review editor: Beth Sher
Address: same as above
Seeking reviewers: yes
Unsolicited reviews accepted: yes
How to apply: send in review
Materials reviewed: books

Additional notes

Royalties are negotiated on a case-to-case basis.

ORBIS: A JOURNAL OF WORLD AFFAIRS

Focus: international relations and foreign policy
Institutional affiliation: Foreign Policy Research Institute and the Graduate Program in International Relations, University of Pennsylvania
Editors: Nils H. Wessell, Alan Ned Sabrosky
Editorial address:
3508 Market Street
Suite 350
Philadelphia, PA 19104
Frequency: 4/year
Circulation: 3,078

Subscription rate(s): student $10, individual $15, institutional $25
Pages/issue: 285
Readership: policymakers, academics, informed public
Indexed/abstracted in: PAIS, Soc Sci Ind, Curr Cont, ABC POL SCI, Hist Abstr, Int Polit Sci Abstr

Manuscripts
Query: no
Abstract: no
Style guide: MOS
Preferred length: 30–40 pages
Number of copies: 3, double-spaced
Notes: end of manuscript
Blind referee: yes
Time to consider manuscript: 6–8 weeks
Proportion of manuscripts accepted: 10 percent
Illustrations accepted: tables, graphs, charts, photos, drawings
Foreign languages: no

Reviews
Book review editor: Charles B. Purrenhage
Address: same as above
Seeking reviewers: yes
Unsolicited reviews accepted: yes
How to apply: letter of inquiry
Include in application: professional degrees, institutional affiliation, areas of expertise, published works, foreign languages, current research, sample review
Materials reviewed: books
Length of review: 5–8 pages (reviews), 15–25 pages (review essays)

Additional notes
Orbis seeks articles that are concise and, though well-informed, unmarred by jargon and gobbledygook. Authors should have something important to say, and be able to say it in clear, direct, and elegant prose. Simultaneous submission is not permitted. Articles appear 3–6 months after acceptance.

OTTAWA LAW REVIEW

Focus: legal articles
Institutional affiliation: Faculty of Law, University of Ottawa
Editor: R. Paul Nadin-Davis
Editorial address:
Faculty of Law
University of Ottawa
Ottawa, Ontario K1N 6N5
CANADA
Frequency: 3/year
Circulation: 850
Subscription rate(s): $15
Pages/issue: 225
Readership: academics, legal practitioners, general public
Indexed/abstracted in: Ind Can Leg Per Lit, Leg Per, CCLP

Manuscripts
Query: no
Abstract: no
Style guide: Ottawa Law Review Citation Manual
Preferred length: 20–100 pages
Number of copies: 1
Notes: end of manuscript
Blind referee: no
Time to consider manuscript: 2–4 weeks
Proportion of manuscripts accepted: not given
Illustrations accepted: tables, charts
Foreign languages: French

Reviews
Book review editor: Barbara Wieczorek
Address: same as above
Seeking reviewers: yes
Unsolicited reviews accepted: yes
How to apply: letter of inquiry
Include in application: institutional affiliation, areas of expertise
Materials reviewed: books
Length of review: 8–12 pages

Additional notes
The *Ottawa Law Review* has a Board of Contributing Editors who write annual surveys on various areas of law. Usually

three to four surveys are published each year. Simultaneous submission is not allowed. Articles are published 3–6 months after acceptance.

PACIFIC AFFAIRS

Focus: contemporary social, economic, political, and international affairs of Asia and the Pacific
Institutional affiliation: University of British Columbia
Editor: H.B. Chamberlain
Editorial address:
University of British Columbia
2021 West Mall
Vancouver, British Columbia
V6T 1K8
CANADA
Frequency: 4/year
Circulation: 3,000
Subscription rate(s): $15
Pages/issue: 200
Readership: academics, government personnel, business people
Indexed/abstracted in: PAIS, Soc Sci and Human Ind, Curr Cont, Hist Abstr, Amer Hist and Life, Int Polit Sci Abstr

Manuscripts
Query: no
Abstract: yes
Style guide: MLA
Preferred length: 25 pages
Number of copies: 2
Notes: end of manuscript
Blind referee: yes
Time to consider manuscript: 8–10 weeks
Proportion of manuscripts accepted: 20 percent
Illustrations accepted: tables, graphs, charts, drawings
Foreign languages: no

Reviews
Book review editor: H.B. Chamberlain
Address: same as above
Seeking reviewers: yes
Unsolicited reviews accepted: yes
How to apply: letter of inquiry

Include in application: professional degrees, institutional affiliation, areas of expertise, foreign languages, current research
Materials reviewed: books
Length of review: 500 words

Additional notes
Submission of a manuscript implies that it has not previously been published, and that it is not currently on offer to another publisher. Articles are published 6–9 months after acceptance.

PACIFIC HISTORICAL REVIEW

Focus: American diplomatic history; American expansion to the Pacific and developments in the American West in the 20th century
Editor: Norris Hundley, Jr.
Editorial address:
Ralph Bunche Hall
University of California
Los Angeles, CA 90024
Frequency: 4/year
Circulation: 3,000
Subscription rate(s): $12
Pages/issue: 150
Readership: academics
Indexed/abstracted in: Hist Abstr, Amer Hist and Life, Hum Ind, SSCI

Manuscripts
Query: no
Abstract: no
Style guide: MOS
Preferred length: 25 pages
Number of copies: 3
Notes: end of manuscript
Blind referee: yes
Time to consider manuscript: 2–5 months
Proportion of manuscripts accepted: 15 percent
Illustrations accepted: camera-ready tables, graphs, charts, photos
Foreign languages: no

Reviews
Book review editor: Craig Cunningham
Address: same as above
Seeking reviewers: no
Unsolicited reviews accepted: no

Additional notes
Simultaneous submission is not allowed. Articles appear within 1 year of acceptance.

PACIFIC RESEARCH

Focus: U.S. foreign policy in, and the political economy of, Asia and the Pacific
Institutional affiliation: Pacific Studies Center
Editor: submit to the Editor
Editorial address:
867 West Dana, #204
Mountain View, CA 94041
Frequency: 4/year
Circulation: 2,000
Subscription rate(s): $10
Pages/issue: not given
Readership: academics, social activists
Indexed/abstracted in: not given

Manuscripts
Query: no, but preferable
Abstract: no
Style guide: see current issue or write for guidelines
Preferred length: 2,000–8,000 words
Number of copies: 1
Notes: not given
Blind referee: no
Time to consider manuscript: 1 month
Proportion of manuscripts accepted: not given
Illustrations accepted: not given
Foreign languages: no

Reviews
Book review editor: submit to the Editor
Address: same as above
Materials reviewed: books

Additional notes
Articles are published 1–3 months after acceptance.

PACIFIC SOCIOLOGICAL REVIEW

Focus: general sociology
Institutional affiliation: Pacific Sociological Association
Editor: David Gold
Editorial address:
Department of Sociology
University of California
Santa Barbara, CA 93106
Frequency: 4/year
Circulation: 2,000
Subscription rate(s): individual $20, institutional $42
Pages/issue: 135
Readership: social scientists
Indexed/abstracted in: ABC POL SCI, Abstr Crim and Pen, Curr Cont, Human Resour Abstr, Int Bibl Sociol, Sage Urb Stud Abstr, SSCI, Sociol Abstr, Sociol Educ Abstr, USPSD

Manuscripts
Query: no
Abstract: yes
Style guide: available on request
Preferred length: 20–30 pages
Number of copies: 3
Notes: end of manuscript
Blind referee: yes
Time to consider manuscript: 3 months
Proportion of manuscripts accepted: 10 percent
Illustrations accepted: tables, graphs, charts
Foreign languages: no

Reviews
Seeking reviewers: no
Unsolicited reviews accepted: no

Additional notes
Review essays covering a number of related books are accepted. A brief biographical paragraph, describing each author's current affiliation, research

interests, and recent publications should accompany the manuscript. A processing fee of $10 is required for each paper submitted; such fees will be waived for students. A check, payable to the Pacific Sociological Association, must be in hand for each submission in order for the review process to begin. Simultaneous submission is not allowed. Articles are published 6–9 months after acceptance.

PACIFIC VIEWPOINT

Focus: interdisciplinary studies of economic growth and social change in developed and developing societies of the Pacific region; intersection of geography with the social sciences
Editor: R. F. Watters
Editorial address:
Department of Geography
Victoria University of Wellington
Private Bag, Wellington
NEW ZEALAND
Frequency: 2/year
Circulation: 1,200
Subscription rate(s): $6 (New Zealand)
Pages/issue: 100
Readership: geographers, social scientists
Indexed/abstracted in: not given

Manuscripts
Query: no
Abstract: yes, 250 words maximum
Style guide: see current issue or write for guidelines
Preferred length: 6,000 words maximum
Number of copies: 1
Notes: end of manuscript
Blind referee: no
Time to consider manuscript: not given
Proportion of manuscripts accepted: not given
Illustrations accepted: tables, graphs, charts, photos, drawings
Foreign languages: no

Reviews
Book review editor: S. H. Franklin
Address: same as above
Materials reviewed: books
Length of review: 5–10 pages

PARAMETERS: JOURNAL OF THE U.S. ARMY WAR COLLEGE

Focus: a forum for the expression of mature professional thought on national and international security affairs, military strategy, military leadership and management, the art and science of land warfare, military history, and other topics of significant and current interest to the U.S. Army and Department of Defense
Institutional affiliation: U.S. Army War College
Editor: Colonel Roland R. Sullivan
Editorial address:
U.S. Army War College
Carlisle Barracks, PA 17013
Frequency: 4/year
Circulation: 9,000
Subscription rate(s): no-cost distribution to qualified subscribers
Pages/issue: 100
Readership: senior officials of the defense establishment, both uniformed and civilian; government; academics; press; study institutes; university and public libraries
Indexed/abstracted in: ABC POL SCI, Abstr Mil Bibl, Air Un Lib Ind, Universal Ref Syst, Monthly Catalog of U.S. Government Publications, Ulrich's Ind Per Dir

Manuscripts
Query: no
Abstract: no
Style guide: available on request
Preferred length: 5,000–6,000 words
Number of copies: 1
Notes: end of manuscript
Blind referee: no
Time to consider manuscript: 4–6 weeks

**Proportion of manuscripts
accepted:** 25 percent
Illustrations accepted: tables,
graphs, charts, photos, drawings
(only if essential)
Foreign languages: no

Reviews
Book review editor: Captain Scott T.
Albro
Address: same as above
Seeking reviewers: yes
Unsolicited reviews accepted: yes
How to apply: letter of inquiry
Include in application: send vita
Materials reviewed: books
Length of review: 300–500 words

Additional notes
An honorarium of up to $200 is paid for
accepted articles. Simultaneous
submission is not permitted. Articles
appear 3–6 months after acceptance.

PARLIAMENTARY AFFAIRS: A JOURNAL OF COMPARATIVE POLITICS

Focus: all aspects of government and
politics connected to parliamentary
systems in Great Britain and
throughout the world
Institutional affiliation: The Hansard
Society for Parliamentary
Government
Editor: submit to the Editors
Editorial address:
Department of Political Theory and
Institutions
The University
Liverpool L69 3BX
ENGLAND
Frequency: 4/year
Circulation: 2,000
Subscription rate(s): $45
Pages/issue: 100
Readership: political scientists
Indexed/abstracted in: ABC POL
SCI, Hist Abstr

Manuscripts
Query: no
Abstract: no
Style guide: none required
Preferred length: no preference
Number of copies: 2
Notes: end of manuscript
Blind referee: no
Time to consider manuscript: not
given
**Proportion of manuscripts
accepted:** not given
Illustrations accepted: tables, graphs
Foreign languages: no

Reviews
Book review editor: submit to the
Editors
Address: same as above
Materials reviewed: books
Length of review: 2–3 pages

PARLIAMENTARY JOURNAL

Focus: educational articles, both
practical and scholarly on
parliamentary procedure and the
group decision-making process
Institutional affiliation: American
Institute of Parliamentarians
Editor: H.W. Farwell
Editorial address:
Department of Speech
Communication and Theatre
University of Southern Colorado
Pueblo, CO 81001
Frequency: 4/year
Circulation: 1,400
Subscription rate(s): $5 (included in
AIP membership dues)
Pages/issue: 40
Readership: those interested in the
use, development, literature, and
training of parliamentarians and the
teaching of parliamentary procedure
Indexed/abstracted in: not given

Manuscripts
Query: no
Abstract: no
Style guide: MLA
Preferred length: 2,000 words

Number of copies: 2
Notes: end of manuscript
Blind referee: no
Time to consider manuscript: 1 month
Proportion of manuscripts accepted: 90 percent
Illustrations accepted: tables, graphs, charts, drawings
Foreign languages: no

Reviews

Book review editor: H.W. Farwell
Address: same as above
Seeking reviewers: yes
Unsolicited reviews accepted: yes
How to apply: letter of inquiry
Include in application: anything which will establish qualifications in parliamentary practice
Materials reviewed: books
Length of review: 1,500 words

Additional notes

Simultaneous submission is not allowed. Articles appear within 2–3 months of acceptance.

PEACE AND CHANGE: A JOURNAL OF PEACE RESEARCH

Focus: militarism, pacifism, social justice, conflict resolution, racism, sexism, and other topics, from a historical and educational perspective
Institutional affiliation: Kent State University
Editor: Dennis P. Carey
Editorial address:
Kent State University
Center for Peaceful Change
Kent, OH 44242
Frequency: 3/year
Circulation: 1,000
Subscription rate(s): student $7.50, individual $12, institutional $18, foreign add $3.00/issue
Pages/issue: 85–125

Readership: educators, activists, scholars, sociologists, theologians, pastors, students, historians, political scientists, curriculum developers, mediators, community organizers, psychologists, peace organization members, philosophers
Indexed/abstracted in: Int Polit Sci Abstr, Peace Res Abstr, Sage Urb Stud Abstr, Hist Abstr, Amer Hist and Life, PAIS, Int Bibl Per Lit, Int Bibl Book Rev

Manuscripts

Query: yes
Abstract: yes
Style guide: MFW
Preferred length: 15–20 pages
Number of copies: 3
Notes: end of manuscript
Blind referee: no
Time to consider manuscript: 2–3 months
Proportion of manuscripts accepted: 33 percent
Illustrations accepted: tables, graphs, charts, photos
Foreign languages: yes, we have published translations of author's work

Reviews

Book review editor: Dennis P. Carey
Address: same as above
Seeking reviewers: yes
Unsolicited reviews accepted: yes
How to apply: letter of inquiry
Include in application: cover letter stating topic/title of the work and 3 copies of the work
Materials reviewed: books
Length of review: 2–3 pages

Additional notes

Peace and Change is co-sponsored by the Consortium on Peace Research, Education and Development (COPRED), and the Conference on Peace Research in History (CPRH). Please do not exceed desired manuscript length; please follow style required by journal. Please be patient in awaiting editor's reply. Simultaneous submission is not allowed. Articles are published 6–12 months after acceptance.

PEACE RESEARCH

Focus: peace research, political science, psychology, history, quantitative analysis
Institutional affiliation: Canadian Peace Research and Education Association and Peace Research Laboratory
Editor: William Eckhardt
Editorial address:
800 Kingsland
University City
St. Louis, MO 63130
Frequency: 4/year
Circulation: 600
Subscription rate(s): individual $5, institutional $10
Pages/issue: 60
Readership: academics
Indexed/abstracted in: Peace Res Abstr

Manuscripts
Query: yes
Abstract: yes
Style guide: available on request
Preferred length: 6 pages
Number of copies: 2
Notes: end of manuscript
Blind referee: not given
Time to consider manuscript: 2 weeks
Proportion of manuscripts accepted: not given
Illustrations accepted: tables, graphs, charts, drawings
Foreign languages: no

Additional notes
Tables, graphs, and charts must be ready for reproduction. Maximum length 19 cm. (7½ ''), maximum width 14 cm (4½ '') drawn with black ink pen or typed with black ribbon. Simultaneous submission is permitted. Articles published 1 month after acceptance.

PEACE RESEARCH ABSTRACTS JOURNAL

Focus: abstracts of articles, books, etc. which are relevant to the peace/war question; intradisciplinary and often contains abstracts of articles or concepts not found in other abstracting journals
Institutional affiliation: Peace Research-Institute-Dundas with some financial assistance from UNESCO, Canadian International Development Agency, Canadian Commission for UNESCO, Institute for World Order, the West German Commission for Peace Research
Editors: Alan Newcombe, Hanna Newcombe
Editorial address:
25 Dundana Avenue
Dundas, Ontario
L9H 4E5
CANADA
Frequency: 12/year
Circulation: 360
Subscription rate(s): $140
Pages/issue: 170
Readership: University faculty and students, diplomats, politicians, military professionals, general public
Indexed/abstracted in: not applicable

Manuscripts
Query: no
Abstract: yes
Style guide: available on request
Preferred length: 300 words
Number of copies: 1
Blind referee: no
Time to consider manuscript: 1 week
Proportion of manuscripts accepted: most
Foreign languages: German, French

Reviews
Seeking reviewers: seeking new volunteer abstractors constantly
Unsolicited reviews accepted: no
How to apply: letter of inquiry
Materials reviewed: books, films, tapes, articles in learned journals
Length of review: 300 words

Additional notes

Many of our abstractors are already reading learned journals on a professional basis and volunteer to abstract such material. Students have found that abstracting teaches them how to study.

PEACE RESEARCH REVIEWS

Focus: a monograph series which reviews material published in a given area of peace research
Institutional affiliation: Canadian Peace Research & Education Association
Editor: Alan Newcombe
Editorial address:
25 Dundana Avenue
Dundas, Ontario
L9H 4E5
CANADA
Frequency: 3/year
Circulation: 500
Subscription rate(s): $20/volume of 6 issues (discount if payment sent with order)
Pages/issue: 90–100
Readership: Canadian citizens, academics, universities, U.S. citizens, diplomats, military professionals, politicians
Indexed/abstracted in: Peace Res Abstr

Manuscripts

Query: yes
Abstract: no
Style guide: available on request
Preferred length: 35,000–40,000 words, 100 pages
Number of copies: 1
Notes: bottom of page, references at end of article
Blind referee: no
Time to consider manuscript: varies
Proportion of manuscripts accepted: very high
Illustrations accepted: tables, graphs, charts, photos, drawings

Reviews

Seeking reviewers: yes
Unsolicited reviews accepted: occasionally
How to apply: letter of inquiry
Length of review: 80–100 pages maximum

Additional notes

Look at copies of *Peace Research Reviews* in order to understand what we are doing.

PERSPECTIVES: THE CIVIL RIGHTS QUARTERLY

Focus: civil rights
Institutional affiliation: U.S. Commission on Civil Rights
Editor: Samuel I. Eskenazi
Editorial address:
U.S. Commission on Civil Rights
1121 Vermont Avenue, NW
(Room 505)
Washington, DC 20425
Frequency: 4/year
Circulation: 23,000
Pages/issue: 40–48
Readership: persons working in the field of civil rights, general public
Indexed/abstracted in: not given

Manuscripts

Query: no
Abstract: no
Style guide: AP
Preferred length: 2,000 words
Number of copies: 1
Notes: end of manuscript
Blind referee: no
Time to consider manuscript: 6–8 weeks
Proportion of manuscripts accepted: not given
Illustrations accepted: tables, graphs, charts, photos, drawings
Foreign languages: no

Reviews

Book review editor: Samuel I. Eskenazi
Address: same as above

Seeking reviewers: yes
Unsolicited reviews accepted: yes
How to apply: letter of inquiry
Include in application: institutional affiliation, areas of expertise, published works
Materials reviewed: books
Length of review: 1,500–2,000 words (review essays covering 3–4 related books)

Additional notes
Simultaneous submission is permitted. Articles appear 3–9 months after acceptance.

PHILIPPINE JOURNAL OF PUBLIC ADMINISTRATION

Focus: all aspects of public administration
Institutional affiliation: Philippine Society for Public Administration and the College of Public Administration, University of the Philippines
Editor: submit to the Managing Editor
Editorial address:
P.O. Box 474
Manila
THE PHILIPPINES
Frequency: 4/year
Circulation: 420
Subscription rate(s): $25
Pages/issue: 100
Readership: academics, public administrators
Indexed/abstracted in: PAIS, ABC POL SCI

Manuscripts
Query: no
Abstract: yes, 100 words
Style guide: see current issue
Preferred length: 5,000 words
Number of copies: 1
Notes: bottom of page
Blind referee: no
Time to consider manuscript: not given
Proportion of manuscripts accepted: not given

Illustrations accepted: tables, graphs, charts
Foreign languages: no

Reviews
Book review editor: submit to the Managing Editor
Address: same as above
Materials reviewed: books
Length of review: review essays of 5–10 pages

Additional notes
Include a brief biographical sketch with submitted manuscript.

PHILOSOPHY AND PUBLIC AFFAIRS

Focus: moral philosophy
Institutional affiliation: Princeton University Press
Editor: Krysia Kolodziej
Editorial address:
Princeton University Press
41 William Street
Princeton, NJ 08540
Frequency: 4/year
Circulation: 3,100
Subscription rate(s): student $7.50, individual $12.50, institutional $18.50
Pages/issue: 96
Readership: political scientists, lawyers, economists, medical doctors, sociologists, philosophers
Indexed/abstracted in: USPSD, Ulrich's Int Per Dir

Manuscripts
Query: no
Abstract: no
Style guide: MOS
Preferred length: 20–40 pages
Number of copies: 1
Notes: end of manuscript
Blind referee: no
Time to consider manuscript: 3 months maximum
Proportion of manuscripts accepted: not given

Illustrations accepted: tables, graphs, charts, drawings
Foreign languages: no

Additional notes

Simultaneous submission is not permitted. Articles are published 3–9 months after acceptance.

PHILOSOPHY OF SCIENCE

Focus: topics of general philosophic interest such as scientific method, knowledge, and causality
Institutional affiliation: Michigan State University, University of Western Ontario
Editor: Robert Butts
Editorial address:
Philosophy, Talbot College
University of Western Ontario
London, Ontario, N6A 3K7
CANADA
Frequency: 4/year
Circulation: 2,250
Subscription rate(s): domestic $32.50, foreign $33.50
Pages/issue: 165
Readership: academics
Indexed/abstracted in: ABC POL SCI, Biol Abstr, Curr Ind Stat, Hum Ind, Ind Bk Rev Hum, Phil Ind, Psychol Abstr, SSCI, Sociol Abstr, Sci Cit Ind

Manuscripts

Query: no
Abstract: yes
Style guide: available on request
Preferred length: 35 pages maximum
Number of copies: 3
Notes: end of manuscript
Blind referee: no
Time to consider manuscript: 6 months
Proportion of manuscripts accepted: 25 percent
Illustrations accepted: not given
Foreign languages: not given

Reviews

Book review editor: William Demopoulos
Address: same as above
Seeking reviewers: no
Unsolicited reviews accepted: no
Materials reviewed: books

Additional notes

Simultaneous submission is not allowed. Articles are published 1 year after acceptance.

PHYLON: THE ATLANTA UNIVERSITY REVIEW OF RACE AND CULTURE

Focus: sociology and social science in general
Institutional affiliation: Atlanta University
Editor: submit to the Editor
Editorial address:
223 Chestnut Street, SW
Atlanta University
Atlanta, GA 30314
Frequency: 4/year
Circulation: 2,000
Subscription rate(s): $16
Pages/issue: 96–100
Readership: academics, school libraries, other agencies, general public
Indexed/abstracted in: PAIS, Soc Sci Ind, SSCI

Manuscripts

Query: no
Abstract: no
Style guide: MOS
Preferred length: 20 pages maximum
Number of copies: 3
Notes: end of manuscript
Blind referee: yes
Time to consider manuscript: 4–6 weeks
Proportion of manuscripts accepted: not given
Illustrations accepted: tables, charts
Foreign languages: no

Reviews

Book review editor: submit to the Editor

Address: same as above

Seeking reviewers: no

Unsolicited reviews accepted: yes

How to apply: letter of inquiry

Include in application: institutional affiliation

Materials reviewed: books

Length of review: 5–6 pages

Additional notes

Phylon does not publish articles that are too specialized or journalistic. It seeks articles that appeal to social scientists and/or humanists in general. Simultaneous submission is not permitted. Publishing time varies after acceptance.

PLANNING AND ADMINISTRATION

Focus: the policy-making and implementing procedures of local and regional governments; relations between regional and local governments

Institutional affiliation: International Union of Local Authorities

Editor: submit to the Editor

Editorial address:
IULA
Wassenaarscweg 45
2596 CG
The Hague
THE NETHERLANDS

Frequency: 2/year

Circulation: not given

Subscription rate(s): IULA members 42 Dutch guilders, nonmembers 70 Dutch guilders

Pages/issue: 115

Readership: academics, public administrators and planners, local government officers

Indexed/abstracted in: SSCI, ABC POL SCI

Manuscripts

Query: no, but preferable

Abstract: no

Style guide: see current issue or write for guidelines

Preferred length: 3,000 words

Number of copies: 2

Notes: end of manuscript

Blind referee: no

Time to consider manuscript: not given

Proportion of manuscripts accepted: not given

Illustrations accepted: tables, graphs, charts, figures

Foreign languages: no

Reviews

Book review editor: submit to Editor

Address: same as above

Materials reviewed: books

Length of review: 2–3 pages

PLURAL SOCIETIES

Focus: the study of problems inherent to states and communities with plural social structures

Institutional affiliation: Foundation for the Study of Plural Societies

Editor: submit to the Editor

Editorial address:
P.O. Box 13566
2501 EN
The Hague
THE NETHERLANDS

Frequency: 4/year

Circulation: 1,500

Subscription rate(s): $25

Pages/issue: 120

Readership: academics

Indexed/abstracted in: ABC POL SCI, Hist Abstr

Manuscripts

Query: no

Abstract: no

Style guide: write for guidelines

Preferred length: no preference

Number of copies: 1

Notes: end of manuscript

Blind referee: no

Time to consider manuscript: not given
Proportion of manuscripts accepted: not given
Illustrations accepted: tables
Foreign languages: no

Reviews
Book review editor: submit to the Editor
Address: same as above
Materials reviewed: books
Length of review: 4–5 pages

POLICY AND POLITICS

Focus: theoretical insights into policy studies; current policy concerns and initiatives of the making and implementation of policy
Institutional affiliation: School for Advanced Urban Studies, University of Bristol
Editor: submit to the Managing Editor
Editorial address:
School for Advanced Urban Studies
Rodney Lodge
Grange Road
Bristol BS8 4EA
ENGLAND
Frequency: 4/year
Circulation: not given
Subscription rate(s): individual £12.50, institutional £28
Pages/issue: 125
Readership: political and social scientists
Indexed/abstracted in: ABC POL SCI, Hist Abstr, Amer Hist and Life

Manuscripts
Query: no
Abstract: no
Style guide: see current issue or write for guidelines
Preferred length: no preference
Number of copies: 2
Notes: end of manuscript
Blind referee: no
Time to consider manuscript: not given

Proportion of manuscripts accepted: not given
Illustrations accepted: tables
Foreign languages: no

Reviews
not applicable

Additional notes
Policy and Politics publishes abstracts of articles from other journals which may be of interest to its readers.

POLICY REVIEW

Focus: public policy, both foreign and domestic
Institutional affiliation: The Heritage Foundation
Editor: Philip F. Lawler
Editorial address:
513 C St. NE
Washington, DC 20002
Frequency: 4/year
Circulation: 17,000
Subscription rate(s): $15
Pages/issue: 184
Readership: academics, members of Congress and staff, general public, corporate heads
Indexed/abstracted in: ABC POL SCI, Int Polit Sci Abstr, USPSD

Manuscripts
Query: no
Abstract: not required, but preferred
Style guide: MOS
Preferred length: 5,000 words
Number of copies: 1
Notes: end of manuscript
Blind referee: no
Time to consider manuscript: 6–8 weeks
Proportion of manuscripts accepted: 15 percent
Illustrations accepted: tables, graphs
Foreign languages: no

Reviews
Book review editor: Robert Blake
Address: same as above
Seeking reviewers: yes

Unsolicited reviews accepted: yes
How to apply: letter of inquiry, send review
Include in application: professional degrees, institutional affiliation, areas of expertise, published works
Materials reviewed: books, films
Length of review: 2,000 words

Additional notes

We also publish short book reviews of 200–500 words. The Heritage Foundation retains copyright on all selected manuscripts. We do not reprint articles that have appeared elsewhere. Include tables/graphs only when absolutely necessary. Author should be willing to rewrite according to our suggestions. Timely consideration of topics is encouraged. Royalties depend upon the article, but are generally $100 per 1,000 words. Simultaneous submission is allowed. Articles appear 3–6 months after acceptance.

POLICY SCIENCES

Focus: the development and analysis of policy and the policymaking process
Editor: Peter deLeon
Editorial address:
Political Science Department
The Rand Corporation
1700 Main Street
Santa Monica, CA 90406
Frequency: 6/year
Circulation: 1,300
Subscription rate(s): $22.50
Pages/issue: 100
Readership: academics, policy analysts, government officials
Indexed/abstracted in: ABC POL SCI, Curr Cont, Econ Abstr, Int Polit Sci Abstr, Sage Urb Stud Abstr, Sociol Abstr, Urb Aff Abstr

Manuscripts

Query: no
Abstract: yes, 150 words maximum
Style guide: available on request
Preferred length: 5,000–10,000 words

Number of copies: 3, double-spaced
Notes: end of manuscript
Blind referee: no
Time to consider manuscript: not given
Proportion of manuscripts accepted: not given
Illustrations accepted: tables, charts, figures
Foreign languages: no

Reviews

Book review editor: Peter deLeon
Address: same as above
Materials reviewed: books
Length of review: 4–6 pages

Additional notes

Simultaneous submission is not permitted. Articles are published 4–5 months after acceptance.

POLICY STUDIES JOURNAL

Focus: the application of political and social science to important policy problems by way of symposia, non-symposium articles, literature reviews, and policy studies news
Institutional affiliation: University of Illinois, Florida State University
Editors: Stuart Nagel, Thomas Dye
Editorial address:
361 Lincoln Hall
University of Illinois
Urbana, IL 61801
Frequency: 4/year
Circulation: 2,500
Subscription rate(s): individual $12, institutional $29
Pages/issue: 180
Readership: academics (mainly social science), government and research institutes
Indexed/abstracted in: ABC POL SCI, Amer Hist and Life, Comm Devel Abstr, Gov Ind, Hist Abstr, Human Resour Abstr, Inform Sci Abstr, Int Bibl Book Rev, Int Bibl Per Lit, Int Polit Sci Abstr, Policy Pub Rev, PAIS, Sage Pub Admin Abstr, Sage Urb Stud Abstr, SSCI, Sociol Abstr, USPSD, Universal Ref Syst

Manuscripts

Query: no
Abstract: no
Style guide: none required
Preferred length: 15–20 pages
Number of copies: 3
Notes: end of manuscript
Blind referee: no
Time to consider manuscript: 2 months
Proportion of manuscripts accepted: 20 percent
Illustrations accepted: tables, graphs, charts, drawings
Foreign languages: no

Reviews

Book review editors: Jarol Manheim, Richard Rich,
Address: same as above
Seeking reviewers: yes
Unsolicited reviews accepted: no
How to apply: letter of inquiry
Materials reviewed: books
Length of review: 6–12 pages

Additional notes

Simultaneous submission is allowed if the editors are informed of such at the time of submission. Articles appear 3 months after acceptance.

POLICY STUDIES REVIEW

Focus: articles and symposia of an interdisciplinary nature and/or pieces emphasizing policy analysis, implementation, and evaluation
Institutional affiliation: University of Kansas
Editor: Dennis J. Palumbo
Editorial address:
Center for Public Affairs
607 Blake Hall
University of Kansas
Lawrence, KS 66045
Frequency: 4/year
Circulation: 2,300
Subscription rate(s): student $8, individual $12, institutional $24
Pages/issue: 170

Readership: academics, policy analysts, government officials
Indexed/abstracted in: ABC POL SCI, Amer Hist and Life, Comm Devel Abstr, Curr Cont, Educ Admin Abstr, Gov Ind, Hist Abstr, Human Resour Abstr, Inform Sci Abstr, Int Bibl Book Rev, Int Bibl Per Lit, Int Polit Sci Abstr, Policy Pub Rev, PAIS, Sage Pub Admin Abstr, Sage Urb Stud Abstr, SSCI, Sociol Abstr, USPSD, Universal Ref Syst

Manuscripts

Query: no
Abstract: yes
Style guide: APA
Preferred length: 15–20 pages
Number of copies: 4
Notes: end of manuscript
Blind referee: yes
Time to consider manuscript: 6–8 weeks
Proportion of manuscripts accepted: 20 percent
Illustrations accepted: tables, graphs, charts, photos, drawings
Foreign languages: no

Reviews

Book review editor: Mel Dubnick
Address: same as above
Seeking reviewers: yes
Unsolicited reviews accepted: yes
How to apply: letter of inquiry
Include in application: professional degrees, institutional affiliation, areas of expertise, published works, current research
Materials reviewed: books
Length of review: 10 pages maximum

Additional notes

The *Policy Studies Review*, along with the *Policy Studies Journal*, is one of two official journals of the Policy Studies Organization.

POLITICAL BEHAVIOR

Focus: independent, cross-disciplinary journal publishing studies on the cognitive, affective, evaluative, and behavioral dimensions of political conduct
Editor: Heinz Eulau
Editorial address:
Department of Political Science
Stanford University
Stanford, CA 94305
Frequency: 4/year
Circulation: not given
Subscription rate(s): individual $17.50, institutional $38, foreign add $3
Pages/issue: 96
Readership: academics, political scientists, psychologists, sociologists
Indexed/abstracted in: Int Polit Sci Abstr, USPSD, ABC POL SCI

Manuscripts
Query: no
Abstract: yes
Style guide: APA
Preferred length: 20–30 pages
Number of copies: 3
Notes: end of manuscript
Blind referee: yes
Time to consider manuscript: 1–2 months
Proportion of manuscripts accepted: 20 percent
Illustrations accepted: tables, graphs, charts
Foreign languages: no

Reviews
not applicable

POLITICAL COMMUNICATION AND PERSUASION

Focus: examines the roles of governmental, intergovernmental, and nongovernmental organizations as political communicators
Editor: Yonah Alexander

Editorial address:
c/o Center for Strategic & International Studies
Georgetown University
1800 K Street, NW
Washington, DC 20006
Frequency: 4/year
Circulation: 1,000
Subscription rate(s): $48
Pages/issue: 100
Readership: professionals, graduate students
Indexed/abstracted in: PAIS, Sociol Abstr, USPSD

Manuscripts
Query: no
Abstract: yes, 150 words maximum
Style guide: MOS, HLRA for legal articles
Preferred length: no preference
Number of copies: 3
Notes: not given
Blind referee: not given
Time to consider manuscript: not given
Proportion of manuscripts accepted: not given
Illustrations accepted: tables, graphs, charts, drawings
Foreign languages: no

Reviews
not applicable

POLITICAL METHODOLOGY

Focus: the process of political inquiry
Editors: George E. Marcus, John L. Sullivan
Editorial address:
George E. Marcus
Department of Political Science
Williams College
Williamstown, MA 01267
or
John L. Sullivan
Department of Sociology
University of Minnesota
Minneapolis, MN 55455
Frequency: 4/year
Circulation: 650

Subscription rate(s): individual $19, institutional $35
Pages/issue: 120
Readership: political and social scientists
Indexed/abstracted in: ABC POL SCI

Manuscripts
Query: no
Abstract: yes, 100–150 words
Style guide: available on request
Preferred length: 20–30 pages
Number of copies: 3
Notes: bottom of page
Blind referee: yes
Time to consider manuscript: 3 months
Proportion of manuscripts accepted: 15 percent
Illustrations accepted: tables, graphs, charts, drawings
Foreign languages: no

Reviews
not applicable

Additional notes
Footnotes are to be used only for substantive observations and not for the purpose of citation.

POLITICAL QUARTERLY

Focus: all aspects of political studies
Editor: submit to the Editors
Editorial address:
4 Bloomsburg Square
London WC1
ENGLAND
Frequency: 4/year
Circulation: 3,500
Subscription rate(s): student $32.50, individual $41.60
Pages/issue: 100
Readership: political scientists
Indexed/abstracted in: ABC POL SCI, PAIS, SSCI

Manuscripts
Query: no
Abstract: no

Style guide: see current issue or write for guidelines
Preferred length: no preference
Number of copies: 2
Notes: bottom of page
Blind referee: no
Time to consider manuscript: not given
Proportion of manuscripts accepted: not given
Illustrations accepted: tables
Foreign languages: no

Reviews
Book review editor: submit to the Editors
Address: same as above
Materials reviewed: books
Length of review: 2–3 pages

POLITICAL SCIENCE

Focus: all aspects of politics; special emphasis is given to the politics of New Zealand, Australia, the South Pacific, and Asia
Editor: submit to the Editor
Editorial address:
School of Political Science and Public Administration
Victoria University of Wellington
Private Bag, Wellington 1
NEW ZEALAND
Frequency: 2/year
Circulation: 700
Subscription rate(s): individual $9.50, institutional $12.50
Pages/issue: 110
Readership: political scientists
Indexed/abstracted in: SSCI, ABC POL SCI, Int Polit Sci Abstr

Manuscripts
Query: no, but preferable
Abstract: yes, 100–150 words
Style guide: see current issue
Preferred length: 4,500–5,000 words maximum
Number of copies: 2
Notes: end of manuscript
Blind referee: yes

Time to consider manuscript: not given

Proportion of manuscripts accepted: not given

Illustrations accepted: tables, graphs, charts, drawings

Foreign languages: no

Reviews

Book review editor: submit to Book Review Editor

Address: same as above

Materials reviewed: books

Length of review: 2–3 pages

Additional notes

Simultaneous submission is not allowed.

POLITICAL SCIENCE QUARTERLY

Focus: contemporary and historical aspects of government, politics, public affairs, and political economy

Institutional affiliation: The Academy of Political Science

Editor: Lesley A. Rimmel

Editorial address:
2852 Broadway
New York, NY 10025

Frequency: 4/year

Circulation: 12,071

Subscription rate(s): student $14, others $18.50 (with membership)

Pages/issue: 216

Readership: academics, government officials, educated general public

Indexed/abstracted in: Hist Abstr, PAIS, SSCI, Soc Sci Ind, ABC POL SCI, Amer Hist and Life, Int Polit Sci Abstr

Manuscripts

Query: no

Abstract: yes

Style guide: MOS

Preferred length: 30 pages

Number of copies: 3

Notes: end of manuscript

Blind referee: yes

Time to consider manuscript: 1–3 months

Proportion of manuscripts accepted: 15 percent

Illustrations accepted: tables, graphs, charts, drawings

Foreign languages: no

Reviews

Book review editor: Demetrios Caraley

Address: same as above

Seeking reviewers: yes

Unsolicited reviews accepted: no

How to apply: letter of inquiry

Include in application: professional degrees, institutional affiliation, areas of expertise, published works, current research

Materials reviewed: books

Length of review: 600 words

Additional notes

Papers submitted should say something original, and should say it well. Authors receive complimentary copies, subscription, and reprints. Simultaneous submission is not permitted. Articles appear 3 months after acceptance.

THE POLITICAL SCIENCE REVIEWER

Focus: review essays of major works (including textbooks), thinkers, and subject areas of political science and closely related fields (law, public administration, philosophy—especially strong in political theory and American government)

Institutional affiliation: Intercollegiate Studies Institute

Editor: Robert A. Schadler

Editorial address:
14 South Bryn Mawr Avenue
Bryn Mawr, PA 19010

Frequency: 1/year

Circulation: 2,000

Subscription rate(s): $8

Pages/issue: 300–400

Readership: academics

Indexed/abstracted in: not given

Manuscripts

Query: not required, but helpful
Abstract: no
Style guide: MOS
Preferred length: 20–50 pages
Number of copies: 2
Notes: end of manuscript
Blind referee: no
Time to consider manuscript: 6 months
Proportion of manuscripts accepted: 30 percent
Illustrations accepted: tables, graphs, charts
Foreign languages: no

Reviews

Book review editor: Robert A. Schadler
Address: same as above
Seeking reviewers: yes
Unsolicited reviews accepted: yes
How to apply: letter of inquiry
Include in application: professional degrees, institutional affiliation, areas of expertise, published works
Materials reviewed: books
Length of review: 20–50 pages

Additional notes

Simultaneous submission is not allowed. Articles are published 6 months after acceptance.

POLITICAL STUDIES

Focus: all aspects of the study of politics
Institutional affiliation: Political Studies Association of the United Kingdom
Editor: L. J. Sharpe
Editorial address:
Nuffield College
Oxford OX1 1NF
ENGLAND
Frequency: 4/year
Circulation: 2,400
Subscription rate(s): $36
Pages/issue: 180
Readership: political scientists
Indexed/abstracted in: Br Hum Ind, PAIS, SSCI, Soc Sci Ind, Sociol Abstr

Manuscripts

Query: no
Abstract: yes, 130 words maximum
Style guide: available on request
Preferred length: 8,000 words
Number of copies: 3
Notes: end of manuscript
Blind referee: no
Time to consider manuscript: not given
Proportion of manuscripts accepted: not given
Illustrations accepted: tables, graphs, charts
Foreign languages: no

Reviews

Book review editor: Steven Lukes
Address:
Balliol College
Oxford OX1 1NF
ENGLAND
Materials reviewed: books
Length of review: approximately 150–250 words

POLITICAL THEORY: AN INTERNATIONAL JOURNAL OF POLITICAL PHILOSOPHY

Focus: the history of political thought and modern political philosophy
Editor: Thomas A. Horne
Editorial address:
732 SIA Columbia University
New York, NY 10027
Frequency: 4/year
Circulation: 1,500
Subscription rate(s): individual $18, institutional $36
Pages/issue: 160
Readership: academics
Indexed/abstracted in: Phil Ind, Int Polit Sci Abstr, Sage Urb Stud Abstr, SSCI, Curr Cont, PAIS, ABC POL SCI

Manuscripts

Query: no
Abstract: no
Style guide: available on request
Preferred length: 25 pages

Number of copies: 2
Notes: end of manuscript
Blind referee: yes
Time to consider manuscript: 3
months
Proportion of manuscripts
accepted: 10 percent
Illustrations accepted: none
Foreign languages: no

Reviews
Book review editor: Richard
Flathman
Address:
Department of Political Science
Johns Hopkins University
Baltimore, MD 21218
Seeking reviewers: no
Unsolicited reviews accepted: no
How to apply: letter of inquiry
Include in application: professional
degrees, institutional affiliation, areas
of expertise, published works
Materials reviewed: books
Length of review: 5 pages

Additional notes
Simultaneous submission is not
permitted. Articles are published 1 year
after acceptance.

POLITICS AND SOCIETY

Focus: theoretical essays, historical
investigations, and theoretically
structured empirical research which
develop Marxist and other radical
frameworks for understanding the
social roots and consequences of
politics
Editor: Fred Block
Editorial address:
Department of Sociology
University of Pennsylvania
Philadelphia, PA 19104
Frequency: 4/year
Circulation: 1,100
Subscription rate(s): individual $19,
institutional $35
Pages/issue: 120
Readership: academics
Indexed/abstracted in: ABC POL
SCI, Amer Hist and Life, Hist Abstr

Manuscripts
Query: no
Abstract: no
Style guide: MOS
Preferred length: 20–45 pages
Number of copies: 2
Notes: end of manuscript
Blind referee: no
Time to consider manuscript: 5
months
Proportion of manuscripts
accepted: not given
Illustrations accepted: tables,
graphs, charts
Foreign languages: no

Reviews
not applicable

POLITY: THE JOURNAL OF THE NORTHEASTERN POLITICAL SCIENCE ASSOCIATION

Focus: all fields of political science
Institutional affiliation: University of
Massachusetts
Editor: Anwar H. Syed
Editorial address:
426 Thompson Hall
University of Massachusetts
Amherst, MA 01003
Frequency: 4/year
Circulation: 1500
Subscription rate(s): individual $12,
institutional $15, foreign add $.50
Pages/issue: 180
Readership: academics, general
public
Indexed/abstracted in: ABC POL
SCI; Int Polit Sci Abstr, USPSD, Sage
Pub Admin Abstr

Manuscripts
Query: no
Abstract: yes
Style guide: MOS
Preferred length: 30–40 pages
Number of copies: 4
Notes: end of manuscript
Blind referee: yes

Time to consider manuscript: 3–4
months
**Proportion of manuscripts
accepted:** 50 percent
Illustrations accepted: tables,
graphs, charts, drawings
Foreign languages: no

Reviews
Book review editor: James A. Riedel
Address: same as above
Seeking reviewers: yes
Unsolicited reviews accepted: yes
How to apply: letter of inquiry
Include in application: professional
degrees, institutional affiliation, areas
of expertise, published works,
current research
Materials reviewed: books
Length of review: 20–25 pages

Additional notes
Please be patient when your manuscript
is being considered. Sometimes these
manuscripts take more time than
desired. Persons reviewing should please
do so promptly. Publishing time after
acceptance varies.

POPULATION AND
DEVELOPMENT REVIEW

Focus: interrelationships between
population and socio-economic
development; related issues of
public policy
Institutional affiliation: Center for
Policy Studies of the Population
Council
Editor: Ethel P. Churchill
Editorial address:
The Population Council
One Dag Hammarskjold Plaza
New York, NY 10017
Frequency: 4/year
Circulation: 4,600
Subscription rate(s): $14
Pages/issue: 180
Readership: academics
Indexed/abstracted in: ABC POL SCI

Manuscripts
Query: no
Abstract: yes
Style guide: MOS
Preferred length: 20–40 pages
Number of copies: 2
Notes: end of manuscript
Blind referee: no
Time to consider manuscript: 2
months
**Proportion of manuscripts
accepted:** 20 percent
Illustrations accepted: tables,
graphs, charts, drawings, maps
Foreign languages: French, Spanish

Reviews
Book review editor: Ethel P. Churchill
Address: same as above
Seeking reviewers: yes
Unsolicited reviews accepted: yes
How to apply: letter of inquiry
Include in application: professional
degrees, institutional affiliation
Materials reviewed: books
Length of review: 2–6 pages

POTOMAC REVIEW

Focus: graduate studies in history and
the social sciences
Institutional affiliation: Washington-
area Consortium of Universities
Editor: Diane Gerros
Editorial address:
430 Marvin Center
George Washington University
Washington, DC 20052
Frequency: 2/year
Circulation: 250–300
Subscription rate(s): individual $6,
institutional $8
Pages/issue: 75
Readership: academic libraries,
university professors, graduate
students
Indexed/abstracted in: PAIS, ABC
POL SCI, Sociol Abstr, Bk Rev Ind,
Soc Sci Ind, Hum Ind

Manuscripts
Query: no
Abstract: yes

Style guide: MOS
Preferred length: 15–25 pages
Number of copies: 3
Notes: end of manuscript
Blind referee: no
Time to consider manuscript: 1 month for initial review
Proportion of manuscripts accepted: 60 percent
Illustrations accepted: tables, graphs, charts, drawings (line drawings only)
Foreign languages: Spanish

Reviews

Book review editor: William D. Myers
Address: same as above
Seeking reviewers: yes
Unsolicited reviews accepted: yes
How to apply: letter of inquiry
Include in application: professional degrees, institutional affiliation, areas of expertise, foreign languages
Materials reviewed: books
Length of review: 4–5 pages, 8–12 pages for review essays

Additional notes

Topics covered in past issues of *Potomac Review* include international relations, Black studies, women's studies, journalism, urban affairs, social behavior, public administration, political theory, and area studies. Books for review should have been published within last 2 years. Authors receive 3 copies of the journal. Simultaneous submission is not permitted.

PRESIDENTIAL STUDIES QUARTERLY

Focus: American presidency and public policy with particular reference to organizational decision making and relations with Congress, historical, present, and projective
Institutional affiliation: Center for the Study of the Presidency
Editor: R. Gordon Hoxie

Editorial address:
Center for the Study of the Presidency
208 East 75th Street
New York, NY 10021
Frequency: 4/year
Circulation: 10,000
Subscription rate(s): $3
Pages/issue: 160
Readership: academics, government officials, libraries
Indexed/abstracted in: ABC POL SCI, Sage Pub Admin Abstr, Int Polit Sci Abstr, PAIS

Manuscripts

Query: no
Abstract: yes
Style guide: MOS
Preferred length: 6,000 words maximum
Number of copies: 2
Notes: end of manuscript
Blind referee: no
Time to consider manuscript: 2 months
Proportion of manuscripts accepted: 40 percent
Illustrations accepted: tables, graphs, charts, photos, drawings
Foreign languages: no

Reviews

Book review editors: Thomas E. Cronin, Kenneth E. Davidson
Address: same as above
Seeking reviewers: yes
Unsolicited reviews accepted: no
How to apply: letter of inquiry
Include in application: professional degrees, institutional affiliation, areas of expertise, published works
Materials reviewed: books
Length of review: 1,500 words maximum

Additional notes

Although only about 40 percent of manuscripts are accepted for publication, over 75 percent of the authors have had at least 1 or more of their works accepted for publication.

PROBLEMS OF COMMUNISM

Focus: contemporary affairs of the Soviet Union, China, and comparable states and political movements
Editor: Paul A. Smith, Jr.
Editorial address:
International Communication Agency
1776 Pennsylvania Avenue, NW
Washington, DC 20547
Frequency: 6/year
Circulation: 26,000
Subscription rate(s): $14
Pages/issue: 75
Readership: academics
Indexed/abstracted in: ABC POL SCI, Curr Cont, Econ Abstr, Hist Abstr, Ind US Gov Per, Int Polit Sci Abstr, PAIS, SSCI, Soc Sci Ind, USPSD

Manuscripts
Query: no
Abstract: no, but helpful
Style guide: GPO
Preferred length: 5,000–6,000 words
Number of copies: 1
Notes: end of manuscript
Blind referee: no
Time to consider manuscript: 4–6 weeks
Proportion of manuscripts accepted: 25 percent
Illustrations accepted: photos
Foreign languages: yes, any language

Reviews
Book review editor: William Freeman
Address: same as above
Seeking reviewers: yes
Unsolicited reviews accepted: yes
How to apply: letter of inquiry
Include in application: professional degrees, institutional affiliation, areas of expertise, published works, current research
Materials reviewed: books
Length of review: 2,500–3,000 words

PROCEEDINGS OF THE AMERICAN PHILOSOPHICAL SOCIETY

Focus: history, science
Editor: Whitfield J. Bell, Jr
Editorial address:
104 South Fifth Street
Philadelphia, PA 19106
Frequency: 6/year
Circulation: 1,350
Subscription rate(s): $20
Pages/issue: 75
Readership: academics
Indexed/abstracted in: not given

Manuscripts
Query: yes
Abstract: no
Style guide: MOS
Preferred length: 100 pages maximum
Number of copies: 1
Notes: bottom of page
Blind referee: no
Time to consider manuscript: 6–9 months
Proportion of manuscripts accepted: 40 percent
Illustrations accepted: tables, graphs, charts, photos, drawings
Foreign languages: some short passages allowed

Reviews
not applicable

PROCEEDINGS OF THE UNITED STATES NAVAL INSTITUTE

Focus: professional magazine of naval and maritime affairs; foreign and military policy
Institutional affiliation: United States Naval Institute
Editor: submit to the Editor
Editorial address:
United States Naval Institute
Annapolis, MD 21402
Frequency: 12/year

Circulation: 73,000
Subscription rate(s): $24
Pages/issue: 120
Readership: naval personnel, those interested in naval/military studies, academics
Indexed/abstracted in: not given

Manuscripts
Query: no, but preferred
Abstract: no
Style guide: see current issue or write for guidelines
Preferred length: 4,000 words maximum
Number of copies: 1
Notes: not given
Blind referee: no
Time to consider manuscript: 2–3 months
Proportion of manuscripts accepted: not given
Illustrations accepted: tables, graphs, charts, photos, drawings, maps
Foreign languages: no

Reviews
Book review editor: submit to the Editor
Address: same as above
Materials reviewed: books
Length of review: 1–3 pages

Additional notes
Authors are paid upon acceptance of article. Simultaneous submission is not allowed. Publishing time after acceptance varies.

THE PROGRESSIVE

Focus: political, economic, and social reporting, analysis and commentary
Editor: Erwin Knoll
Editorial address:
409 East Main Street
Madison, WI 53703
Frequency: 12/year
Circulation: 50,000
Subscription rate(s): $20
Pages/issue: 64

Readership: politically aware and committed members of general public
Indexed/abstracted in: RG, Alt Press Ind

Manuscripts
Query: not required, but preferable
Abstract: no
Style guide: none required
Preferred length: no preference
Number of copies: 1
Notes: none
Blind referee: no
Time to consider manuscript: 3 weeks
Proportion of manuscripts accepted: 2 percent
Illustrations accepted: tables, graphs, charts, photos, drawings
Foreign languages: no

Reviews
Book review editor: Mary Sheridan
Address: same as above
Seeking reviewers: yes
Unsolicited reviews accepted: rarely
How to apply: letter of inquiry
Include in application: institutional affiliation, published works
Materials reviewed: books, films
Length of review: varies

Additional notes
The Progressive is a magazine, not a journal; it publishes articles, not papers. Query before submitting an article, and read the magazine before querying.

PS

Focus: political analysis; articles, news, and information on the profession of political science
Institutional affiliation: American Political Science Association
Editor: Catherine E. Rudder
Editorial address:
1527 New Hampshire Avenue, NW
Washington, DC 20036
Frequency: 4/year
Circulation: 12,000

Subscription rate (s): $5/issue ($6 spring issue), free to APSA members
Pages/issue: 150
Readership: political scientists, both academics and nonacademics
Indexed/abstracted in: ABC POL SCI

Manuscripts
Query: no
Abstract: no
Style guide: MFW
Preferred length: 10 pages (news items 1 page)
Number of copies: 1
Notes: bottom of page
Blind referee: no
Time to consider manuscript: 2 months
Proportion of manuscripts accepted: not given
Illustrations accepted: tables, graphs, charts, photos, drawings
Foreign languages: no

Reviews
Seeking reviewers: no
Unsolicited reviews accepted: no

Additional notes
Simultaneous submission is permitted if editors are notified of such at the time of submission. Articles are published 1 year after acceptance.

PUBLIC ADMINISTRATION

Focus: public administration and the policy-making process
Institutional affiliation: Royal Institute of Public Administration
Editors: J. M. Lee, Christopher Pollitt

Editorial address:
J. M. Lee
Department of Politics
University of Bristol
77–79 Woodland Road
Bristol BS8 1US
ENGLAND
or
Christopher Pollitt
Faculty of Social Sciences
Open University
Walton Hall
Milton Keynes MK7 6AA
ENGLAND
Frequency: 4/year
Circulation: 7,300
Subscription rate(s): $50
Pages/issue: 120
Readership: academics, public administrators
Indexed/abstracted in: Br Hum Ind, Curr Cont, Hist Abstr, PAIS, SSCI, ABC POL SCI, Amer Hist and Life, Educ Admin Abstr, Int Polit Sci Abstr

Manuscripts
Query: no
Abstract: yes, 150 words maximum
Style guide: write for guidelines
Preferred length: 9,000 words maximum
Number of copies: 2
Notes: end of manuscript
Blind referee: yes
Time to consider manuscript: 3 months
Proportion of manuscripts accepted: not given
Illustrations accepted: tables
Foreign languages: no

Reviews
Book review editors: J. M. Lee, Christopher Pollitt
Address: same as above
Materials reviewed: books
Length of review: 1–2 pages

Additional notes
Simultaneous submission is not permitted. Articles are published 6 months after acceptance.

PUBLIC ADMINISTRATION REVIEW

Focus: management in the public sector; public policy issues and processes
Institutional affiliation: American Society for Public Administration
Editor: Charles Wise
Editorial address:
School of Public and Environmental Affairs
Indiana University
Bloomington, IN 47401
Frequency: 6/year
Circulation: 22,000
Subscription rate(s): $40 (institutions, libraries only), rates for ASPA members vary according to income
Pages/issue: 104
Readership: academics, public administrators
Indexed/abstracted in: PAIS, Soc Sci Ind, Bk Rev Ind

Manuscripts
Query: no
Abstract: no
Style guide: MOS
Preferred length: 25 pages
Number of copies: 3
Notes: end of manuscript
Blind referee: yes
Time to consider manuscript: 2 months
Proportion of manuscripts accepted: 10 percent
Illustrations accepted: tables, graphs, charts, photos, drawings
Foreign languages: no

Reviews
Book review editor: Michael White
Address:
School of Public Affairs
University of Southern California
Los Angeles, CA 90007
Seeking reviewers: yes
Unsolicited reviews accepted: no
How to apply: letter of inquiry
Materials reviewed: books
Length of review: 20 pages

Additional notes
Simultaneous submission is not permitted. Articles are published 6–12 months after acceptance.

PUBLIC AFFAIRS

Focus: state and local government, policy and administration; particular emphasis on South Dakota
Institutional affiliation: Government Research Bureau, University of South Dakota
Editor: Mitchel Beville
Editorial address:
Governmental Research Bureau
University of South Dakota
Vermillion, SD 57069
Frequency: 4/year
Circulation: 2,000
Subscription rate(s): none
Pages/issue: 8
Readership: general public, academics
Indexed/abstracted in: not given

Manuscripts
Query: no
Abstract: no
Style guide: MFW
Preferred length: 20–25 pages
Number of copies: 2
Notes: end of manuscript
Blind referee: no
Time to consider manuscript: 2 months
Proportion of manuscripts accepted: not given
Illustrations accepted: tables, graphs, charts, drawings
Foreign languages: no

Reviews
not applicable

PUBLIC AFFAIRS REPORT

Focus: to contribute to informed discussion of public affairs by presenting relevant, accurate background information based upon recent research or upon long-term specialization of the author

Institutional affiliation: Institute of Governmental Studies, University of California

Editors: Stanley Scott, Harriet Nathan

Editorial address:
109 Moses Hall
University of California
Berkeley, CA 94720

Frequency: 6/year

Circulation: 4,000

Subscription rate(s): single issue free

Pages/issue: 8–10

Readership: policymakers, interested nonexperts, general readers

Indexed/abstracted in: PAIS

Manuscripts

Query: no

Abstract: no

Style guide: available on request

Preferred length: 4,000–6,000 words

Number of copies: 2

Notes: end of manuscript

Blind referee: no

Time to consider manuscript: varies

Proportion of manuscripts accepted: not given

Illustrations accepted: tables, graphs, charts

Foreign languages: no

Additional notes

Writing should be clear, direct, and understandable to a nonexpert audience.

PUBLIC CHOICE

Focus: the intersection between economics and political science

Institutional affiliation: Center for Study of Public Choice

Editor: Gordon Tullock

Editorial address:
Center for Study of Public Choice
Virginia Polytechnic Institute and State University
Blacksburg, VA 24061

Frequency: 6/year

Circulation: 1,400

Subscription rate(s): student $12.50, individual $22.50, institutional $65

Pages/issue: 125

Readership: economists, political scientists, sociologists

Indexed/abstracted in: ABC POL SCI

Manuscripts

Query: no

Abstract: yes

Style guide: available on request

Preferred length: 30 pages maximum

Number of copies: 2

Notes: end of manuscript

Blind referee: no

Time to consider manuscript: 2–30 days

Proportion of manuscripts accepted: 20 percent

Illustrations accepted: tables, graphs, charts, line drawings

Foreign languages: no

Reviews

Seeking reviewers: no

Unsolicited reviews accepted: no

Additional notes

Simultaneous submission is permitted. Articles may be submitted by members of the Public Choice Society only. Include with your manuscript a $22.50 check for membership or a $25 check for manuscript submission. If your article is longer than 30 pages, you will be charged $30 for each extra page. Articles are published 3 months after acceptance.

PUBLIC FINANCE/FINANCES PUBLIQUES

Focus: problems and issues in the fields of public finance, public administration, and economics
Institutional affiliation: Institut für Öffentliche Wirtschaft, Geld und Währung
Editor: Dieter Biehl
Editorial address:
Johann Wolfgang Goethe Universität
Postfach 111932
D-6000 Frankfurt am Main 11
FEDERAL REPUBLIC OF GERMANY
Frequency: 3/year
Circulation: 1,800
Subscription rate(s): 90 (West German marks)
Pages/issue: 140
Readership: economists, academics, government officials
Indexed/abstracted in: PAIS, SSCI, J of Econ Lit

Manuscripts
Query: no
Abstract: yes
Style guide: available on request
Preferred length: 30 pages maximum
Number of copies: 3
Notes: end of manuscript
Blind referee: no
Time to consider manuscript: 6–9 months
Proportion of manuscripts accepted: not given
Illustrations accepted: tables, graphs, charts, figures
Foreign languages: French, German

Reviews
not applicable

Additional notes
Also submit a summary of the article and an abstract for the *Journal of Economic Literature*. Simultaneous submission is permitted.

PUBLIC FINANCE QUARTERLY

Focus: theoretical and quantitative studies of the problems and functions of the public sectors of national economies
Editor: submit to the Editor
Editorial address:
Department of Economics
University of Florida
Gainesville, FL 32611
Frequency: 4/year
Circulation: not given
Subscription rate(s): $22
Pages/issue: 120
Readership: economists, business people, academics
Indexed/abstracted in: Curr Cont, PAIS, SSCI, J of Econ Lit, Sage Pub Admin Abstr, Sage Urb Stud Abstr, USPSD

Manuscripts
Query: no
Abstract: yes, 175 words maximum
Style guide: available on request
Preferred length: 25–30 pages
Number of copies: 3
Notes: end of manuscript
Blind referee: not given
Time to consider manuscript: 6–8 weeks
Proportion of manuscripts accepted: not given
Illustrations accepted: tables, charts
Foreign languages: no

Reviews
Write to the Editor for information on how to become a reviewer.

Additional notes
A $10 submission fee is required. Simultaneous submission is allowed, but discouraged. Articles are published 6–9 months after acceptance.

THE PUBLIC HISTORIAN

Focus: applied history in government, business, cultural resources management, and planning
Institutional affiliation: University of California, Santa Barbara
Editor: submit to the Editor
Editorial address:
Department of History
University of California
Santa Barbara, CA 93106
Frequency: 4/year
Circulation: 1,000
Subscription rate(s): individual $12, institutional $16
Pages/issue: 96
Readership: historians, policy analysts, cultural resource managers, museum personnel, administrators in government and business
Indexed/abstracted in: not given

Manuscripts
Query: no
Abstract: no
Style guide: MOS
Preferred length: issue and analysis, 8–12 pages; research and case studies, 15–20 pages
Number of copies: 2
Notes: end of manuscript
Blind referee: yes
Time to consider manuscript: 6–10 weeks
Proportion of manuscripts accepted: not given
Illustrations accepted: camera-ready tables, graphs, charts, photos (only those vital to the article are accepted)
Foreign languages: no

Reviews
Book review editor: submit to the Editor
Address: same as above
Seeking reviewers: yes
Unsolicited reviews accepted: no
How to apply: letter of inquiry

Include in application: professional degrees, institutional affiliation, areas of expertise, published works, current research
Materials reviewed: books, films
Length of review: 2–3 pages

Additional notes
Author must notify editors of simultaneous submission at the time of submission. Articles are published 2 months after acceptance.

THE PUBLIC INTEREST

Focus: domestic political/cultural thought and policy
Editor: Thomas Main
Editorial address:
10 East 53rd Street
New York, NY 10022
Frequency: 4/year
Circulation: 16,000
Subscription rate(s): $14
Pages/issue: 150
Readership: academics, general public
Indexed/abstracted in: ABC POL SCI, Amer Hist and Life

Manuscripts
Query: no
Abstract: no
Style guide: none required
Preferred length: 20–25 pages
Number of copies: 1
Notes: bottom of page
Blind referee: no
Time to consider manuscript: 4–6 weeks
Proportion of manuscripts accepted: 1 percent
Illustrations accepted: tables, graphs, charts
Foreign languages: no

Reviews
Book review editor: Thomas Main
Address: same as above
Seeking reviewers: no
Unsolicited reviews accepted: no
How to apply: letter of inquiry

Include in application: professional degrees, institutional affiliation, areas of expertise, published works, current research
Materials reviewed: books
Length of review: 10 pages

Additional notes

Contributors should read three or four back issues of the journal in order to get a better idea of the type of manuscripts accepted. Simultaneous submission is not permitted. Most articles appear 2–6 months after acceptance.

PUBLIC MANAGEMENT

Focus: local government
Editor: Elizabeth K. Kellar
Editorial address:
ICM4
1120 G Street, NW
Washington, DC 20005
Frequency: 12/year
Circulation: 17,000
Subscription rate(s): $15
Pages/issue: 24
Readership: city and county managers and their staffs
Indexed/abstracted in: not given

Manuscripts

Query: no
Abstract: no
Style guide: MOS
Preferred length: not given
Number of copies: 1
Notes: not given
Blind referee: not given
Time to consider manuscript: 3 months
Proportion of manuscripts accepted: less than 5 percent
Illustrations accepted: tables, graphs, charts, photos, drawings
Foreign languages: no

Reviews

Book review editor: Janice L. Hontz
Address: same as above
Seeking reviewers: yes
Unsolicited reviews accepted: yes

Materials reviewed: books
Length of review: 3–5 pages

Additional notes

Simultaneous submission is not permitted. Articles appear 6–7 months after acceptance.

PUBLIC OPINION

Focus: opinion polls and survey research
Institutional affiliation: American Enterprise Institute
Editor: Karlyn H. Keene
Editorial address:
1150 17th Street NW
Washington, DC 20036
Frequency: 6/year
Circulation: 16,000
Subscription rate(s): $18
Pages/issue: 60
Readership: academics, members of Congress and staff, business people
Indexed/abstracted in: not given

Manuscripts

Query: yes
Abstract: no
Style guide: MOS
Preferred length: 1,000–3,000 words
Number of copies: 2
Notes: end of manuscript
Blind referee: no
Time to consider manuscript: varies
Proportion of manuscripts accepted: not given
Illustrations accepted: tables, graphs, charts
Foreign languages: no

Reviews

Seeking reviewers: no
Unsolicited reviews accepted: no

PUBLIC OPINION QUARTERLY

Focus: public opinion research
Institutional affiliation: Columbia University
Editor: Ina C. Jaeger

Editorial address:
500 Journalism Building
Columbia University
New York, NY 10027
Frequency: 4/year
Circulation: 5,000
Subscription rate(s): individual $16, institutional $32
Pages/issue: 144
Readership: academics, commercial researchers
Indexed/abstracted in: PAIS, Soc Sci Ind, USPSD, CRIS

Manuscripts
Query: no
Abstract: yes
Style guide: available on request
Preferred length: 20 pages
Number of copies: 3
Notes: end of manuscript
Blind referee: yes
Time to consider manuscript: 3 months
Proportion of manuscripts accepted: 15 percent
Illustrations accepted: tables, graphs, charts
Foreign languages: no

Reviews
Book review editor: Marc B. Glassman
Address: same as above
Seeking reviewers: no
Unsolicited reviews accepted: no
Materials reviewed: books

PUBLIC PERSONNEL MANAGEMENT

Focus: all aspects of public personnel management
Institutional affiliation: International Personnel Management Association
Editor: Kenneth A. Fisher
Editorial address:
1850 K Street, NW
Suite 870
Washington, DC 20006
Frequency: 4/year
Circulation: 9,700

Subscription rate(s): $25
Pages/issue: 80
Readership: professionals in public personnel management, academics
Indexed/abstracted in: BPI, Psychol Abstr, SSCI, Pers Manage Abstr, Work Rel Abstr

Manuscripts
Query: no
Abstract: no
Style guide: see current issue or write for guidelines
Preferred length: no preference
Number of copies: 1
Notes: end of manuscript
Blind referee: not given
Time to consider manuscript: not given
Proportion of manuscripts accepted: not given
Illustrations accepted: tables, figures
Foreign languages: no

Reviews
not applicable

PUBLIUS: THE JOURNAL OF FEDERALISM

Focus: federalism and intergovernmental relations
Institutional affiliation: Center for the Study of Federalism
Editor: John Kincaid
Editorial address:
Department of Political Science
North Texas State University
Denton, TX 76203
Frequency: 4/year
Circulation: 1,300
Subscription rate(s): student and retired $15, individual $20, institutional $30
Pages/issue: 170
Readership: academics, students
Indexed/abstracted in: ABC POL SCI, Amer Hist and Life, Hist Abstr, Int Polit Sci Abstr, PAIS, SSCI, Sociol Abstr

Manuscripts

Query: no
Abstract: no
Style guide: MOS
Preferred length: 20–25 pages
Number of copies: 3
Notes: end of manuscript
Blind referee: yes
Time to consider manuscript: 3–4 months
Proportion of manuscripts accepted: 15 percent
Illustrations accepted: tables, graphs, charts
Foreign languages: no

Reviews

Book review editor: Donald S. Lutz
Address:
Department of Political Science
University of Houston
Houston, TX 77004
Seeking reviewers: yes
Unsolicited reviews accepted: no
How to apply: letter of inquiry
Include in application: professional degrees, institutional affiliation, areas of expertise, published works, foreign languages
Materials reviewed: books
Length of review: 3 pages

QUALITY AND QUANTITY: EUROPEAN-AMERICAN JOURNAL OF METHODOLOGY

Focus: quantification in sociology and related social sciences
Editor: Vittorio Capecchi
Editorial address:
Elsevier Scientific Publishing Company
P.O. Box 211
1000 AE Amsterdam
THE NETHERLANDS
Frequency: 6/year
Circulation: not given
Subscription rate(s): $90
Pages/issue: 100

Readership: sociologists, other social scientists
Indexed/abstracted in: Curr Cont, SSCI, Sociol Abstr

Manuscripts

Query: no
Abstract: yes
Style guide: write for guidelines
Preferred length: no preference
Number of copies: 1
Notes: end of manuscript
Blind referee: not given
Time to consider manuscript: not given
Proportion of manuscripts accepted: not given
Illustrations accepted: tables, graphs
Foreign languages: French

Reviews

Book review editor: P. M. Coxon
Address: same as above
Materials reviewed: books
Length of review: 1–2 pages

QUARTERLY JOURNAL OF IDEOLOGY

Focus: significant articles in social science and humanities which have an ideological thesis
Editors: Alex S. Freedman, Harry H. Bash
Editorial address:
406 Greenwood Drive
Tahlequah, OK 74464
Frequency: 4/year
Circulation: 335
Subscription rate(s): individual $8, institutional $10, foreign $14
Pages/issue: 64
Readership: academics
Indexed/abstracted in: not given

Manuscripts

Query: yes
Abstract: no
Style guide: available on request
Preferred length: 10 pages
Number of copies: 3, double-spaced
Notes: end of manuscript

Blind referee: no
Time to consider manuscript: 3 months
Proportion of manuscripts accepted: 35 percent
Illustrations accepted: tables, graphs, charts, photos, drawings
Foreign languages: no

Reviews

Book review editor: Charles E. Marske
Address:
Department of Sociology
St. Louis University
St. Louis, MO 63103
Seeking reviewers: yes
Unsolicited reviews accepted: yes
How to apply: letter of inquiry
Include in application: institutional affiliation, areas of expertise, current research.
Materials reviewed: books, rejoinders to articles in *QJI* or other scholarly journals
Length of review: 1,500 words maximum

Additional notes

QJI is always open to new ideas and inputs. Short, well-written articles with a minimum of footnotes and quotations are preferred. *QJI* invites graduate students and foreign students and professors to submit their work. Simultaneous submission is not permitted. Articles appear 3 months after acceptance.

RADICAL AMERICA

Focus: radical history, analysis of current trends in Marxism, socialism, feminism, grassroots and community organizing, workplace and shopfloor organizing
Institutional affiliation: Alternative Education Project
Editor: John Demeter
Editorial address:
38 Union Square, #14
Somerville, MA 02143

Frequency: 6/year
Circulation: 5,000
Subscription rate(s): $12
Pages/issue: 80
Readership: general public, academics, community and women activists
Indexed/abstracted in: Amer Hist and Life, Sociol Abstr, Wom Stud Abstr, Alt Press Ind

Manuscripts

Query: yes
Abstract: yes
Style guide: MOS
Preferred length: 5,000–8,000 words
Number of copies: 2
Notes: end of manuscript
Blind referee: no
Time to consider manuscript: 4–6 weeks
Proportion of manuscripts accepted: 20 percent
Illustrations accepted: tables, graphs, charts, photos, drawings
Foreign languages: no

Reviews

Book review editor: James Stark
Address: same as above
Unsolicited reviews accepted: yes
How to apply: letter of inquiry
Include in application: areas of expertise
Materials reviewed: books, films
Length of review: 500–2,500 words

REGIONAL SCIENCE AND URBAN ECONOMICS

Focus: interdisciplinary studies of regional and urban planning, policy development, and economics
Editor: Urs Schweizer
Editorial address:
Department of Economics
University of Bielefeld
P.O. Box 8640
D-4800 Bielefeld 1
FEDERAL REPUBLIC OF GERMANY
Frequency: 4/year
Circulation: not given

Subscription rate(s): individual $40, institutional $102
Pages/issue: 140
Readership: local and civic officials, regional and urban planners, social scientists
Indexed/abstracted in: Curr Cont, Geo Abstr, J of Econ Lit

Manuscripts
Query: no
Abstract: yes, 100 word maximum
Style guide: see current issue
Preferred length: 30 pages maximum
Number of copies: 3
Notes: end of manuscript
Blind referee: yes
Time to consider manuscript: 6 months
Proportion of manuscripts accepted: not given
Illustrations accepted: tables, graphs, figures, maps, drawings
Foreign languages: no

Reviews
not applicable

Additional notes
Simultaneous submission is not permitted. Articles are published 6 months after acceptance.

RES PUBLICA: BELGIAN JOURNAL FOR POLITICAL SCIENCE

Focus: all aspects of political science and related fields
Institutional affiliation: Belgian Ministry of Public Education
Editor: Wilfried Dewachter
Editorial address:
Van Evenstraat 2B
B-3000 Leuven
BELGIUM
Frequency: 4/year
Circulation: not given
Subscription rate(s): not given
Pages/issue: 110–120

Readership: political and social scientists
Indexed/abstracted in: ABC POL SCI, SSCI, Sociol Abstr

Manuscripts
Query: no
Abstract: yes, 150 words maximum
Style guide: see current issue or write for guidelines
Preferred length: no preference
Number of copies: 2
Notes: bottom of page
Blind referee: no
Time to consider manuscript: not given
Proportion of manuscripts accepted: not given
Illustrations accepted: tables, graphs, charts, diagrams
Foreign languages: French, other West European

Reviews
not applicable

REVIEW OF INTERNATIONAL STUDIES

Focus: interdisciplinary studies of international society
Institutional affiliation: British International Studies Association
Editor: J. E. Spence
Editorial address:
University of Leicester
Leicester LE1 7RH
ENGLAND
Frequency: 4/year
Circulation: not given
Subscription rate(s): $50
Pages/issue: 80–100
Readership: social scientists
Indexed/abstracted in: Hist Abstr, Amer Hist and Life, Int Polit Sci Abstr

Manuscripts
Query: no
Abstract: no
Style guide: available on request
Preferred length: 8,000 words

Number of copies: 3
Notes: end of manuscript
Blind referee: no
Time to consider manuscript: not given
Proportion of manuscripts accepted: not given
Illustrations accepted: tables, graphs, charts, drawings, maps
Foreign languages: no

Reviews
not applicable

THE REVIEW OF POLITICS

Focus: study of political realities and political community in its Aristotelian sense; emphasis is on philosophical and historical aspects of current problems
Institutional affiliation: University of Notre Dame
Editor: Frederick J. Crosson
Editorial address:
Box B
University of Notre Dame
Notre Dame, IN 46556
Frequency: 4/year
Circulation: 1,700
Subscription rate(s): individual $10, institutional $15 (domestic); individual $11, institutional $16 (foreign)
Pages/issue: 160
Readership: academics
Indexed/abstracted in: Int Ind Per, Cath Ind, Int Polit Sci Abstr, ABC POL SCI, Soc Sci Ind

Manuscripts
Query: no
Abstract: no
Style guide: MOS
Preferred length: 25–30 pages
Number of copies: 3
Notes: end of manuscript
Blind referee: no
Time to consider manuscript: 3 months
Proportion of manuscripts accepted: not given

Illustrations accepted: none
Foreign languages: yes

Reviews
Book review editor: Dennis William Moran
Address: same as above
Seeking reviewers: no
Unsolicited reviews accepted: no
How to apply: letter of inquiry
Include in application: professional degrees, institutional affiliation, areas of expertise, published works, current research
Materials reviewed: books

Additional notes
Simultaneous submission is not allowed. Articles are published 6–9 months after acceptance.

REVIEW OF PUBLIC DATA USE

Focus: the production, distribution, and use of publicly available statistical data
Editor: Charles G. Renfro
Editorial address:
11 East Princeton Road
Bala Cynwyd, PA 19004
Frequency: 4/year
Circulation: not given
Subscription rate(s): $72
Pages/issue: 90–100
Readership: researchers, social scientists
Indexed/abstracted in: not given

Manuscripts
Query: no
Abstract: yes, 150 words maximum
Style guide: American Sociological Association format
Preferred length: 24 pages maximum
Number of copies: 3
Notes: 3
Blind referee: end of manuscript
Time to consider manuscript: not given
Proportion of manuscripts accepted: not given

Illustrations accepted: tables, figures
Foreign languages: no

Reviews
not applicable

Additional notes
Submit 2 copies of a brief biography of the author(s). The editors should be informed of simultaneous submission.

ROYAL UNITED SERVICES INSTITUTE FOR DEFENCE STUDIES JOURNAL

Focus: military and defense studies; foreign and military policy, both British and foreign
Institutional affiliation: Royal United Services Institute for Defence Studies
Editor: submit to the Editor
Editorial address:
Royal United Services Institute
Whitehall
London SW1A 2ET
ENGLAND
Frequency: 4/year
Circulation: 6,500
Subscription rate(s): £18
Pages/issue: 75
Readership: those interested in defense or working in a defense-related industry, academics
Indexed/abstracted in: not given

Manuscripts
Query: no
Abstract: no
Style guide: see current issue
Preferred length: 3,000–5,000 words
Number of copies: 2
Notes: end of manuscript
Blind referee: no
Time to consider manuscript: 4–8 weeks
Proportion of manuscripts accepted: not given
Illustrations accepted: tables, graphs, charts, photos, drawings
Foreign languages: no

Reviews
Book review editor: submit to the Editor
Address: same as above
Materials reviewed: books
Length of review: 2–3 pages

Additional notes
Simultaneous submission is not permitted. Articles are published 3 months or more after acceptance. Published authors receive £12.50 per 1,000 words.

RURAL AFRICANA

Focus: scholarly social science research on sub-Saharan Africa
Institutional affiliation: African Studies Center, Michigan State University
Editors: Assefa Mehretu, David Wiley
Editorial address:
African Studies Center
Michigan State University
East Lansing, MI 48824
Frequency: 3/year
Circulation: 250
Subscription rate(s): individual $12, institutional $18
Pages/issue: 90
Readership: academics, government and research agencies
Indexed/abstracted in: not given

Manuscripts
Query: no
Abstract: no
Style guide: MOS
Preferred length: 30 pages maximum
Number of copies: 1
Notes: end of manuscript
Blind referee: no
Time to consider manuscript: 2 weeks
Proportion of manuscripts accepted: 50 percent
Illustrations accepted: camera-ready tables, graphs, charts, line illustrations
Foreign languages: no

Reviews
Book review editor: submit to the Editors
Address: same as above
Seeking reviewers: no
Unsolicited reviews accepted: yes
How to apply: letter of inquiry
Materials reviewed: books, films, tapes
Length of review: 3 pages

THE RUSSIAN REVIEW

Focus: Russia/Soviet Union, past and present
Institutional affiliation: Hoover Institution
Editor: Terence Emmons
Editorial address:
Hoover Institution
Stanford, CA 94305
Frequency: 4/year
Circulation: 1,850
Subscription rate(s): $12
Pages/issue: 140
Readership: academics, general public
Indexed/abstracted in: Hist Abstr, Hum Ind, PAIS, Peace Res Abstr

Manuscripts
Query: no
Abstract: no
Style guide: MOS
Preferred length: 25 pages
Number of copies: 2
Notes: end of manuscript
Blind referee: no
Time to consider manuscript: 6–8 weeks
Proportion of manuscripts accepted: not given
Illustrations accepted: tables, graphs, charts, photos
Foreign languages: occasionally, French, Russian

Reviews
Book review editor: submit to the Editor
Address: same as above
Unsolicited reviews accepted: no

How to apply: letter of inquiry
Include in application: professional degrees, institutional affiliation, areas of expertise, published works, foreign languages, current research
Materials reviewed: books
Length of review: 150–800 words

SAIS REVIEW

Focus: policy implications of current international developments
Institutional affiliation: The School of Advanced International Studies, Johns Hopkins University
Editor: Lisa M. Buttenheim
Editorial address:
1740 Massachusetts Avenue, NW
Washington, DC 20036
Frequency: 2/year
Circulation: 2,000
Subscription rate(s): student $6, individual $8, institutional $15
Pages/issue: 200
Readership: academics
Indexed/abstracted in: ABC POL SCI, PAIS

Manuscripts
Query: no
Abstract: no
Style guide: available on request
Preferred length: 3,000–5,000 words
Number of copies: 1
Notes: end of manuscript
Blind referee: no
Time to consider manuscript: see additional notes
Proportion of manuscripts accepted: 50 percent
Illustrations accepted: tables, graphs
Foreign languages: no

Reviews
Book review editors: Rolf Lundberg, Masara Tamamoto
Address: same as above
Seeking reviewers: yes
Unsolicited reviews accepted: yes
Materials reviewed: books, periodical articles
Length of review: 1,000–1,500 words

Additional notes

Simultaneous submission is permitted. Essay format is preferred as opposed to paper format. Include two or three lines of biographical data (positions held, recent publications) with the manuscript. When choosing a topic, keep in mind that the *Review* is published only twice per year. The winter deadline falls in early October, and the spring deadline falls in early April. Some subjects or issues may be too transient to remain current until publication. The time required for consideration of a manuscript is dependent upon the proximity of the submission deadline.

SCANDINAVIAN POLITICAL STUDIES

Focus: all aspects of political science
Institutional affiliation: Nordic Political Science Association
Editor: submit to the Editors
Editorial address:
Institutt for Sosiologi og Statsvitenskape lige Fag Universitetet i Bergen Christiesgate 15–17 N-5014 Bergen-U NORWAY
Frequency: 4/year
Circulation: 500
Subscription rate(s): $28
Pages/issue: 100
Readership: political scientists
Indexed/abstracted in: ABC POL SCI, Hist Abstr

Manuscripts
Query: no
Abstract: yes, 150 words maximum
Style guide: see current issue
Preferred length: 5,000 words
Number of copies: 3
Notes: end of manuscript
Blind referee: no
Time to consider manuscript: not given
Proportion of manuscripts accepted: not given

Illustrations accepted: tables, graphs, diagrams, drawings
Foreign languages: no

Reviews
not applicable

SCIENCE AND SOCIETY

Focus: independent Marxist journal
Editor: David Goldway
Editorial address:
445 West 59th Street New York, NY 10019
Frequency: 4/year
Circulation: 3,800
Subscription rate(s): individual $15, institution $25 (domestic); individual $19, institutional $30 (foreign)
Pages/issue: 130
Readership: academics
Indexed/abstracted in: Soc Sci and Human Ind, PAIS, Universal Ref Syst, Bk Rev Ind, ABC POL SCI, Hist Abstr, Amer Hist and Life, Int Polit Sci Abstr, Alt Press Ind

Manuscripts
Query: no
Abstract: no
Style guide: MFW
Preferred length: 6,000–8,000 words
Number of copies: 3
Notes: bottom of page
Blind referee: no
Time to consider manuscript: 4–12 months
Proportion of manuscripts accepted: not given
Illustrations accepted: tables, graphs, photos
Foreign languages: no

Reviews
Book review editor: submit to Book Review Editor
Address: same as above
Seeking reviewers: yes
Unsolicited reviews accepted: yes
How to apply: letter of inquiry

Include in application: professional
degrees, institutional affiliation, areas
of expertise, published works,
current research
Materials reviewed: books
Length of review: 1,000–1,200 words

Additional notes
Simultaneous submission is not
permitted. Articles are published 3
months after acceptance.

SCOTTISH JOURNAL OF POLITICAL ECONOMY

Focus: political economy
Institutional affiliation: Scottish
Economic Society
Editor: submit to the Editors
Editorial address:
Department of Social and Economic
Research
Adam Smith Building
University of Glasgow
Glasgow G12 8RT SCOTLAND
Frequency: 3/year
Circulation: not given
Subscription rate(s): $18
Pages/issue: 120
Readership: economists, other social
scientists
Indexed/abstracted in: Br Hum Ind,
PAIS, SSCI, J of Econ Lit, Work Rel
Abstr

Manuscripts
Query: no
Abstract: no
Style guide: available on request
Preferred length: no preference
Number of copies: 2
Notes: end of manuscript
Blind referee: no
Time to consider manuscript: not
given
**Proportion of manuscripts
accepted:** not given
Illustrations accepted: tables, figures
Foreign languages: no

Reviews
Book review editor: Gavin Reid
Address:
Department of Economics
William Robertson Building
George Square
University of Edinburgh
Edinburgh EH8 9JY
SCOTLAND
Materials reviewed: books

THE SEARCH: JOURNAL FOR ARAB AND ISLAMIC STUDIES

Focus: various aspects of Arab and
Islamic affairs (cultural, political,
economic, legal, etc.)
Institutional affiliation: Center for
Arab and Islamic Studies, Inc.
Editor: Samir Abde-Rabbo
Editorial address:
P.O. Box 543
Brattleboro, VT 05301
Frequency: 4/year
Circulation: 2,000
Subscription rate(s): student $12,
individual $15, institutional $25
Pages/issue: 120
Readership: academics, business
people, and general public
Indexed/abstracted in: Hist Abstr

Manuscripts
Query: no
Abstract: no
Style guide: none required
Preferred length: 5,000 words or 25
pages
Number of copies: 3
Notes: end of manuscript
Blind referee: no
Time to consider manuscript: 1
month
**Proportion of manuscripts
accepted:** not given
Illustrations accepted: tables,
graphs, charts
Foreign languages: Arabic

Reviews
Book review editor: Richard Pfau
Address: same as above

Seeking reviewers: yes
Unsolicited reviews accepted: yes
How to apply: letter of inquiry
Include in application: professional degrees, institutional affiliation, areas of expertise, published works
Materials reviewed: books, films, tapes
Length of review: 2–5 pages

SIGNS: JOURNAL OF WOMEN IN CULTURE AND SOCIETY

Focus: new scholarship about women
Institutional affiliation: Barnard College
Editor: Elsa Dixler
Editorial address:
Barnard Hall
Barnard College
New York, NY 10027
Frequency: 4/year
Circulation: 7,500
Subscription rate(s): $18
Pages/issue: 200
Readership: academics
Indexed/abstracted in: ABC POL SCI

Manuscripts
Query: yes
Abstract: no
Style guide: available on request
Preferred length: 35 pages
Number of copies: 3
Notes: end of manuscript
Blind referee: yes
Time to consider manuscript: 4–6 months
Proportion of manuscripts accepted: not given
Illustrations accepted: tables, graphs, charts, photos
Foreign languages: occasionally, Western European languages only

Reviews
Book review editor: Joan Burstyn
Address: same as above
Seeking reviewers: no
Unsolicited reviews accepted: rarely
How to apply: letter of inquiry

Include in application: professional degrees, institutional affiliation, areas of expertise, published works, foreign languages, current research
Materials reviewed: books
Length of review: 300 words

Additional notes
Simultaneous submission is not permitted. Articles are published 12–18 months after acceptance.

SIMULATION AND GAMES

Focus: theory, design, and research in all aspects of gaming and simulation, especially in social science and business
Institutional affiliation: Sage Publications
Editor: Cathy Stein Greenblat
Editorial address:
Department of Sociology
Rutgers University
New Brunswick, NJ 08903
Frequency: 4/year
Circulation: 1,200
Subscription rate(s): individual $22, institutional $46, foreign add $2
Pages/issue: 125
Readership: academics, public policy and business education people
Indexed/abstracted in: not given

Manuscripts
Query: no
Abstract: yes
Style guide: APA
Preferred length: 10–35 pages
Number of copies: 3
Notes: end of manuscript
Blind referee: yes
Time to consider manuscript: 2–3 months
Proportion of manuscripts accepted: 30 percent
Illustrations accepted: tables, graphs, charts, photos, drawings
Foreign languages: no

Reviews

Book review editor: R. Garry Shirts
Address:
   c/o Simile II
   Del Mar, CA 93014
Seeking reviewers: yes
Unsolicited reviews accepted: yes
How to apply: letter of inquiry
Include in application: professional
   degrees, institutional affiliation, areas
   of expertise, published works,
   current research
Materials reviewed: books on games/
   simulations
Length of review: 2-8 pages

Additional notes

Simultaneous submission is permitted,
but discouraged. Articles appear 6-9
months after acceptance.

SLAVIC REVIEW

Focus: Russian and East European
   studies, past and present
Institutional affiliation: American
   Association for the Advancement of
   Slavic Studies
Editor: David L. Ransel
Editorial address:
   University of Illinois
   911 West High Street, Room 200
   Urbana, IL 61801
Frequency: 4/year
Circulation: 3,800
Subscription rate(s): student $15,
   individual $40
Pages/issue: 190
Readership: specialists in Slavic
   studies
Indexed/abstracted in: ABC POL
   SCI, Hist Abstr

Manuscripts

Query: yes
Abstract: no
Style guide: MOS
Preferred length: 25 pages maximum
Number of copies: 4
Notes: end of manuscript
Blind referee: yes

Time to consider manuscript: 3-4
   months
**Proportion of manuscripts
   accepted:** 10 percent
Illustrations accepted: tables,
   graphs, charts
Foreign languages: no

Reviews

Book review editor: David L. Ransel
Address: same as above
Seeking reviewers: yes
Unsolicited reviews accepted: no
How to apply: letter of inquiry, letter of
   recommendation
Include in application: professional
   degrees, institutional affiliation, areas
   of expertise, published works,
   current research
Materials reviewed: books
Length of review: 1-2 pages

Additional notes

Publication of articles in the *Slavic
Review* is ordinarily limited to those
submitted by members of the AAASS.
Nonmembers wishing to submit
manuscripts are asked to request a
membership application. Simultaneous
submission is not permitted. Articles
appear 9 months after acceptance.

SOCIAL ACTION AND THE LAW

Focus: brings relevant social science
   information to the attention of
   persons in the legal, judicial, and
   correction fields
Institutional affiliation: Center for
   Responsive Psychology, Brooklyn
   College, City University of New York
Editor: Robert Buckhout
Editorial address:
   Center for Responsive Psychology
   Brooklyn College
   Brooklyn, NY 11210
Frequency: 4/year
Circulation: 1,500
Subscription rate(s): individual $10,
   institutional $25
Pages/issue: 32

Readership: lawyers, law libraries, academics (social psychology, law, forensic psychology), law enforcement
Indexed/abstracted in: NCJRS

Manuscripts
Query: no
Abstract: no
Style guide: available on request
Preferred length: 10–12 pages
Number of copies: 2, double-spaced
Notes: end of manuscript
Blind referee: no
Time to consider manuscript: 3 weeks
Proportion of manuscripts accepted: varies
Illustrations accepted: tables, graphs, charts, photos, drawings
Foreign languages: no

Reviews
Book review editor: Robert Buckhout
Address: same as above
Seeking reviewers: yes
Unsolicited reviews accepted: yes
How to apply: letter of inquiry
Include in application: professional degrees, institutional affiliation, areas of expertise
Materials reviewed: books, films
Length of review: 4–8 pages, double-spaced

Additional notes
Simultaneous submission is allowed. Articles are published 3 months after acceptance.

SOCIAL FORCES

Focus: highlights sociological inquiry; papers also explore realms shared with social psychology, anthropology, political science, history, and economics
Institutional affiliation: University of North Carolina at Chapel Hill
Editor: Norma C. Scofield

Editorial address:
Department of Sociology
168 Hamilton Hall 070A
University of North Carolina
Chapel Hill, NC 27514
Circulation: 5,100–5,200
Subscription rate(s): individual $16, institutional $20
Pages/issue: 350
Readership: social scientists
Indexed/abstracted in: Soc Sci Ind, Popul Ind, CIJE, Sociol Abstr, Psychol Abstr, Abstr Anthropol

Manuscripts
Query: no
Abstract: yes
Style guide: available on request
Preferred length: 15–20 pages
Number of copies: 4
Notes: end of manuscript
Blind referee: yes
Time to consider manuscript: 1 month
Proportion of manuscripts accepted: 11–12 percent
Illustrations accepted: tables, graphs, charts
Foreign languages: no

Reviews
Book review editor: John Shelton Reed
Address: same as above
Seeking reviewers: yes
Unsolicited reviews accepted: no
How to apply: letter of inquiry
Include in application: professional degrees, institutional affiliation, areas of expertise
Materials reviewed: books
Length of review: 500 words

Additional notes
Simultaneous submission is not allowed. Articles are published 1 year after acceptance.

SOCIALIST REVIEW

Focus: political analysis of American politics and culture, socialist theory, political economy, the international left, feminist theory, and new social movements
Institutional affiliation: Center for Social Research and Education
Editor: Jeffrey Escoffier
Editorial address:
4228 Telegraph Avenue
Oakland, CA 94609
Frequency: 6/year
Circulation: 8,500
Subscription rate(s): $18
Pages/issue: 144
Readership: academics, political activists
Indexed/abstracted in: Sociol Abstr, SSCI, Alt Press Ind, Int Polit Sci Abstr

Manuscripts
Query: yes
Abstract: no
Style guide: MOS
Preferred length: 30 pages
Number of copies: 3
Notes: end of manuscript
Blind referee: no
Time to consider manuscript: 2 months
Proportion of manuscripts accepted: 10 percent
Illustrations accepted: tables, graphs, charts, photos, drawings
Foreign languages: no

Reviews
Book review editor: Joel Krieger
Address: same as above
Seeking reviewers: yes
Unsolicited reviews accepted: yes
How to apply: letter of inquiry
Include in application: sample of written work
Materials reviewed: books, films
Length of review: 8-10 pages

Additional notes
Simultaneous submission is not permitted. Articles appear 4-6 months after acceptance.

SOCIAL POLICY

Focus: political and social alternatives in today's society
Editor: Audrey Gartner
Editorial address:
33 West 42nd Street
Room 1212
New York, NY 10036
Frequency: 4/year
Circulation: 8,500
Subscription rate(s): $15
Pages/issue: 64
Readership: academics
Indexed/abstracted in: Soc Sci Ind, Curr Cont, SSCI, Sage Urb Stud Abstr

Manuscripts
Query: no
Abstract: no
Style guide: MOS
Preferred length: 3,000-5,000 words
Number of copies: 2
Notes: end of manuscript
Blind referee: no
Time to consider manuscript: 3 weeks
Proportion of manuscripts accepted: 33 percent
Illustrations accepted: tables, photos, drawings
Foreign languages: no

Reviews
Book review editor: Audrey Gartner
Address: same as above
Seeking reviewers: yes
Unsolicited reviews accepted: yes
Materials reviewed: books, films
Length of review: 2,000 words

Additional notes
Simultaneous submission is not allowed. Articles appear 2-12 months after acceptance.

SOCIAL RESEARCH

Focus: interdisciplinary approach to issues in the social sciences
Institutional affiliation: New School for Social Research

Editor: Arien Mack
Editorial address:
New School for Social Research
66 West 12th Street
New York, NY 10011
Frequency: 4/year
Circulation: 3,500
Subscription rate(s): individual $20,
institutional $35
Pages/issue: 200
Readership: social scientists
Indexed/abstracted in: ABC POL
SCI, Amer Hist and Life, Hist Abstr

Manuscripts
Query: no
Abstract: no
Style guide: available on request
Preferred length: 20–25 pages
Number of copies: 2
Notes: end of manuscript
Blind referee: no
Time to consider manuscript: 3
months
**Proportion of manuscripts
accepted:** 5 percent
Illustrations accepted: none
Foreign languages: no

Reviews
not applicable

Additional notes
Simultaneous submission is permitted.
Articles are published 3–12 months after
acceptance.

SOCIAL SCIENCE

Focus: political science, economics,
sociology
Institutional affiliation: Pi Gamma Mu
Editor: Panos D. Bardis
Editorial address:
Department of Sociology
Toledo University
Toledo, OH 43606
Frequency: 4/year
Circulation: 10,000
Subscription rate(s): $4
Pages/issue: 64

Readership: social scientists, general
public
Indexed/abstracted in: Curr Cont,
Hist Abstr, PAIS, SSCI, Social Abstr,
Int Polit Sci Abstr

Manuscripts
Query: no
Abstract: yes
Style guide: available on request
Preferred length: 10–20 pages
Number of copies: 1
Notes: end of manuscript
Blind referee: no
Time to consider manuscript: 2
weeks
**Proportion of manuscripts
accepted:** 40 percent
Illustrations accepted: tables,
graphs, charts, photos
Foreign languages: no

Reviews
Book review editor: Panos D. Bardis
Address: same as above
Seeking reviewers: yes
Unsolicited reviews accepted: yes
How to apply: letter of inquiry
Include in application: professional
degrees, institutional affiliation, areas
of expertise, published works
Materials reviewed: books
Length of review: 500–1,500 words

Additional notes
Social Science is an interdisciplinary
journal that stresses both the past and
the present, and seeks qualitative as well
as quantitative studies. Simultaneous
submission is not allowed. Articles are
published 6 months after acceptance.

SOCIAL SCIENCE HISTORY

Focus: the study of social theory
within an empirical, historical context
to make a valuable contribution to
understanding societies of the past
and present
Editors: James O. Graham, Jr., Robert
P. Swierenga

Editorial address:
Department of History
Bowling Green State University
111 Williams Hall
Bowling Green, OH 43403
Frequency: 4/year
Circulation: 1,000
Subscription rate(s): not given
Pages/issue: 128
Readership: social scientists
Indexed/abstracted in: Hist Abstr

Manuscripts
Query: no
Abstract: no
Style guide: available on request
Preferred length: 15–30 pages
Number of copies: 3
Notes: in-text citations, references at
end
Blind referee: yes
Time to consider manuscript: 4
months
**Proportion of manuscripts
accepted:** 33 percent
Illustrations accepted: tables,
graphs, charts, photos
Foreign languages: no

Reviews
Book review editor: Alan M. Kraut
Address:
Department of History
American University
Washington, DC 20016
Seeking reviewers: yes
Unsolicited reviews accepted: no
How to apply: letter of inquiry
Include in application: professional
degrees, institutional affiliation, areas
of expertise, published works,
foreign languages, current research
Materials reviewed: books
Length of review: 500 words
maximum

SOCIAL SCIENCE INFORMATION/INFORMATION SUR LES SCIENCES SOCIALES

Focus: international, cross-disciplinary
analysis and debate concerning
trends and approaches in social
science research and teaching;
includes studies in new areas, cross-
cultural comparison, problems of
research organization, and social
studies of science
Institutional affiliation: International
Social Science Council/Conseil
international des Sciences Sociales
Editor: Elina Almasy
Editorial address:
Unesco House/Maison de l'Unesco
1 Rue Miollis
Paris 75015
FRANCE
Frequency: 6/year
Circulation: not given
Subscription rate(s): individual $27,
institutional $64
Pages/issue: 161
Readership: social scientists
Indexed/abstracted in: ABC POL
SCI, Curr Cont, Human Resour
Abstr, Sage Pub Admin Abstr

Manuscripts
Query: no
Abstract: no
Style guide: available on request
Preferred length: 20–30 pages
Number of copies: 1
Notes: end of manuscript
Blind referee: no
Time to consider manuscript: not
given
**Proportion of manuscripts
accepted:** not given
Illustrations accepted: tables,
graphs, charts
Foreign languages: French, German,
Italian, Dutch, Spanish, and the
Scandinavian and Slavic languages;
all articles will eventually be
translated into either English or
French

Reviews
not applicable

THE SOCIAL SCIENCE JOURNAL

Focus: the social sciences
Institutional affiliation: Colorado State University, Western Social Science Association
Editor: D. Stanley Eitzen
Editorial address:
Department of Sociology
Colorado State University
Fort Collins, CO 80523
Frequency: 4/year
Circulation: 1,400
Subscription rate(s): domestic $15, foreign $20
Pages/issue: 140
Readership: anthropologists, economists, geographers, historians, political scientists, sociologists, related social science disciplines
Indexed/abstracted in: Soc Work Res and Abstr, Amer Hist and Life, Curr Cont, Econ Abstr, Hist Abstr, Human Resour Abstr, Int Polit Sci Abstr, Peace Res Abstr, PAIS, Sage Pub Admin Abstr, Sage Urb Stud Abstr, Social Abstr, Social Educ Abstr, Universal Ref Syst

Manuscripts
Query: no
Abstract: yes
Style guide: MOS
Preferred length: 25 pages
Number of copies: 4
Notes: end of manuscript
Blind referee: yes
Time to consider manuscript: 45 days
Proportion of manuscripts accepted: 15 percent
Illustrations accepted: tables, graphs, charts, photos
Foreign languages: no

Reviews
Book review editor: Fred Erisman
Address:
Department of English
Texas Christian University
Fort Worth, TX 76129
Seeking reviewers: yes
Unsolicited reviews accepted: yes
How to apply: letter of inquiry
Include in application: professional degrees, institutional affiliation, areas of expertise, current research
Materials reviewed: books
Length of review: 3–4 pages

Additional notes
Simultaneous submission is not permitted. Articles are published 6 months after acceptance.

SOCIAL SCIENCE QUARTERLY

Focus: social science and public policy
Institutional affiliation: Southwestern Social Science Association
Editor: Charles M. Bonjean
Editorial address:
W.C. Hogg Building
Room 310
University of Texas
Austin, TX 78712
Frequency: 4/year
Circulation: 3,000
Subscription rate(s): student $10 individual $16, institutional $32
Pages/issue: 204
Readership: political scientists, sociologists, economists, historians, geographers
Indexed/abstracted in: ABC POL SCI, Amer Hist and Life, Bk Rev Ind, CRIS, Curr Cont, Curr Ind Stat, Educ Admin Abstr, Hist Abstr, Ind Econ J, Int Bibl Polit Sci, Int Bibl Sociol, Int Ind, Int Polit Sci Abstr, J Econ Abstr, PAIS, Soc Sci Ind, Sociol Abstr, USPSD

Manuscripts
Query: no
Abstract: yes
Style guide: MOS
Preferred length: 25 pages maximum
Number of copies: 4
Notes: end of manuscript
Blind referee: yes
Time to consider manuscript: 6 weeks
Proportion of manuscripts accepted: 12.5 percent
Illustrations accepted: tables, graphs, charts, photos, drawings
Foreign languages: no

Reviews
Book review editor: H. Malcolm Macdonald
Address:
Department of Government
University of Texas
Austin, TX 78712
Seeking reviewers: yes
Unsolicited reviews accepted: no
How to apply: letter of inquiry (with vita)
Include in application: professional degrees, institutional affiliation, areas of expertise, published works, current research
Materials reviewed: books

Additional notes
Simultaneous submission is not permitted. Articles appear 5–8 months after acceptance.

SOCIAL SCIENCE RESEARCH

Focus: social science methodology and quantitative research
Editors: Peter H. Rossi, James D. Wright
Editorial address:
Department of Sociology
University of Massachusetts
Amherst, MA 01002
Frequency: 4/year
Circulation: 900
Subscription rate(s): $62
Pages/issue: 100–125

Readership: social scientists
Indexed/abstracted in: ABC POL SCI

Manuscripts
Query: no
Abstract: yes, 100–150 words
Style guide: available on request
Preferred length: 20–30 pages
Number of copies: 3
Notes: end of manuscript
Blind referee: no
Time to consider manuscript: 3–6 months
Proportion of manuscripts accepted: 18 percent
Illustrations accepted: tables, graphs, charts, photos, drawings
Foreign languages: no

Reviews
not applicable

Additional notes
Articles dealing with issues or methods that cut across traditional disciplinary lines are especially welcome.

SOCIAL THEORY AND PRACTICE

Focus: studies of contemporary and controversial social and political issues
Institutional affiliation: Department of Philosophy, Florida State University
Editor: Jayne A. Moneysmith
Editorial address:
Department of Philosophy
Florida State University
Tallahassee, FL 32306
Frequency: 3/year
Circulation: 850
Subscription rate(s): individual $12, institutional $27
Pages/issue: 130
Readership: social scientists
Indexed/abstracted in: ABC POL SCI, Abstr Crim and Pen, Lang and Lang Behav Abstr, Phil Ind, SSCI, Soc Sci Ind, Social Abstr

Manuscripts
Query: no
Abstract: no
Style guide: MOS
Preferred length: 20–30 pages
Number of copies: 2
Notes: end of manuscript
Blind referee: yes
Time to consider manuscript: 3–4 months
Proportion of manuscripts accepted: 10 percent
Illustrations accepted: tables, graphs
Foreign languages: no

Reviews
Book review editor: Russell Davey
Address: same as above
Seeking reviewers: yes
Unsolicited reviews accepted: yes
How to apply: letter of inquiry
Include in application: professional degrees, institutional affiliation, areas of expertise, published works, current research, availability (long or short term)
Materials reviewed: books
Length of review: 2–8 pages

Additional notes
Simultaneous submission is not allowed. Articles are published 6–12 months after acceptance.

SOCIO-ECONOMIC PLANNING SCIENCES

Focus: quantitative analysis of interdisciplinary problems arising in the area of socio-economic planning; applications of systems analysis to the planning of public welfare and community services
Editor: Summer N. Levine
Editorial address:
P.O. Box 116
Setauket, NY 11733
Frequency: 6/year
Circulation: not given
Subscription rate(s): individual $45, institutional $125
Pages/issue: 50

Readership: academics, mathematicians
Indexed/abstracted in: ABC POL SCI

MANUSCRIPTS
Query: no
Abstract: yes
Style guide: available on request
Preferred length: 10–30 pages
Number of copies: 2
Notes: end of manuscript
Blind referee: no
Time to consider manuscript: not given
Proportion of manuscripts accepted: not given
Illustrations accepted: tables, graphs, charts, photos (glossy finish), drawings
Foreign languages: no

REVIEWS
not applicable

SOCIOLOGICAL INQUIRY

Focus: general sociology and other social science
Institutional affiliation: Virginia Polytechnic Institute and State University
Editor: James K. Skipper, Jr
Editorial address:
Department of Sociology
Virginia Polytechnic Institute and State University
Blacksburg, VA 24061
Frequency: 4/year
Circulation: 3,650
Subscription rate(s): individual $12, institutional $20
Pages/issue: 100
Readership: academics
Indexed/abstracted in: Sociol Abstr, Psychol Abstr, Curr Cont

Manuscripts
Query: no
Abstract: yes
Style guide: available on request
Preferred length: 15–25 pages
Number of copies: 3

Notes: end of manuscript
Blind referee: yes
Time to consider manuscript: 6–8 weeks
Proportion of manuscripts accepted: 14 percent
Illustrations accepted: tables, graphs, charts, drawings
Foreign languages: no

Reviews
Seeking reviewers: no
Unsolicited reviews accepted: no
How to apply: reviewers are appointed

Additional notes
Sociological Inquiry is the official journal of Alpha Kappa Delta, the International Sociology Honor Society. Simultaneous submission is not allowed.

THE SOCIOLOGICAL QUARTERLY

Focus: articles relevant to sociology
Institutional affiliation: Department of Sociology, Southern Illinois University at Carbondale
Editors: Thomas G. Eynon, Herman Lantz
Editorial address:
Department of Sociology
Southern Illinois University
Carbondale, IL 62901
Frequency: 4/year
Circulation: 2,500
Subscription rate(s): individual $12, institutional $18
Pages/issue: 150–200
Readership: academic sociologists
Indexed/abstracted in: not given

Manuscripts
Query: no
Abstract: yes
Style guide: none required
Preferred length: 20 pages
Number of copies: 4
Notes: no notes
Time to consider manuscript: 6 weeks

Proportion of manuscripts accepted: 10 percent
Illustrations accepted: tables, graphs, charts
Foreign languages: no

Reviews
Book review editors: Herman Lantz, Thomas G. Eynon
Address: same as above
Seeking reviewers: yes
Unsolicited reviews accepted: no
How to apply: letter of inquiry
Include in application: professional degrees, institutional affiliation, areas of expertise, published works, current research
Materials reviewed: books

Additional notes
Non-sociologists will be published if the articles are significant for sociology. Simultaneous submission is not allowed. Articles are published 6–9 months after acceptance.

SOUTH ATLANTIC QUARTERLY

Focus: humanities, social sciences, general interest
Institutional affiliation: Duke University
Editor: Oliver W. Ferguson
Editorial address:
P.O. Box 6697
College Station
Durham, NC 27706
Frequency: 4/year
Circulation: 1,200
Subscription rate(s): individual $10, institutional $14
Pages/issue: 150
Readership: academics
Indexed/abstracted in: Hum Ind, PAIS, Amer Hist and Life

Manuscripts
Query: no
Abstract: no
Style guide: none required

Preferred length: 4,500 words
maximum
Number of copies: 1
Notes: end of manuscript
Blind referee: no
Time to consider manuscript: 4–6
weeks
**Proportion of manuscripts
accepted:** 5 percent
Illustrations accepted: tables,
graphs, charts, photos, but
discouraged
Foreign languages: no

Reviews
Book review editor: Oliver W.
Ferguson
Address: same as above
Seeking reviewers: no
Unsolicited reviews accepted: no
How to apply: letter of inquiry
Materials reviewed: books
Length of review: 100–350 words

SOUTHEAST ASIA
CHRONICLE

Focus: political economy of Southeast
Asia; interests of U.S. government
and business in Southeast Asia
Institutional affiliation: Southeast
Asia Resource Center
Editor: Joel Rocamora
Editorial address:
P.O. Box 4000-D
Berkeley, CA 94704
Frequency: 6/year
Circulation: 3,000
Subscription rate(s): low income $9,
regular $12, foreign $15, institutional
$25, foreign airmail add $10
Pages/issue: 24
Readership: academics, university
students, general public
Indexed/abstracted in: Alt Press Ind

Manuscripts
Query: yes
Abstract: no
Style guide: available on request
Preferred length: 8–12 pages
Number of copies: 1

Notes: end of manuscript
Blind referee: no
Time to consider manuscript: 1
month
**Proportion of manuscripts
accepted:** nct given
Illustrations accepted: tables,
graphs, charts, photos
Foreign languages: no

Reviews
Book review editor: Joel Rocamora
Address: same as above
Seeking reviewers: yes
Unsolicited reviews accepted: no
How to apply: letter of inquiry
Include in application: professional
degrees, institutional affiliation, areas
of expertise, current research
Materials reviewed: books, films
Length of review: 1–2 pages

Additional notes
Potential contributors should write a one-
page letter of inquiry, since each issue is
on a single theme.

THE SOUTH EAST ASIAN
REVIEW

Focus: all aspects of South Asian
culture, with emphasis on the
humanities and social sciences
Institutional affiliation: Centre for
South East Asian Studies
Editor: Sachchidanand Sahai
Editorial address:
Ramsagar Road
Gaya 823001
Bihar
INDIA
Frequency: 2/year
Circulation: 500
Subscription rate(s): individual $12,
institutional $20
Pages/issue: 64
Readership: academics
Indexed/abstracted in: not given

Manuscripts
Query: no
Abstract: no

Style guide: see current issue
Preferred length: 30 pages maximum
Number of copies: 2
Notes: bottom of page
Blind referee: no
Time to consider manuscript: not given
Proportion of manuscripts accepted: not given
Illustrations accepted: tables
Foreign languages: no

Reviews
Book review editor: B. J. Terwiel
Address: same as above
Materials reviewed: books
Length of review: see current issue

Additional notes
Indications about the professional position of the author and acknowledgments, if any, should precede the first footnote. Contributors will be offered 25 free reprints and a copy of the journal.

SOUTHEASTERN EUROPE/ L'EUROPE DU SUD-EST

Focus: humanities and social sciences pertaining to the Balkans, Yugoslavia, Romania, Bulgaria, Albania, Greece, and European Turkey
Editor: Charles Schlacks, Jr.
Editorial address:
Russian and East European Publications
Arizona State University
120B McAllister Avenue
Tempe, AZ 85281
Frequency: 2–4/year
Circulation: 500
Subscription rate(s): student $12, faculty $15, institutional $20
Pages/issue: 130–160
Readership: academics, diplomats
Indexed/abstracted in: Hist Abstr

Manuscripts
Query: no
Abstract: no

Style guide: MLA
Preferred length: 15–25 pages
Number of copies: 3
Notes: end of manuscript
Blind referee: no
Time to consider manuscript: 3 months
Proportion of manuscripts accepted: not given
Illustrations accepted: tables, graphs, charts, photos
Foreign languages: French, German, Russian

Reviews
Seeking reviewers: yes
Unsolicited reviews accepted: no
How to apply: letter of inquiry
Include in application: areas of expertise
Materials reviewed: books
Length of review: 600–800 words

Additional notes
Simultaneous submission is not allowed. Articles are published 6–12 months after acceptance.

SOUTHEASTERN POLITICAL REVIEW

Focus: eclectic
Institutional affiliation: West Georgia College
Editor: Elmo Roberds
Editorial address:
Department of Political Science
West Georgia College
Carrollton, GA 30118
Frequency: 2/year
Circulation: 355
Subscription rate(s): individual $6, institutional $12
Pages/issue: 200–225
Readership: academics
Indexed/abstracted in: Int Polit Sci Abstr

Manuscripts
Query: no
Abstract: yes
Style guide: MFW

Preferred length: 20–25 pages
Number of copies: 4
Notes: end of manuscript
Blind referee: yes
Time to consider manuscript: 3 months
Proportion of manuscripts accepted: 20 percent
Illustrations accepted: tables, graphs, charts, drawings
Foreign languages: no

Reviews
Book review editor: James D. McBrayer, Jr
Address:
Department of Political Science
Georgia State University
Atlanta, GA 30328
Seeking reviewers: yes
Unsolicited reviews accepted: yes
How to apply: letter of inquiry
Include in application: professional degrees, areas of expertise, published works, current research
Materials reviewed: books

SOUTHERN REVIEW OF PUBLIC ADMINISTRATION

Focus: scholarly and opinion articles focusing on public administration and public policy concerns
Institutional affiliation: Rider College and Auburn University at Montgomery
Editors: Jack Rabin, Thomas Vocino
Editorial address:
Center for Public Policy and Administration
Rider College
Lawrenceville, NJ 08648
or
Department of Government
Auburn University
Montgomery, AL 36193
Frequency: 4/year
Circulation: 875
Subscription rate(s): $16
Pages/issue: 136

Readership: academics, public administrators
Indexed/abstracted in: not given

Manuscripts
Query: no
Abstract: no
Style guide: available on request
Preferred length: 20–25 pages
Number of copies: 3
Notes: end of manuscript
Blind referee: yes
Time to consider manuscript: 6–9 weeks
Proportion of manuscripts accepted: 20 percent
Illustrations accepted: tables, graphs, charts, drawings
Foreign languages: no

Reviews
Book review editor: Gerald J. Miller
Address:
Department of Political Science
University of Kansas
Lawrence, KS 66045
Seeking reviewers: yes
Unsolicited reviews accepted: no
How to apply: letter of inquiry
Include in application: professional degrees, institutional affiliation, areas of expertise
Materials reviewed: books
Length of review: 500 words

SOVIET STUDIES

Focus: Soviet and East European studies
Institutional affiliation: British National Association for Soviet and East European Studies
Editor: submit to the Editor
Editorial address:
10 Southpark Terrace
Glasgow G12 8LQ
SCOTLAND
Frequency: 4/year
Circulation: 1,700
Subscription rate(s): $48
Pages/issue: 150

Readership: academics
Indexed/abstracted in: Br Hum Ind, Hum Ind, PAIS, ABC POL SCI, Hist Abstr

Manuscripts
Query: no
Abstract: no
Style guide: see current issue or write for guidelines
Preferred length: no preference
Number of copies: 1
Notes: end of manuscript
Blind referee: no
Time to consider manuscript: not given
Proportion of manuscripts accepted: not given
Illustrations accepted: tables
Foreign languages: Russian

Reviews
Book review editor: submit to the Editor
Address: same as above
Materials reviewed: books
Length of review: 1–2 pages

SOVIET UNION/UNION SOVIETIQUE

Focus: interdisciplinary studies of the Soviet Union
Editor: Ellen Michiewicz
Editorial address:
Graduate School of Arts and Sciences
Emory University
Atlanta, GA 30322
Frequency: 2/year
Circulation: 4,000
Subscription rate(s): student $12, faculty $15, institutional $20
Pages/issue: 150
Readership: academics
Indexed/abstracted in: Hist Abstr

Manuscripts
Query: no
Abstract: no
Style guide: MLA
Preferred length: 25–35 pages

Number of copies: 3
Notes: end of manuscript
Blind referee: no
Time to consider manuscript: 3–6 weeks
Proportion of manuscripts accepted: not given
Illustrations accepted: tables, graphs
Foreign languages: no

Reviews
Book review editor: Thomas Remington
Address:
Department of Political Science
Emory University
Atlanta, GA 30322
Seeking reviewers: yes
How to apply: letter of inquiry
Materials reviewed: books
Length of review: 1–2 pages

Additional notes
Simultaneous submission is not allowed. Articles appear 6–12 months after acceptance.

STANFORD JOURNAL OF INTERNATIONAL LAW

Focus: international law, politics, and economics
Institutional affiliation: Stanford University School of Law
Editor: submit to the Editors
Editorial address:
Stanford Law School
Stanford, CA 94305
Frequency: 2/year
Circulation: 600
Subscription rate(s): $18
Pages/issue: 235
Readership: law professors, law students, government officials (U.S. and foreign), lawyers, business people
Indexed/abstracted in: Leg Per, ABC POL SCI, Int Polit Sci Abstr

Manuscripts
Query: no
Abstract: no

Style guide: none required
Preferred length: 75–125 pages
Number of copies: 2, triple-spaced
Notes: end of manuscript
Blind referee: no
Time to consider manuscript: 10 days–1 month
Proportion of manuscripts accepted: 12 percent
Illustrations accepted: tables, graphs, charts
Foreign languages: no

Reviews
Book review editor: submit to Book Review Editor
Address: same as above
Seeking reviewers: yes
Unsolicited reviews accepted: yes
How to apply: letter of inquiry
Include in application: professional degrees, institutional affiliation, areas of expertise, published works, current research, description of professional career
Materials reviewed: books
Length of review: 35–50 pages, triple-spaced

Additional notes
At least one of the two yearly issues is related to a single topic of current interest. Such issues include articles, student submissions, and an annotated bibliography on the topic. Each issue, including such ''theme '' issues, contains articles of general interest as well. Be familiar with the format of legal periodicals. This would include some basic knowledge of legal reasoning. Propositions must be soundly documented and arguments should proceed logically and avoid technocratic/bureaucratic/academic jargon.

STATE AND LOCAL GOVERNMENT REVIEW

Focus: applied research, service, training, and policymaking in state and local government
Institutional affiliation: Institute of Government, University of Georgia

Editor: Joseph W. Whorton
Editorial address:
Institute of Government
Terrell Hall
University of Georgia
Athens, GA 30602
Frequency: 3/year
Circulation: 1,000
Subscription rate(s): $8
Pages/issue: 48
Readership: academics, professionals
Indexed/abstracted in: PAIS, ABC POL SCI

Manuscripts
Query: no
Abstract: yes
Style guide: MOS
Preferred length: 11–20 pages
Number of copies: 4
Notes: end of manuscript
Blind referee: yes
Time to consider manuscript: 6–8 weeks
Proportion of manuscripts accepted: 20 percent
Illustrations accepted: tables, graphs, charts, drawings
Foreign languages: no

Reviews
not applicable

Additional notes
Simultaneous submission is not allowed. Most articles appear within 18 months of acceptance.

STATE GOVERNMENT

Focus: all aspects of state government—legislative, electoral, administrative, policy, judicial, fiscal, and anything else
Institutional affiliation: The Council of State Governments
Editor: L. Edward Purcell
Editorial address:
P.O. Box 11910
Lexington, KY 40578
Frequency: 4/year
Circulation: 7,000

Subscription rate(s): $15
Pages/issue: 32
Readership: academics, elected and appointed state government officials
Indexed/abstracted in: ABC POL SCI, Soc Sci Ind, CIS Ind, Pub Admin Info

Manuscripts
Query: no
Abstract: no
Style guide: MOS
Preferred length: 8–12 pages
Number of copies: 2
Notes: end of manuscript
Blind referee: no
Time to consider manuscript: 4–6 weeks
Proportion of manuscripts accepted: 30–50 percent
Illustrations accepted: tables, graphs, charts, photos, drawings
Foreign languages: no

Additional notes
Simultaneous submission is not allowed. Articles are published 3 months after acceptance.

STATE GOVERNMENT NEWS

Focus: state innovations in programs, services, and legislation
Institutional affiliation: The Council of State Governments
Editor: Elaine Knapp
Editorial address:
P.O. Box 11910
Iron Works Pike
Lexington, KY 40578
Frequency: 12/year
Circulation: 30,000
Subscription rate(s): $15
Pages/issue: 24
Readership: governors, legislators, state administrators and staff
Indexed/abstracted in: not given

Manuscripts
Query: no
Abstract: no
Style guide: AP

Preferred length: 1,000–1,500 words
Number of copies: 1
Notes: end of manuscript
Blind referee: no
Time to consider manuscript: 3 months
Proportion of manuscripts accepted: 50 percent
Illustrations accepted: tables, graphs, charts, photos, drawings
Foreign languages: no

Reviews
Book review editor: Jennifer Stoffel
Address: same as above
Seeking reviewers: no
Unsolicited reviews accepted: no

Additional notes
Write for a sample copy first.

STATE LEGISLATURES

Focus: national source of information on current developments in the states
Institutional affiliation: National Conference of State Legislatures
Editor: Steve Millard
Editorial address:
Publications Department
National Conference of State Legislatures
1125 17th Street
Denver, CO 80202
Frequency: 10/year
Circulation: 12,200
Subscription rate(s): $30
Pages/issue: 32
Readership: corporations, public and university libraries, associations, state legislators, legislative staff, press, federal VIP's, members of Congress, governors
Indexed/abstracted in: PAIS

Manuscripts
Query: yes
Abstract: no
Style guide: MOS
Preferred length: 10–12 pages
Number of copies: 1

Notes: end of manuscript
Blind referee: no
Time to consider manuscript: 2–4 weeks
Proportion of manuscripts accepted: 1 percent
Illustrations accepted: tables, graphs, charts, photos
Foreign languages: no

Reviews
not applicable

Additional notes
Because the editorial focus of the magazine is to provide state legislators with information on current issues on the state level, it is advisable for prospective writers to contact the editor regarding subject matter. Royalties of up to $400 are paid for accepted articles.

STRATEGIC REVIEW

Focus: those principles and practices—political and military—which serve the vital interests and security of the United States
Institutional affiliation: United States Strategic Institute
Editor: Walter F. Hahn
Editorial address:
United States Strategic Institute
20 Memorial Drive
Cambridge, MA 02142
Frequency: 4/year
Circulation: 4,000
Subscription rate(s): $15
Pages/issue: 100
Readership: those interested in American foreign and military policy, academics
Indexed/abstracted in: not given

Manuscripts
Query: no
Abstract: no, but preferred
Style guide: see current issue
Preferred length: 3,000–5,000 words
Number of copies: 2
Notes: end of manuscript
Blind referee: no

Time to consider manuscript: 6 weeks
Proportion of manuscripts accepted: not given
Illustrations accepted: tables, graphs, charts, photos
Foreign languages: no

Reviews
Book review editor: Walter F. Hahn
Address: same as above
Materials reviewed: books
Length of review: 3–5 pages

Additional notes
Published authors are paid $200 per article. Submit a brief biography with each manuscript. Simultaneous submission is not permitted. Articles appear 2–12 months after acceptance.

STUDIES IN COMPARATIVE COMMUNISM: AN INTERNATIONAL INTERDISCIPLINARY JOURNAL

Focus: scholarly analyses of political, economic, social, military, cultural, and other developments in Communist countries; all disciplines; all ruling and nonruling Communist parties
Institutional affiliation: Von KleinSmid Institute of International Affairs, School of International Relations, University of Southern California
Editor: Peter Berton
Editorial address:
School of International Relations
VKC Room 330
University of Southern California
University Park
Los Angeles, CA 90007
Frequency: 4/year
Circulation: not given
Subscription rate(s): individual $15, institutional $25, foreign add $2
Pages/issue: 100

Readership: academics, libraries, government agencies
Indexed/abstracted in: Soc Sci Ind, PAIS, ABC POL SCI, SSCI, Curr Cont, CRIS, Hist Abstr, Int Polit Sci Abstr, Universal Ref Syst, USPSD

Manuscripts
Query: no
Abstract: yes
Style guide: available on request
Preferred length: 6,000–9,000 words
Number of copies: 3, double-spaced
Notes: end of manuscript
Blind referee: yes
Time to consider manuscript: 1–3 months
Proportion of manuscripts accepted: 10–20 percent
Illustrations accepted: tables, graphs, charts, photos, drawings
Foreign languages: no

Reviews
Book review editor: Rudolf L. Tőkes
Address:
Department of Political Science
University of Connecticut
Storrs, CT 06268
Seeking reviewers: yes
Unsolicited reviews accepted: yes
How to apply: letter of inquiry
Include in application: professional degrees, institutional affiliation, areas of expertise, published works, foreign languages, current research
Materials reviewed: books
Length of review: 2,000–5,000 words

Additional notes
The editors encourage advanced graduate students to submit manuscripts for publication in the *Journal*'s Graduate Student Essays. Comparative studies, including comparisons across political and social systems are given preference. Only review articles are accepted. Proposals for review articles should describe the issues to be dealt with and provide a list of books to be reviewed (full bibliographical citations, including pagination). Simultaneous submission is not allowed. Articles appear 3–18 months after acceptance.

STUDIES IN COMPARATIVE INTERNATIONAL DEVELOPMENT

Focus: interdisciplinary approach to comparative international development
Institutional affiliation: Georgia Institute of Technology
Editor: Jay Weinstein
Editorial address:
Department of Social Sciences
Georgia Institute of Technology
Atlanta, GA 30332
Frequency: 4/year
Circulation: 35,000
Subscription rate(s): student $12, individual $18, institutional $24
Pages/issue: 95
Readership: academics, professionals
Indexed/abstracted in: ABC POL SCI, Hist Abstr

Manuscripts
Query: no
Abstract: no
Style guide: MOS
Preferred length: 20–25 pages
Number of copies: 3
Notes: end of manuscript
Blind referee: yes
Time to consider manuscript: 4–6 weeks
Proportion of manuscripts accepted: 33 percent
Illustrations accepted: tables, graphs, charts, drawings, maps
Foreign languages: no

Reviews
Book review editor: John Weinstein
Address:
Strategic Studies Institute
U.S. Army War College
Carlisle Barracks, PA 17013
Seeking reviewers: yes
Unsolicited reviews accepted: yes
How to apply: letter of inquiry
Include in application: professional degrees, institutional affiliation, areas of expertise, foreign languages, current research, overseas travel relative to the subject

Materials reviewed: books
Length of review: 1,000 words maximum

Additional notes

Simultaneous submission is not permitted. Articles appear 6–12 months after acceptance.

STUDIES IN SOVIET THOUGHT

Focus: Marxist-Leninist philosophy in the Soviet Union, as well as the historical sources from Hegel to Mao
Institutional affiliation: Institute of East-European Studies, University of Fribourg (Switzerland); Center for East Europe, Russia and Asia at Boston College; Seminar for Political Theory and Philosophy, University of Munich
Editor: J. O'Rourke, A. Sarlemijn
Editorial address:
  For North America:
  T. Blakeley
  Philosophy Department
  Boston College
  Chestnut Hill, MA 02167
  For Europe and Asia:
  G. Küng
  Université, Miséricorde
  CH-1700
  Fribourg
  SWITZERLAND
Frequency: 4/year
Circulation: 650
Subscription rate(s): $15
Pages/issue: 80
Readership: philosophers, sociologists, political scientists
Indexed/abstracted in: Phil Ind

Manuscripts

Query: no
Abstract: yes
Style guide: available on request
Preferred length: 20 pages
Number of copies: 3
Notes: end of manuscript
Blind referee: yes
Time to consider manuscript: 1–2 months

Proportion of manuscripts accepted: 65 percent
Illustrations accepted: none
Foreign languages: French, German, Spanish, Italian

Reviews

Book review editor: William Gavin
Address:
  Philosophy Department
  University of Southern Maine
  Portland, ME 04103
Seeking reviewers: yes
Unsolicited reviews accepted: yes
How to apply: letter of inquiry
Include in application: type of books to be reviewed
Materials reviewed: books
Length of review: 1,000–1,500 words

Additional notes

Simultaneous submission is not permitted. Articles appear 6 months after acceptance.

SURVEY: A JOURNAL OF EAST AND WEST STUDIES

Focus: interdisciplinary study of East–West relations
Institutional affiliation: London School of Economics, Freedom House of New York
Editor: Leopold Labedz
Editorial address:
  Ilford House
  133 Oxford Street
  London W1R 1TD
  ENGLAND
Frequency: 4/year
Circulation: 3,000
Subscription rate(s): $27
Pages/issue: 150
Readership: academics, politicians, informed general public
Indexed/abstracted in: ABC POL SCI, Hist Abstr

Manuscripts

Query: no, but preferable
Abstract: no
Style guide: see current issue

Preferred length: 4,000 words
Number of copies: 2
Notes: bottom of page
Blind referee: no
Time to consider manuscript: varies
**Proportion of manuscripts
accepted:** not given
Illustrations accepted: not given
Foreign languages: not given

Reviews
not applicable

Additional notes
Simultaneous submission is not allowed.
Publication time after acceptance varies.

TEACHING POLITICAL SCIENCE

Focus: social science with a bearing
on the educational process affecting
the study of politics, e.g., application
of economic rationality models to
political analysis, history of public
attitudes toward the cold war,
philosophy of law, and academic
environment
Editor: Kay Lueje
Editorial address:
HELDREF Publications
4000 Albemarle Street, NW
Washington, DC 20016
Frequency: 4/year
Circulation: not given
Subscription rate(s): $36
Pages/issue: 48
Readership: academics (especially in
junior colleges)
Indexed/abstracted in: Curr Cont, Int
Polit Sci Abstr, Human Resour Abstr,
Sage Urb Stud Abstr, SSCI, ABC
POL SCI

Manuscripts
Query: no
Abstract: yes, 100 words
Style guide: MOS
Preferred length: 25–30 pages
maximum
Number of copies: 3
Notes: end of manuscript

Blind referee: yes
Time to consider manuscript: 6–8
weeks
**Proportion of manuscripts
accepted:** not given
Illustrations accepted: tables,
graphs, charts
Foreign languages: no

Reviews
Book review editor: Dean C. Myers
Address:
Department of Political Science
Indiana State University
Terre Haute, IN 47809
Unsolicited reviews accepted: yes
Include in application: professional
degrees, institutional affiliation, areas
of expertise
Materials reviewed: books
Length of review: 500–1,500 words

Additional notes
Simultaneous submission is permitted
but discouraged. Articles are published
12–18 months after acceptance.

TECHNOLOGY AND CULTURE

Focus: technology and the relations of
technology to society and culture
Institutional affiliation: Society for the
History of Technology
Editor: Melvin Kranzberg
Editorial address:
Georgia Institute of Technology
Atlanta, GA 30332
Frequency: 4/year
Circulation: 2,400
Subscription rate(s): individual $20,
institutional $27
Pages/issue: 225
Readership: academics
Indexed/abstracted in: not given

Manuscripts
Query: no
Abstract: no
Style guide: MOS
Preferred length: 3,000 words
Number of copies: 2
Notes: end of manuscript

Blind referee: yes
Time to consider manuscript: 4 months
Proportion of manuscripts accepted: 30 percent
Illustrations accepted: tables, graphs, charts, photos
Foreign languages: no

Reviews
Book review editor: Melvin Kranzberg
Address: same as above
Seeking reviewers: yes
Unsolicited reviews accepted: yes
How to apply: letter of inquiry
Include in application: professional degrees, institutional affiliation, areas of expertise, published works, foreign languages, current research
Materials reviewed: books, museum exhibits
Length of review: 800 words

Additional notes
Simultaneous submission is not permitted. Articles are published 8 months after acceptance.

TELOS: A QUARTERLY JOURNAL OF RADICAL THOUGHT

Focus: a journal of left-wing social and political thought
Editor: Paul Piccone
Editorial address:
Box 3111
St. Louis, MO 63130
Frequency: 4/year
Circulation: 3,000
Subscription rate(s): individual $18, institutional $38
Pages/issue: 225
Readership: academics, left-wing activists
Indexed/abstracted in: Social Abstr, Alt Press Ind, Phil Ind

Manuscripts
Query: no
Abstract: no

Style guide: see current issue or write for guidelines
Preferred length: no preference
Number of copies: 3
Notes: bottom of page
Blind referee: no
Time to consider manuscript: 3 months minimum
Proportion of manuscripts accepted: not given
Illustrations accepted: not given
Foreign languages: no

Reviews
Book review editor: Paul Breines
Address: same as above
Materials reviewed: books
Length of review: 10–20 pages

TERRORISM: AN INTERNATIONAL JOURNAL

Focus: examines the types, causes, consequences, control, and meaning of all forms of terrorist action
Editor: Yonah Alexander
Editorial address:
Center for Strategic & International Studies
Georgetown University
1800 K Street, NW
Washington, DC 20006
Frequency: 4/year
Circulation: 1,000
Subscription rate(s): $40
Pages/issue: 100
Readership: academics, graduate students
Indexed/abstracted in: Abstr Mil Bibl, Amer Hist and Life, Curr Cont, Hist Abstr, Mon List Sel Art, NCJRS, Int Polit Sci Abstr, SSCI, Sociol Abstr

Manuscripts
Query: no
Abstract: yes, 150 words
Style guide: MOS, HLRA
Preferred length: no preference
Number of copies: 3
Notes: not given
Blind referee: not given

Time to consider manuscript: not given
Proportion of manuscripts accepted: not given
Illustrations accepted: tables, graphs, charts, drawings
Foreign languages: no

Reviews
not applicable

TEXAS INTERNATIONAL LAW JOURNAL

Focus: public and private international law; law of international organizations; comparative and foreign law; domestic law that has international implications (nonjudicial governmental decisions of international significance, aviation, commercial, anti-trust, constitutional, customs, energy, environmental, immigration, maritime, tax)
Institutional affiliation: University of Texas at Austin
Editor: Rebecca Yee
Editorial address:
727 East 26th Street
Austin, Texas 78705
Frequency: 3/year
Circulation: 525
Subscription rate(s): domestic $16, foreign $18
Pages/issue: 200
Readership: academics, foreign and U.S.; firms with international law sections
Indexed/abstracted in: Leg Per, Curr Law Ind

Manuscripts
Query: no
Abstract: no
Style guide: HLRA, Texas Law Review Manual on Style
Preferred length: no preference
Number of copies: 1, triple-spaced
Notes: end of manuscript
Blind referee: no
Time to consider manuscript: 2 weeks

Proportion of manuscripts accepted: not given
Illustrations accepted: tables, graphs, charts, photos, drawings
Foreign languages: no

Reviews
Book review editor: Chester Beattie
Address: same as above
Seeking reviewers: yes
Unsolicited reviews accepted: no
How to apply: letter of inquiry
Include in application: professional degrees, institutional affiliation, areas of expertise, published works, foreign languages, current research
Materials reviewed: books

Additional notes
Simultaneous submission is permitted. Articles are published 1–6 months after acceptance.

TEXAS JOURNAL OF POLITICAL STUDIES

Focus: political studies
Institutional affiliation: Sam Houston State University
Editor: Edwin S. Davis
Editorial address:
Box 2149
Huntsville, TX 77341
Frequency: 2/year
Circulation: 135
Subscription rate(s): individual $7.50, institutional $10
Pages/issue: 75
Readership: academics, political scientists, libraries
Indexed/abstracted in: not given

Manuscripts
Query: no
Abstract: yes
Style guide: available on request
Preferred length: 20 pages, research notes 10 pages
Number of copies: 3
Notes: end of manuscript
Blind referee: yes

Time to consider manuscript: 2 months
Proportion of manuscripts accepted: 25 percent
Illustrations accepted: tables, graphs, charts, drawings
Foreign languages: no

Reviews
Book review editor: James Dickson
Address:
Box 13045 SFA
Nacogdoches, TX 75962
Seeking reviewers: yes
Unsolicited reviews accepted: yes
How to apply: letter of inquiry
Include in application: professional degrees, institutional affiliation, areas of expertise, published works
Materials reviewed: books
Length of review: 2 pages

Additional notes
A majority of manuscripts have been on Texas but that is a result of submissions. One piece in each edition will be on Texas. A submitted manuscript should be well written and free of methodological errors. Simultaneous submission is not permitted. Articles are published 1–4 months after acceptance.

TEXAS LAW REVIEW

Focus: legal issues
Institutional affiliation: University of Texas School of Law
Editor: submit to the Editor
Editorial address:
727 East 26th Street
Austin, TX 78705
Frequency: 8/year
Circulation: 2,750
Subscription rate(s): $25
Pages/issue: 225
Readership: lawyers, law students, law professors, judges
Indexed/abstracted in: not given

Manuscripts
Query: yes
Abstract: no

Style guide: HLRA, GPO
Preferred length: no preference
Number of copies: 1
Notes: end of manuscript
Blind referee: no
Time to consider manuscript: 1 month
Proportion of manuscripts accepted: not given
Illustrations accepted: tables, graphs, charts
Foreign languages: no

Reviews
Book review editor: submit to Book Review Editor
Address: same as above
Seeking reviewers: yes
Unsolicited reviews accepted: yes
How to apply: letter of inquiry
Include in application: professional degrees, institutional affiliation
Material reviewed: books

THEORY AND DECISION: AN INTERNATIONAL JOURNAL FOR PHILOSOPHY AND METHODOLOGY OF THE SOCIAL SCIENCES

Focus: the application of philosophy of science methodology to the social sciences
Editor: H. Berghel
Editorial address:
University of Nebraska
Department of Computer Science
Lincoln, NB 68588
Frequency: 4/year
Circulation: not given
Subscription rate(s): individual $23.50, institutional $79.50
Pages/issue: 100
Readership: social scientists
Indexed/abstracted in: Psychol Abstr, SSCI, Sociol Abstr, Phil Ind

Manuscripts
Query: no
Abstract: no
Style guide: see current issue

Preferred length: no preference
Number of copies: 3
Notes: end of manuscript
Blind referee: no
Time to consider manuscript: not given
Proportion of manuscripts accepted: not given
Illustrations accepted: figures
Foreign languages: not given

Reviews
not applicable

THEORY AND SOCIETY

Focus: critical analysis of contemporary society using a broad social science perspective
Editor: submit to the Editors
Editorial address:
Box 1113
Washington University
St. Louis, MO 63130
Frequency: 6/year
Circulation: 1,500
Subscription rate(s): individual $26.40, institutional $79.20
Pages/issue: 120
Readership: social scientists
Indexed/abstracted in: Curr Cont, Sociol Abstr

Manuscripts
Query: yes
Abstract: yes
Style guide: MOS
Preferred length: no preference
Number of copies: 3
Notes: end of manuscript
Blind referee: yes
Time to consider manuscript: not given
Proportion of manuscripts accepted: not given
Illustrations accepted: tables, figures, drawings
Foreign languages: articles in other languages may be translated

Reviews
Book review editor: Charles Lemert
Address:
Department of Sociology
Wesleyan University
Middletown, CT 06457
Seeking reviewers: yes
Unsolicited reviews accepted: yes
Materials reviewed: books
Length of review: 2,000 words

Additional notes
Simultaneous submission is not permitted.

THE THIRD WORLD REVIEW

Focus: interdisciplinary: political, historical, sociological, and economic interface of developing and developed societies
Institutional affiliation: State University of New York at Cortland
Editor: Ilyas Ba-Yunus
Editorial address:
Department of Sociology
State University of New York
Cortland, NY 13045
Frequency: 2/year
Circulation: 700
Subscription rate(s): student $6, institutional $8
Pages/issue: 100
Readership: social scientists
Indexed/abstracted in: not given

Manuscripts
Query: no
Abstract: yes
Style guide: MOS
Preferred length: 20 pages
Number of copies: 3
Notes: end of manuscript
Blind referee: yes
Time to consider manuscript: 3 months
Proportion of manuscripts accepted: 50 percent
Illustrations accepted: tables, graphs, charts, photos
Foreign languages: no

Reviews

Book review editor: Nicolas Gavrielides
Address: same as above
Seeking reviewers: yes
Unsolicited reviews accepted: yes
How to apply: letter of inquiry
Include in application: professional degrees, institutional affiliation, areas of expertise, published works, current research
Materials reviewed: books
Length of review: 4 pages

Additional notes

Simultaneous submission is not permitted. Articles are published 12–18 months after acceptance.

TOWSON STATE JOURNAL OF INTERNATIONAL AFFAIRS

Focus: economic, political, and social effects on international relations
Institutional affiliation: Towson State University
Editors: Brian R. Doster, Donna L. Meyers
Editorial address:
Political Science Department
Towson State University
Towson, MD 21204
Frequency: 2/year
Circulation: not given
Subscription rate(s): $1/issue
Pages/issue: 100
Readership: students, college professors, academic libraries
Indexed/abstracted in: Hist Abstr, Amer Hist and Life, ABC POL SCI

Manuscripts

Query: no
Abstract: no
Style guide: MOS
Preferred length: 20 pages
Number of copies: 2
Notes: no preference
Blind referee: no
Time to consider manuscript: 1 month minimum

Proportion of manuscripts accepted: 66 percent
Illustrations accepted: tables, graphs, charts
Foreign languages: no

Reviews

Book review editor: Glen R. Pryce
Address: same as above
Seeking reviewers: yes
Unsolicited reviews accepted: yes
How to apply: letter of inquiry
Include in application: professional degrees, institutional affiliation, areas of expertise, current research
Materials reviewed: books
Length of review: 3 pages

Additional notes

The *Journal* is published by undergraduate students along with advisors from the political science department. We accept papers from undergraduate and graduate students as well as college professors. We prefer that these student papers come recommended by their instructors.

TRANSACTION/SOCIETY

Focus: the periodical of record in social science and public policy
Institutional affiliation: Rutgers University
Editor: Irving Louis Horowitz
Editorial address:
Rutgers University
New Brunswick, NJ 08903
Frequency: 6/year
Circulation: 25,000–35,000
Subscription rate(s): individual $12, institutional $21
Pages/issue: 100
Readership: academics, policymakers, social analysts
Indexed/abstracted in: not given

Manuscripts

Query: no
Abstract: yes
Style guide: MOS
Preferred length: 20 pages

Number of copies: 3
Notes: no preference
Blind referee: yes
Time to consider manuscript: 1–6
months
Proportion of manuscripts
accepted: 3 percent
Illustrations accepted: tables,
graphs, photos
Foreign languages: no

Reviews
Book review editor: C. Waxman
Address: same as above
Seeking reviewers: no
Unsolicited reviews accepted: no
Materials reviewed: books, films
Length of review: 5–10

Additional notes
Simultaneous submission is not
permitted. Articles are published 6–10
months after acceptance.

TRANSPORTATION JOURNAL

Focus: the management of
transportation; the practice and
techniques of transportation and
related fields
Institutional affiliation: American
Society of Traffic and Transportation
Editor: John C. Spychalski
Editorial address:
College of Business Administration
509 Business Administration Building
Pennsylvania State University
University Park, PA 16802
Frequency: 4/year
Circulation: 3,500
Subscription rate(s): nonmembers in
the U.S. $25, foreign nonmembers
$30
Pages/issue: 75
Readership: academics, professionals
in the field of transportation
Indexed/abstracted in: PAIS, SSCI

Manuscripts
Query: no
Abstract: no
Style guide: see current issue

Preferred length: 1,500–5,000 words
Number of copies: 4
Notes: end of manuscript
Blind referee: no
Time to consider manuscript: not
given
Proportion of manuscripts
accepted: not given
Illustrations accepted: tables, figures
Foreign languages: no

Reviews
Book review editor: E. P. Patton
Address:
College of Business Administration
University of Tennessee
Knoxville, TN 37916
Materials reviewed: books

TRANSPORTATION LAW
JOURNAL

Focus: all political, legal, and economic
issues relating to transportation
Institutional affiliation: University of
Denver College of Law, Motor
Carrier Lawyers Association
Editor: Albert J. Mrozik, Jr.
Editorial address:
200 West 14th Avenue
Denver, CO 80204
Frequency: 2/year
Circulation: 6,000
Subscription rate(s): $6.50/issue
Pages/issue: 250
Readership: academics,
professionals, attorneys
Indexed/abstracted in: G Leg Per

Manuscripts
Query: no
Abstract: no
Style guide: HLRA
Preferred length: 25 pages minimum
Number of copies: 3
Notes: end of manuscript
Blind referee: no
Time to consider manuscript: 4
months
Proportion of manuscripts
accepted: 40 percent

Illustrations accepted: tables, graphs, charts, photos, drawings
Foreign languages: no

Reviews
not applicable

Additional notes
Simultaneous submission is not permitted. Articles appear 2–4 months after acceptance.

TRANSPORTATION RESEARCH

Focus: transportation
Editor: Frank A. Haight
Editorial address:
Research Building B
University Park, PA 16802
Frequency: 12/year
Circulation: not given
Subscription rate(s): $225
Pages/issue: 80
Readership: researchers
Indexed/abstracted in: not given

Manuscripts
Query: no
Abstract: yes
Style guide: HLRA
Preferred length: no preference
Number of copies: 3
Notes: end of manuscript
Blind referee: no
Time to consider manuscript: 3–6 months
Proportion of manuscripts accepted: 50 percent
Illustrations accepted: tables, graphs, charts, drawings
Foreign languages: no

Reviews
Book review editor: Richard de Neufville
Address:
M.I.T.
1-138
Cambridge, MA 02138
Materials reviewed: books

Additional notes
Simultaneous submission is not permitted. Articles are published 5 months after acceptance.

TULANE LAW REVIEW

Focus: general legal
Institutional affiliation: Tulane Law School
Editor: submit to the Editors
Editorial address:
Tulane Law School
New Orleans, LA 70118
Frequency: 4/year
Circulation: 2,600
Subscription rate(s): $17
Pages/issue: 300–350
Readership: academics
Indexed/abstracted in: not given

Manuscripts
Query: no
Abstract: no
Style guide: GPO, HLRA
Preferred length: varies
Number of copies: 1
Notes: end of manuscript
Blind referee: no
Time to consider manuscript: 3 weeks
Proportion of manuscripts accepted: 4 percent
Illustrations accepted: tables, graphs, charts, photos, drawings
Foreign languages: no

Reviews
Book review editor: submit to the Editors
Address: same as above
Seeking reviewers: yes
Unsolicited reviews accepted: yes
How to apply: letter of inquiry
Include in application: professional degrees
Materials reviewed: books
Length of review: 5–10 pages

UCLA LAW REVIEW

Focus: current issues in federal, state, and international law
Institutional affiliation: University of California, Los Angeles
Editor: Lori Huff
Editorial address:
UCLA Law Review
School of Law
405 Hilgard Avenue
Los Angeles, CA 90024
Frequency: 6/year
Circulation: 1,100
Subscription rate(s): $20
Pages/issue: 225
Readership: lawyers, legal academicians, judges, law students
Indexed/abstracted in: Leg Per

Manuscripts

Query: no
Abstract: no
Style guide: HLRA
Preferred length: 75 pages
Number of copies: 1
Notes: end of manuscript
Blind referee: no
Time to consider manuscript: 1 month
Proportion of manuscripts accepted: 3 percent
Illustrations accepted: tables, graphs, charts
Foreign languages: no

Reviews

Book review editor: submit to the Editor
Address: same as above
Seeking reviewers: no
Unsolicited reviews accepted: yes
How to apply: letter of inquiry
Include in application: professional degrees, institutional affiliation published works
Materials reviewed: books
Length of review: 20 pages, triple-spaced

THE UKRAINIAN QUARTERLY: A JOURNAL OF EAST EUROPEAN AND ASIAN AFFAIRS

Focus: East European and Ukrainian studies
Institutional affiliation: Ukrainian Congress Committee of America
Editor: Walter Dushnyck
Editorial address:
203 Second Avenue
New York, NY 10003
Frequency: 4/year
Circulation: 5,000
Subscription rate(s): $15
Pages/issue: 112
Readership: academics
Indexed/abstracted in: PAIS, Hist Abstr

Manuscripts

Query: no
Abstract: no
Style guide: write for guidelines
Preferred length: no preference
Number of copies: 1
Notes: bottom of page
Blind referee: no
Time to consider manuscript: not given
Proportion of manuscripts accepted: not given
Illustrations accepted: tables, charts
Foreign languages: no

Reviews

Book review editor: Walter Dushnyck
Address: same as above
Materials reviewed: books
Length of review: 3–4 pages

THE UNIVERSITY OF CHICAGO LAW REVIEW

Focus: law and the legal system; legal history; political issues in the legal system and politics of legal institutions
Institutional affiliation: University of Chicago Law School

Editor: submit to the Editors
Editorial address:
1111 East 60th Street
Chicago, IL 60637
Frequency: 4/year
Circulation: 3,000
Subscription rate(s): $15
Pages/issue: 250
Readership: academics, lawyers
Indexed/abstracted in: Leg Per

Manuscripts
Query: no
Abstract: no
Style guide: MOS, HLRA for citations
Preferred length: no preference
Number of copies: 1 for
consideration, 3 on acceptance
Notes: no preference
Blind referee: no
Time to consider manuscript: 1–3
weeks
**Proportion of manuscripts
accepted:** 3 percent
Illustrations accepted: tables,
graphs, charts, photos, drawings
Foreign languages: no

Reviews
Book review editor: submit to the
Editors
Address: same as above
Seeking reviewers: yes
Unsolicited reviews accepted: yes
How to apply: special form
Materials reviewed: books
Length of review: prefer essay length
rather than notes

Additional notes
Simultaneous submission is allowed.
Articles appear 3–4 months after
acceptance.

UNIVERSITY OF COLORADO
LAW REVIEW

Focus: legal issues
Institutional affiliation: University of
Colorado
Editor: submit to Editor-in-Chief

Editorial address:
290 Fleming Law Building
School of Law
University of Colorado
Boulder, CO 80309
Frequency: 4/year
Circulation: 1,000
Subscription rate(s): $17.50
Pages/issue: 160
Readership: law libraries, courts,
attorneys, legal and social scholars
Indexed/abstracted in: G Leg Per,
CCLP

Manuscripts
Query: no
Abstract: no
Style guide: HLRA
Preferred length: 40 pages
Number of copies: 2
Notes: end of manuscript
Blind referee: no
Time to consider manuscript: 1
month
**Proportion of manuscripts
accepted:** 5 percent
Illustrations accepted: tables,
graphs, charts
Foreign languages: no

Reviews
Book review editor: submit to Articles
Editor
Address: same as above
Seeking reviewers: yes
Unsolicited reviews accepted: yes
How to apply: letter of inquiry
Include in application: professional
degrees, institutional affiliation, areas
of expertise, published works,
current research
Materials reviewed: books
Length of review: 15 pages

Additional notes
The *Review's* primary readers are
scholars of the law, consequently articles
with a theoretical bent are generally
preferred over those that are more
practically oriented. Check past issues of
this and other law reviews to determine
the content and style of typical articles.
Include a brief but informative cover

letter that stresses the article's timeliness. Simultaneous submission is allowed. Articles appear 2–6 months after acceptance.

UNIVERSITY OF DETROIT JOURNAL OF URBAN LAW

Focus: all facets of the law and legal problems, particularly those relating to the urban setting
Institutional affiliation: University of Detroit
Editor: Edward C. Cutlip
Editorial address:
651 East Jefferson Avenue
Detroit, MI 48226
Frequency: 4/year
Circulation: 950
Subscription rate(s): $15
Pages/issue: 200–250
Readership: law libraries, universities, law firms
Indexed/abstracted in: Cath Ind Leg Per

Manuscripts
Query: yes
Abstract: no
Style guide: HLRA
Preferred length: depends on subject
Number of copies: 2
Notes: end of manuscript
Blind referee: no
Time to consider manuscript: varies
Proportion of manuscripts accepted: 20 percent
Illustrations accepted: tables, graphs, charts
Foreign languages: no

Reviews
Book review editors: Linda G. Sklaren, Linda E. Bloch
Address: same as above
Seeking reviewers: yes
Unsolicited reviews accepted: yes
How to apply: letter of inquiry
Include in application: professional degrees, institutional affiliation, areas of expertise, current research
Materials reviewed: books

Additional notes
To expedite the publication process, the editorial staff requests that both text and footnotes be triple-spaced. Simultaneous submission is permitted. Articles appear 3–9 months after acceptance.

UNIVERSITY OF PENNSYLVANIA LAW REVIEW

Focus: scholarly law articles, case comments, book reviews
Institutional affiliation: University of Pennsylvania
Editorial address:
3400 Chestnut Street
Philadelphia, PA 19174
Frequency: 6/year
Circulation: 1,800
Subscription rate(s): domestic $24, foreign $28
Pages/issue: 250
Readership: academics
Indexed/abstracted in: Leg Per, CCLP

Manuscripts
Query: no
Abstract: no
Style guide: available on request
Preferred length: 150 pages
Number of copies: 1, triple-spaced
Notes: end of manuscript
Blind referee: no
Time to consider manuscript: 1 month
Proportion of manuscripts accepted: 3 percent
Illustrations accepted: tables, graphs, charts, drawings
Foreign languages: no

Reviews
Book review editor: submit to Book Review Editor
Address: same as above
Seeking reviewers: yes
Unsolicited reviews accepted: yes
How to apply: letter of inquiry

Include in application: professional degrees, institutional affiliation, areas of expertise, published works, current research
Materials reviewed: books
Length of review: 30–50 pages including footnotes

URBAN AFFAIRS QUARTERLY

Focus: theoretical and applied urban research; implementation of public policy and programs
Institutional affiliation: Center for Urban Affairs and Policy Research, Northwestern University
Editor: Margaret T. Gordon
Editorial address:
Center for Urban Affairs and Policy Research
Northwestern University
2040 Sheridan Road
Evanston, IL 60201
Frequency: 4/year
Circulation: 3,000
Subscription rate(s): individual $22, institutional $46
Pages/issue: 123
Readership: academics
Indexed/abstracted in: ABC POL SCI, Abstr Soc Work, Amer Hist and Life, Curr Cont, Int Polit Sci Abstr, PAIS, Sage Pub Admin Abstr, Sage Urb Stud Abstr, SSCI, Sociol Abstr, USPSD, Urb Aff Abstr

Manuscripts
Query: no
Abstract: yes, 100 words, 5 copies
Style guide: available on request
Preferred length: 25 pages maximum
Number of copies: 5
Notes: end of manuscript
Blind referee: yes
Time to consider manuscript: 2–4 months
Proportion of manuscripts accepted: 10 percent
Illustrations accepted: tables, graphs, charts
Foreign languages: no

Reviews
Book review editor: Bryon D. Jones
Address:
Department of Political Science
Wayne State University
Detroit, MI 48202
Seeking reviewers: yes
Unsolicited reviews accepted: no
How to apply: letter of inquiry
Include in application: professional degrees, institutional affiliation, areas of expertise, published works, current research
Materials reviewed: books
Length of review: 4–8 pages

Additional notes
The journal includes special issues and symposia on national urban policies, changing demographic trends and their consequences for urban social organization, new technologies, and political economy. All reference to the author's previous work should be omitted in the text. Include a brief biographical paragraph describing each author's current affiliation, research interests, and recent publications. Simultaneous submission is not permitted. Articles appear 6–9 months after acceptance.

THE URBAN AND SOCIAL CHANGE REVIEW

Focus: interdisciplinary, action-oriented approach to urban and social problems
Institutional affiliation: Boston College Graduate School of Social Work Alumni Association
Editor: Karen Wolk Feinstein
Editorial address:
Boston College
McGuinn Hall 202
Chestnut Hill, MA 02167
Frequency: 2/year
Circulation: 2,000
Subscription rate(s): $8
Pages/issue: 32
Readership: human services practitioners, social workers, libraries

Indexed/abstracted in: Sage Urb Stud Abstr, Human Resour Abstr, Pub Admin Abstr, ABC POL SCI, Sociol Abstr

Manuscripts
Query: no
Abstract: no
Style guide: MOS
Preferred length: 12–20 pages
Number of copies: 2
Notes: end of manuscript
Blind referee: no
Time to consider manuscript: 2 months
Proportion of manuscripts accepted: 25 percent
Illustrations accepted: tables, graphs, charts, photos, drawings
Foreign languages: no

Reviews
not applicable

Additional notes
Simultaneous submission is permitted. Articles are published 6 months after acceptance.

URBAN EDUCATION

Focus: the administration, functioning, and economics of city schools
Editor: Warren Button
Editorial address:
Faculty of Educational Studies
Christopher Baldy Hall
State University of New York at Buffalo
Buffalo, NY 14260
Frequency: 4/year
Circulation: not given
Subscription rate(s): individual $20, institutional $42
Pages/issue: 125
Readership: educational administrators, academics
Indexed/abstracted in: Sage Urb Stud Abstr, Educ Admin Abstr, ERIC, Curr Cont, SSCI, Educ Ind

Manuscripts
Query: no
Abstract: no
Style guide: available on request
Preferred length: 1,250–5,000 words
Number of copies: 2
Notes: end of manuscript
Blind referee: no
Time to consider manuscript: 8–12 weeks
Proportion of manuscripts accepted: not given
Illustrations accepted: tables, graphs, charts
Foreign languages: no

Reviews
Book review editor: Eugene L. Gaier
Address: same as above
Materials reviewed: books
Length of review: 5–10 pages

Additional notes
Simultaneous submission is allowed, but not encouraged. Articles are published 6–9 months after acceptance.

URBAN FOCUS

Focus: problems and issues of urban government in a federal system
Institutional affiliation: Queen's University
Editor: Judith M. MacKenzie
Editorial address:
Institute of Local Government
Queen's University
Kingston, Ontario, K7L 3N6
CANADA
Frequency: 5/year
Circulation: 400
Subscription rate(s) $8
Pages/issue: 8
Readership: academics, urban management practitioners
Indexed/abstracted in: not given

Manuscripts
Query: yes
Abstract: no
Style guide: MFW
Preferred length: 1,000–1,500 words

Number of copies: 2
Notes: end of manuscript
Blind referee: no
Time to consider manuscript: 4–6 weeks
Proportion of manuscripts accepted: not given
Illustrations accepted: tables, graphs, charts, photos
Foreign languages: no

Reviews

Book review editor: George Muirhead
Address: same as above
Seeking reviewers: no
Unsolicited reviews accepted: yes
How to apply: letter of inquiry
Include in application: professional degrees, institutional affiliation, areas of expertise
Materials reviewed: books, films
Length of review: 500 words

URBANISM PAST AND PRESENT

Focus: historical and policy issues relating to cities; seeks to promote the exchange of ideas between the people who study cities and those who run them
Institutional affiliation: University of Wisconsin–Milwaukee
Editor: Bruce Fetter
Editorial address:
History Department
University of Wisconsin–Milwaukee
P.O. Box 413
Milwaukee, WI 53201
Frequency: 2/year
Circulation: 2,500
Subscription rate(s): individual $8, institutional $15
Pages/issue: 72
Readership: academics, urban officials
Indexed/abstracted in: Amer Hist and Life, Urb Aff Abstr, Sage Urb Stud Abstr, Sage Pub Admin Abstr, Geo Abstr, Amer Stat Ind

Manuscripts

Query: no
Abstract: no
Style guide: MOS
Preferred length: 12–30 pages
Number of copies: 1
Notes: end of manuscript
Blind referee: yes
Time to consider manuscript: 2 weeks–2 months
Proportion of manuscripts accepted: 25 percent
Illustrations accepted: tables, graphs, charts, photos, drawings
Foreign languages: no

Reviews

Book review editor: Bruce Fetter
Address: same as above
Seeking reviewers: no
Unsolicited reviews accepted: no
Include in application: institutional affiliation, areas of expertise

Additional notes

Style and clarity are at a premium, once academic standards have been met. Simultaneous submission is not allowed. Articles are published within 2 months of acceptance.

URBAN LIFE

Focus: ethnographic social analysis
Institutional affiliation: Northern Illinois University and Michigan State University
Editor: Jim Thomas
Editorial address:
Department of Sociology
Northern Illinois University
DeKalb, IL 60115
Frequency: 4/year
Circulation: 1,200
Subscription rate(s): $15
Pages/issue: 120
Readership: social scientists
Indexed/abstracted in: not given

Manuscripts

Query: no
Abstract: yes

Style guide: MOS
Preferred length: 20 pages
Number of copies: 4
Notes: end of manuscript
Blind referee: yes
Time to consider manuscript: 2 months
Proportion of manuscripts accepted: 8 percent
Illustrations accepted: tables, graphs, charts, photos, drawings
Foreign languages: no

Reviews
Book review editor: John Van Maanen
Address:
Sloan School of Management
Massachusetts Institute of Technology
Cambridge, MA 02139
Seeking reviewers: yes
Unsolicited reviews accepted: no
How to apply: letter of inquiry
Include in application: professional degrees, institutional affiliation, areas of expertise, published works, current research, vita
Materials reviewed: books
Length of review: 3 pages

Additional notes
Simultaneous submission is not permitted. Articles are published 9–12 months after acceptance.

URBAN STUDIES

Focus: interdisciplinary study of urban and regional problems and planning
Editor: submit to the Managing Editor
Editorial address:
Adam Smith Building
University of Glasgow
Glasgow G12 8RT
SCOTLAND
or
U.S. authors send to:
B. Chinitz
ABT Associates
55 Wheeler Street
Cambridge, MA 02138

Frequency: 3/year
Circulation: not given
Subscription rate(s): $32
Pages/issue: 110–120
Readership: academics, professionals
Indexed/abstracted in: SSCI, Soc Sci Ind, Hist Abstr

Manuscripts
Query: no
Abstract: yes, 120 words maximum
Style guide: see current issue
Preferred length: 4,000–12,000 words
Number of copies: 3
Notes: end of manuscript
Blind referee: no
Time to consider manuscript: not given
Proportion of manuscripts accepted: not given
Illustrations accepted: tables, charts, diagrams, maps
Foreign languages: no

Reviews
Book review editor: submit to the Managing Editor or B. Chinitz (for the U.S. and Canada)
Address: same as above
Materials reviewed: books
Length of review: 3–5 pages

Additional notes
Simultaneous submission is not allowed.

VANDERBILT JOURNAL OF TRANSNATIONAL LAW

Focus: private and public international legal developments; primarily of interest to Western practitioners and scholars
Institutional affiliation: Vanderbilt University
Editor: Robert C. Goodrich, Jr.
Editorial address:
Vanderbilt Law School
Vanderbilt University
Nashville, TN 37240
Frequency: 4/year
Circulation: 1,000

Subscription rate(s): domestic $14, foreign $15
Pages/issue: 250
Readership: legal practitioners, legal scholars

Manuscripts
Query: no, but preferred
Abstract: no
Style guide: Texas Law School Style Manual, HLRA
Preferred length: not given
Number of copies: 1
Notes: end of manuscript
Blind referee: no
Time to consider manuscript: 2 weeks
Proportion of manuscripts accepted: not given
Illustrations accepted: graphs, charts
Foreign languages: no

Reviews
Book review editor: William Buechler
Address: same as above
Seeking reviewers: yes
Unsolicited reviews accepted: yes
How to apply: letter of inquiry
Include in application: professional degrees, institutional affiliation, areas of expertise, published works, current research
Materials reviewed: books

Additional notes
Please contact us to discuss publication possibilities. Manuscript should be triple-spaced. Simultaneous submission is allowed. Articles are published 3 months after acceptance.

VIRGINIA JOURNAL OF INTERNATIONAL LAW

Focus: all aspects of international law
Institutional affiliation: Virginia Journal of International Law Association
Editor: submit to the Editor

Editorial address:
Virginia Journal of International Law
University of Virginia School of Law
Charlottesville, VA 22901
Frequency: 4/year
Circulation: 1,000
Subscription rate(s): student $8, individual $16
Pages/issue: 200
Readership: academics
Indexed/abstracted in: ABC POL SCI, Leg Per, SSCI

Manuscripts
Query: no
Abstract: no
Style guide: see current issue
Preferred length: no preference
Number of copies: 1
Notes: bottom of page
Blind referee: no
Time to consider manuscript: not given
Proportion of manuscripts accepted: not given
Illustrations accepted: not given
Foreign languages: no

Reviews
Book review editor: submit to the Editor
Address: same as above
Materials reviewed: books
Length of review: 10–20 pages

VIRGINIA LAW REVIEW

Focus: legal
Institutional affiliation: University of Virginia School of Law
Editor: submit to the Editors
Editorial address:
University of Virginia, School of Law
Charlottesville, VA 22901
Frequency: 8/year
Circulation: not given
Subscription rate(s): domestic $24, foreign $26.50
Readership: libraries, judges, lawyers, academics
Indexed/abstracted in: not given

Manuscripts

Query: no
Abstract: no
Style guide: GPO, EOS
Preferred length: no preference
Number of copies: 1
Notes: end of manuscript
Blind referee: no
Time to consider manuscript: not given
Proportion of manuscripts accepted: not given
Illustrations accepted: tables, graphs, charts, photos, drawings
Foreign languages: no

Reviews

Book review editor: submit to the Editors
Address: same as above
Seeking reviewers: sometimes
Unsolicited reviews accepted: yes
How to apply: letter of inquiry
Include in application: professional degrees, institutional affiliation, areas of expertise, published works, current research
Materials reviewed: books
Length of review: varies, usually very short

THE WASHINGTON MONTHLY

Focus: how our political system works and why it does not work better; special emphasis on the bureaucracy
Editor: Charles Peters
Editorial address:
The Washington Monthly Company
2712 Ontario Road, NW
Washington, DC 20009
Frequency: 11/year
Circulation: 30,000
Subscription rate(s): $22
Pages/issue: 58
Readership: academics, general public
Indexed/abstracted in: Bk Rev Ind, PAIS, RG, Soc Sci Ind

Manuscripts

Query: no
Abstract: yes
Style guide: none required
Preferred length: 2,000–5,000 words
Number of copies: 2
Notes: not given
Blind referee: no
Time to consider manuscript: 1 month
Proportion of manuscripts accepted: not given
Illustrations accepted: photos, drawings
Foreign languages: no

Reviews

Write for information on how to become a reviewer.

Additional notes

Simultaneous submission permitted with knowledge of editor.

THE WASHINGTON PAPERS

Focus: major developments in world affairs
Institutional affiliation: The Center for Strategic and International Studies, Georgetown University
Editor: Nancy B. Eddy
Editorial address:
The Center for Strategic and International Studies
Georgetown University
1800 K Street NW, Suite 400
Washington, DC 20006
Frequency: 8/year
Circulation: 1,000
Subscription rate(s): individual $35, institutional $45
Pages/issue: 110
Readership: academics, government policymakers
Indexed/abstracted in: ABC POL SCI

Manuscripts

Query: no
Abstract: yes
Style guide: MOS
Preferred length: 120–150 pages

Number of copies: 2
Notes: end of manuscript
Blind referee: no
Time to consider manuscript: 1
month
Proportion of manuscripts
accepted: not given
Illustrations accepted: tables,
graphs, charts, drawings
Foreign languages: no

Reviews
not applicable

Additional notes
Inquiries should include a curriculum vita,
synopsis, table of contents, and
estimated manuscript length.

THE WASHINGTON
QUARTERLY: A REVIEW OF
STRATEGIC AND
INTERNATIONAL ISSUES

Focus: international political and
business affairs; foreign policy and
strategic issues
Institutional affiliation: Center for
Strategic and International Studies,
Georgetown University
Editor: submit to the Manuscript Editor
Editorial address:
1800 K Street, NW
Suite 400
Washington, DC 20006
Frequency: 4/year
Circulation: 2,500
Subscription rate(s): individual $16,
institutional $20
Pages/issue: 200
Readership: academics, legislators,
business people
Indexed/abstracted in: not given

Manuscripts
Query: no
Abstract: no
Style guide: MOS or write for
guidelines
Preferred length: no preference
Number of copies: 3
Notes: end of manuscript

Blind referee: no
Time to consider manuscript: 4
months
Proportion of manuscripts
accepted: not given
Illustrations accepted: drawings
Foreign languages: no

Reviews
not applicable

Additional notes
Published authors receive $150 per
article. Simultaneous submission is not
allowed. Articles are published 3–5
months after acceptance.

WESTERN CITY

Focus: local government affairs; city
management
Institutional affiliation: League of
California Cities
Editor: Hal Stemmler
Editorial address:
1400 K Street
Sacramento, CA 95814
Frequency: 12/year
Circulation: 10,000
Subscription rate(s): $15
Pages/issue: 32–64
Readership: council members,
mayors, city managers, department
heads, legislators
Indexed/abstracted in: not given

Manuscripts
Query: yes
Abstract: no
Style guide: none required
Preferred length: 2,500 words
Number of copies: 2
Notes: no preference
Blind referee: no
Time to consider manuscript: not
given
Proportion of manuscripts
accepted: not given
Illustrations accepted: tables,
graphs, charts, photos, drawings
Foreign languages: no

Reviews
not applicable

WESTERN POLITICAL QUARTERLY

Focus: general political science, with articles in all fields; American and comparative politics; international relations; political theory; public law, administration, and policy
Institutional affiliation: Western Political Science Association, University of Utah
Editors: Dean E. Mann, A. J. Wann
Editorial address:
Editor: Department of Political Science
University of California
Santa Barbara, CA 93106
or
Department of Political Science
University of Utah
Salt Lake City, UT 84712
Frequency: 4/year
Circulation: 2,000
Subscription rate(s): $16
Pages/issue: 140
Readership: academics (faculty and students)
Indexed/abstracted in: not given

Manuscripts
Query: no
Abstract: yes
Style guide: available on request
Preferred length: 30 pages
Number of copies: 4
Notes: end of manuscript
Blind referee: yes
Time to consider manuscript: 3 months
Proportion of manuscripts accepted: 15 percent
Illustrations accepted: tables, graphs, photos
Foreign languages: no

Reviews
Book review editor: Bernard Hennessy

Address:
Department of Political Science
California State University
Hayward, CA 94542
Seeking reviewers: yes
Unsolicited reviews accepted: no
How to apply: letter of inquiry
Include in application: professional degrees, institutional affiliation, areas of expertise, published works, current research
Materials reviewed: books
Length of review: 750 words (book review), 2,000 words (review essay)

Additional notes
Simultaneous submission is not permitted. Articles are published 6–12 months after acceptance.

WEST EUROPEAN POLITICS

Focus: political problems and issues of the nations of Western Europe
Editor: submit to the Administrative Editor, *West European Politics*
Editorial address:
Frank Cass and Co. Ltd.
Gainsborough House
Gainsborough Road
London E11 1RS
ENGLAND
Frequency: 4/year
Circulation: 800
Subscription rate(s): individual £22.50, institutional £36
Pages/issue: 110–120
Readership: political and social scientists
Indexed/abstracted in: ABC POL SCI

Manuscripts
Query: no
Abstract: yes, 100 words maximum
Style guide: see current issue or write for guidelines
Preferred length: 6,000 words
Number of copies: 2
Notes: end of manuscript
Blind referee: no
Time to consider manuscript: not given

**Proportion of manuscripts
accepted:** not given
Illustrations accepted: tables,
graphs, charts, diagrams
Foreign languages: no

Reviews
Book review editor: submit to the
Administrative Editor
Address: same as above
Materials reviewed: books
Length of review: 2–3 pages

Additional notes
Simultaneous submission is not allowed.

WIN MAGAZINE

Focus: the nonviolent movement for
social change
Institutional affiliation: War Resisters
League
Editor: five-person editorial collective
Editorial address:
326 Livingston Street
Brooklyn, NY 11217
Frequency: 22/year
Circulation: 5,000
Subscription rate(s): $20
Pages/issue: 36
Readership: academics, political
activists, students, political scientists
Indexed/abstracted in: Alt Press Ind

Manuscripts
Query: yes
Abstract: no
Style guide: none required
Preferred length: 2,000 words
Number of copies: 1
Notes: no notes
Blind referee: no
Time to consider manuscript: varies
**Proportion of manuscripts
accepted:** not given
Illustrations accepted: photos,
drawings
Foreign languages: no

Reviews
Book review editor: Sharon Bray
Address: same as above

Seeking reviewers: yes
Unsolicited reviews accepted: yes
How to apply: letter of inquiry
Include in application: areas of
expertise
Materials reviewed: books, films,
tapes, records, theater
Length of review: 600–800 words

Additional notes
WIN Magazine is primarily a news
publication and not a journal, so the style
of writing should be journalistic,
pertaining to issues of social change,
nuclear disarmament, feminism, and
nonviolence.

WISCONSIN LAW REVIEW

Focus: law topics
Institutional affiliation: University of
Wisconsin
Editor: Sylvan Sobel
Editorial address:
University of Wisconsin
Madison, WI 53706
Frequency: 6/year
Circulation: 2,000
Subscription rate(s): $20
Pages/issue: 200
Readership: academics
Indexed/abstracted in: not given

Manuscripts
Query: no
Abstract: no
Style guide: HLRA
Preferred length: varies
Number of copies: 2
Notes: end of manuscript
Blind referee: no
Time to consider manuscript: varies
**Proportion of manuscripts
accepted:** not given
Illustrations accepted: tables,
graphs, charts, photos, drawings
Foreign languages: no

Reviews
Book review editor: John Hovel
Address: same as above
Seeking reviewers: yes

Unsolicited reviews accepted: yes
How to apply: letter of inquiry
Materials reviewed: books

WOMEN AND POLITICS: A QUARTERLY JOURNAL OF RESEARCH AND POLICY STUDIES

Focus: scholarly
Institutional affiliation: Haworth Press (New York)
Editor: Sarah Slavin
Editorial address:
Economics and Political Science Department
State University College at Buffalo
Buffalo, NY 14222
Frequency: 4/year
Circulation: 450
Subscription rate(s): individual $19, institutional $40, libraries/subscription agencies $48
Pages/issue: 130
Readership: academics, public policy analysts, activists
Indexed/abstracted in: not given

Manuscripts
Query: yes
Abstract: yes
Style guide: MOS
Preferred length: 20 pages
Number of copies: 3
Notes: end of manuscript
Blind referee: yes
Time to consider manuscript: 6 weeks
Proportion of manuscripts accepted: 10–15 percent
Illustrations accepted: tables, graphs, charts
Foreign languages: no

Reviews
Book review editor: Sharon Wolchik
Address:
Sino-Soviet Studies Institute
George Washington University
Washington, DC 20006
Seeking reviewers: yes
Unsolicited reviews accepted: yes

How to apply: letter of inquiry
Include in application: professional degrees, institutional affiliation, areas of expertise, published works, foreign languages, current research
Materials reviewed: books
Length of review: 900 words maximum

Additional notes
Women and Politics invites significant contributions to scholarship in the social sciences and humanities, from all points of view. Articles welcome for review include: articles that assist in describing the behavior, performance, and problems of women who participate in either mass or elite politics; studies that elucidate the manner or way in which such participation occurs; research aimed at identifying pertinent factors which facilitate, discourage, or otherwise influence female political participation; material that addresses political and/or legal issues, problem areas, and policies which primarily or uniquely affect women; articles that trace the impact of women on the political process; contributions aimed at developing a comprehensive theory about women and politics.
Women and Politics encourages, among others, submissions of an interdisciplinary nature, from a wide spectrum of methodological approaches, and with a comparative perspective. The innovative and the traditional are equally welcome. All work will be submitted to appropriate peer review, and most issues will emphasize diversity in the scholarship presented. Simultaneous submission is not permitted. Articles are published 9–12 months after acceptance.

WOMEN ORGANIZING

Focus: a resource for those involved in feminist organizing; deals with feminist theory, organizing projects, evaluation of such projects and tactics, and issues and trends in the women's movement
Institutional affiliation: New American Movement
Editor: submit to the Editors
Editorial address:
3244 North Clark Street
Chicago, IL 60657
Frequency: 4/year
Circulation: 3,000
Subscription rate(s): $5
Pages/issue: 30–40
Readership: feminists, academics
Indexed/abstracted in: not given

Manuscripts

Query: no
Abstract: no
Style guide: none required
Preferred length: 10 pages
Number of copies: 2, double-spaced
Notes: end of manuscript
Blind referee: no
Time to consider manuscript: 1 month
Proportion of manuscripts accepted: 33 percent
Illustrations accepted: tables, drawings
Foreign languages: no

Reviews

Book review editor: Christine Riddiough
Address: same as above
Seeking reviewers: no
Unsolicited reviews accepted: yes
How to apply: letter of inquiry
Include in application: professional degrees, institutional affiliation, areas of expertise, published works, current research
Materials reviewed: books, films
Length of review: 3 pages

Additional notes

The publisher, New American Movement, is a democratic-socialist organization.

WOMEN'S RIGHTS LAW REPORTER

Focus: legal issues affecting women and minority women—discrimination, employment, rape, domestic violence, harassment
Editor: Pat Voger
Editorial address:
15 Washington Street
Newark, NJ 07102
Frequency: 4/year
Circulation: 1,500
Subscription rate(s): $18–28
Pages/issue: 60–80
Readership: lawyers, legal workers, students, social workers
Indexed/abstracted in: Leg Per

Manuscripts

Query: no
Abstract: no
Style guide: HLRA
Preferred length: 40–60 pages
Number of copies: 2, triple-spaced
Notes: end of manuscript
Blind referee: no
Time to consider manuscript: 1–2 months
Proportion of manuscripts accepted: 25–50 percent
Illustrations accepted: tables, graphs, charts, photos, drawings
Foreign languages: no

Reviews

Book review editor: Caaron Willinger
Address: same as above
Seeking reviewers: yes
Unsolicited reviews accepted: yes
How to apply: letter of inquiry
Materials reviewed: books
Length of review: 5–8 pages

Additional notes

Simultaneous submission is not allowed. Articles are published 2–12 months after acceptance.

WORLD AFFAIRS

Focus: international relations, law and organization, foreign policy, comparative politics, theory, diplomatic history; articles that illuminate the issues involved in international conflict
Institutional affiliation: American Peace Society
Editor: Frank C. Turley
Editorial address:
American Peace Society
4000 Albemarle Street, NW
Washington, DC 20037
Frequency: 4/year
Circulation: 900
Subscription rate(s): $15
Pages/issue: 96
Readership: academics, researchers, general public
Indexed/abstracted in: PAIS, Curr Cont, USPSD, ABC POL SCI, Hist Abstr

Manuscripts
Query: no
Abstract: no
Style guide: MOS
Preferred length: 20 pages
Number of copies: 2
Notes: end of manuscript
Blind referee: no
Time to consider manuscript: 3 months
Proportion of manuscripts accepted: 10 percent
Illustrations accepted: tables, graphs, charts, photos, drawings
Foreign languages: no

Reviews
Seeking reviewers: no
Unsolicited reviews accepted: no
Materials reviewed: books

Additional notes
Editorial board headed by Evron M. Kirkpatrick has final say on manuscripts. Simultaneous submission is not permitted. Articles are published 6 months after acceptance.

WORLD DEVELOPMENT

Focus: the study and promotion of world development
Editor: Anne Corden Drabek
Editorial address:
Queen Elizabeth House
21 St Giles
Oxford OX1 3LA
ENGLAND
Frequency: 12/year
Circulation: 2,000
Subscription rate(s): institutional $200
Pages/issue: 100
Readership: academics
Indexed/abstracted in: not given

Manuscripts
Query: no
Abstract: yes, 100 words maximum
Style guide: available on request
Preferred length: 8,000 words
Number of copies: 2
Notes: end of manuscript
Blind referee: not given
Time to consider manuscript: not given
Proportion of manuscripts accepted: not given
Illustrations accepted: tables, graphs, charts
Foreign languages: no

Reviews
not applicable

THE WORLD ECONOMY

Focus: the conduct of international economic affairs
Institutional affiliation: Trade Policy Research Centre
Editor: Hugh Corbet
Editorial address:
Trade Policy Research Centre
1 Gough Square
London EC4A 3DE
ENGLAND
Frequency: 4/year
Circulation: not given
Subscription rate(s): individual $38.50, institutional $72
Pages/issue: 110

Readership: academics
Indexed/abstracted in: ABC POL SCI

Manuscripts
Query: yes
Abstract: no
Style guide: none required
Preferred length: 15–20 pages
Number of copies: 1
Notes: end of manuscript
Blind referee: no
Time to consider manuscript: not given
Proportion of manuscripts accepted: not given
Illustrations accepted: tables, graphs, charts
Foreign languages: no

Reviews
Book review editor: Hugh Corbet
Address: same as above
Seeking reviewers: yes
Unsolicited reviews accepted: no
How to apply: letter of inquiry
Include in application: institutional affiliation, areas of expertise
Materials reviewed: books
Length of review: 1–2 pages

WORLD FEDERALIST: NEWSMAGAZINE OF THE WORLD FEDERALISTS ASSOCIATION

Focus: reviews and discusses events affecting progress toward world order
Institutional affiliation: World Association of World Federalists
Editor: Lawrence Abbott
Editorial address:
259 High Street
Coventry, CT 06238
Frequency: 4/year
Circulation: 6,500
Subscription rate(s): $5
Pages/issue: 8
Readership: academics, professionals, civil servants
Indexed/abstracted in: not given

Manuscripts
Query: no
Abstract: yes
Preferred length: 500–1,000 words
Number of copies: 2
Notes: end of manuscript
Time to consider manuscript: 2 months
Proportion of manuscripts accepted: not given
Illustrations accepted: tables, graphs, charts, photos, drawings
Foreign languages: no

Reviews
Book review editor: Edward Rawson
Address:
1011 Arlington Blvd.
Arlington, VA 22209
Seeking reviewers: no
Unsolicited reviews accepted: yes
How to apply: letter of inquiry
Materials reviewed: books

WORLD POLITICS: A QUARTERLY JOURNAL OF INTERNATIONAL RELATIONS

Focus: multidisciplinary, analytical/theoretical articles on the frontiers of scholarship in international relations, comparative politics, political theory, foreign policy, national development, history, geography, economics, military affairs, and sociology
Institutional affiliation: Center of International Studies, Princeton University
Editor: Elsbeth G. Lewin
Editorial address:
Corwin Hall
Princeton University
Princeton, NJ 08544
Frequency: 4/year
Circulation: 4,000
Subscription rate(s): individual $12.50, institutional $22.50; foreign individual $15.50, foreign institutional $28.25; single issue $6.50
Pages/issue: 160

Readership: social scientists
Indexed/abstracted in: ABC POL
SCI, Bk Rev Ind, CRIS, PAIS, Soc Sci
Ind, USPSD, Hist Abstr, Int Polit Sci
Abstr

Manuscripts
Query: no
Abstract: yes
Style guide: MOS, NYT
Preferred length: 10,000 words
Number of copies: 2
Notes: end of manuscript
Blind referee: yes
Time to consider manuscript: 1–3
months
**Proportion of manuscripts
accepted:** 10–12 percent
Illustrations accepted: tables, graphs
Foreign languages: no

Reviews
Book review editor: Henry S. Bienen
Address: same as above
Seeking reviewers: no
Unsolicited reviews accepted:
occasionally
Materials reviewed: books
Length of review: 10,000 words

Additional notes
Authors are paid $50 per article.
Simultaneous submission is not allowed.
Articles are published 6–12 months after
acceptance.

THE WORLD TODAY

Focus: international issues and events;
internal political and economic
developments of individual countries
by authors with first-hand knowledge
Institutional affiliation: Royal Institute
of International Affairs
Editor: submit to the Editor
Editorial address:
Royal Institute of International Affairs
Chatham House
10 St. James' Square
London SW1Y 4LE
ENGLAND
Frequency: 12/year

Circulation: 5,000
Subscription rate(s): $27
Pages/issue: 30–40
Readership: academics, students,
politicians, business people,
journalists
Indexed/abstracted in: not given

Manuscripts
Query: no, but advisable
Abstract: no
Style guide: available on request
Preferred length: 3,500 words
Number of copies: 1
Notes: bottom of page
Blind referee: no
Time to consider manuscript: 1
month
**Proportion of manuscripts
accepted:** not given
Illustrations accepted: tables
Foreign languages: French, German

Reviews
not applicable

Additional notes
Simultaneous submission is not
permitted. Articles are published 1–4
months after acceptance.

THE YALE LAW JOURNAL

Focus: law
Institutional affiliation: The Yale Law
School
Editor: submit to the Editors
Editorial address:
Box 401A
Yale Station
New Haven, CT 06520
Frequency: 8/year
Circulation: 4,500
Subscription rate(s): $25
Pages/issue: 200
Readership: legal professionals,
libraries
Indexed/abstracted in: G Leg Per

Manuscripts
Query: no
Abstract: no

Style guide: HLRA
Preferred length: no preference
Number of copies: 1
Notes: no preference
Blind referee: no
Time to consider manuscript: 4–6
weeks
**Proportion of manuscripts
accepted:** not given
Illustrations accepted: not given
Foreign languages: yes

Reviews
Book review editor: submit to the
Editors
Address: same as above
Unsolicited reviews accepted: yes
How to apply: letter of inquiry
Materials reviewed: books

Additional notes
Simultaneous submission is allowed.

Subject Index of Journal Titles

African Studies, see Area Studies

American/Canadian Studies, see Area Studies

Area Studies

General
Journal of Area Studies

African Studies
Africa
African Review
African Studies
African Studies Review
African Urban Studies
Africa Quarterly
Africa Report
Africa Today
Canadian Journal of African Studies
Issue: A Quarterly Journal of Africanist Opinion
Journal of African Studies
Journal of Asian and African Studies
The Journal of Modern African Studies
Journal of Southern African Affairs
Journal of Southern African Studies
MERIP Reports
Rural Africana

American/Canadian Studies
American Review of Canadian Studies
American Studies
Canadian Review of American Studies
International Perspectives
Journal of American Culture
Journal of American Studies
Journal of Canadian Studies
Journal of Popular Culture

Asian Studies
Asian Affairs: An American Review
Asian Profile
Asian Survey
Asian Thought and Society: An International Review
Asia Pacific Community: A Quarterly Review
Bulletin of Concerned Asian Scholars
The China Quarterly
Contributions to Asian Studies
Far Eastern Economic Review
Issues and Studies: A Journal of China Studies and International Affairs
The Japan Interpreter: A Journal of Social and Political Ideas
Journal of Asian and African Studies
The Journal of Asian Studies
Journal of Japanese Studies
Journal of South Asian and Middle Eastern Studies
Journal of Southeast Asian Studies
The Korean Journal of International Studies
Modern Asian Studies
Modern China: An International Quarterly of History and Social Science
Pacific Research
Southeast Asia Chronicle
The South East Asian Review
The Ukrainian Quarterly: A Journal of East European and Asian Affairs

Australian/Pacific Studies
Asia Pacific Community: A Quarterly Review
Australian Outlook
The Australian Quarterly
Journal of the Polynesian Society
Pacific Affairs
Pacific Research
Pacific Viewpoint

European Studies
Canadian-American Slavic Studies
Canadian Slavonic Papers
Common Market Law Review
Contemporary French Civilization
Critique: A Journal of Soviet Studies and Socialist Thought
East Central Europe
East European Quarterly
European Studies Review
German Studies Review

Journal of Common Market Studies
The Russian Review
Scandinavian Political Studies
Slavic Review
Southeastern Europe
Soviet Studies
Soviet Union
The Ukrainian Quarterly: A Journal of
    East European and Asian Affairs
West European Politics

Latin American/Caribbean Studies
Caribbean Quarterly
Caribbean Review
Caribbean Studies
Cuban Studies
Inter-American Economic Affairs
Journal of Interamerican Studies and
    World Affairs
Journal of Latin American Studies
Latin American Perspectives: A Journal
    on Capitalism and Socialism
Latin American Research Review
NACLA Report on the Americas

Middle Eastern/Arab Studies
Arab Studies Quarterly
International Journal of Middle East
    Studies
International Problems
Jerusalem Journal of International
    Studies
Journal of Arab Affairs
Journal of Palestine Studies
Journal of South Asian and Middle East-
    ern Studies
MERIP Reports
Middle Eastern Studies
Middle East Journal
Middle East Perspective
Middle East Review
Middle East Studies Association Bulletin
The Search: Journal for Arab and Islamic
    Studies

Asian Studies, see Area Studies

Australian/Pacific Studies, see Area Studies

Behavioral Science, see also Social Science, Sociology
Behavioral Science
The Journal of Applied Behavioral
    Science
Journal of the History of the Behavioral
    Sciences

Black Studies, see Ethnic/Minority Studies

Business, see Economics

Development Studies, see also Economics
Canadian Journal of Development
    Studies
The Developing Economies
Development and Change
Economic Development and Cultural
    Change
International Development Review
International Problems
Journal of Developing Areas
The Journal of Development Studies
Journal of Energy and Development
Population and Development Review
Studies in Comparative International
    Development
The Third World Review
World Development

Economics, see also Development Studies

General
American Economic Review
American Journal of Economics and
    Sociology
The Developing Economies
Economic Development and Cultural
    Change
Far Eastern Economic Review
George Washington Journal of Interna-
    tional Law and Economics
Inter-American Economic Affairs
Journal of Economic History
The Journal of Law and Economics
Regional Science and Urban Economics
Socio-Economic Planning Sciences
The World Economy

Business
Business History Review
Harvard Business Review

Public Finance and Economics
Governmental Finance
Journal of Public Economics
Public Choice
Public Finance
Public Finance Quarterly

Environmental Studies

Alternatives: Journal of Friends of the Earth
Environmental Review
Natural Resources Journal

Ethnic/Minority Studies, see also Human/Civil Rights

General
Canadian Ethnic Studies
The Crisis: A Record of the Darker Races
Ethnic and Racial Studies
Explorations in Ethnic Studies
Focus
International Migration Review
The Journal of Ethnic Studies
Phylon: The Atlanta University Review of Race and Culture

Black Studies
The Black Law Journal
The Black Scholar
Journal of Black Studies

European Studies, see Area Studies

Government/Politics, see also International Studies, Political Science, Urban Studies

General
American Opinion
Campaigns and Elections: The Journal of Political Action
Canadian Review of Studies in Nationalism
Congress and the Presidency
Congress Monthly
Conservative Digest
Dissent

Foreign Service Journal
Governmental Finance
Government and Opposition: A Journal of Comparative Politics
Harvard Journal on Legislation
Journal of Contemporary Studies
Journal of Libertarian Studies–An Interdisciplinary Review
Journal of Legislation
Journal of Public and International Affairs
Legislative Studies Quarterly
Libertarian Forum
The Nation
National Review
New Republic
Presidential Studies Quarterly
The Progressive
Public Affairs
Public Affairs Quarterly
The Public Interest
Publius: The Journal of Federalism
Socialist Review
Studies in Comparative Communism: An International Interdisciplinary Journal
The Washington Monthly
World Federalist: Newsmagazine of the World Federalists Association

State and Local Government
American City and County Magazine
California Journal
State and Local Government Review
State Government
State Government News
State Legislatures

History

American Historical Review
American Journal of Legal History
American Quarterly
Australian Journal of Politics and History
Business History Review
Comparative Studies in Society and History
Diplomatic History
History of Political Economy
History of Political Thought
International Labor and Working Class History
International Review of History and Political Science

Journal of Contemporary History
Journal of Economic History
The Journal of Interdisciplinary History
Journal of the History of the Behavioral
    Sciences
Journal of Urban History
Pacific Historical Review
Potomac Review
Proceedings of the American Philosophi-
    cal Society
The Public Historian
Social Science History

Human/Civil Rights, see also Ethnic/Minority Studies

The Citizen
First Principles
Free Speech Yearbook
Harvard Civil Rights–Civil Liberties Law
    Review
Human Rights Internet Reporter
Human Rights Quarterly
Perspectives: The Civil Rights Quarterly

Industrial Relations, see Labor Studies/Industrial Relations

International Law, see Law

International Studies, see also Government/Politics, Political Science

Alternatives: A Journal of World Policy
The Atlantic Community Quarterly
Aussenpolitik
Australian Outlook
B'nai B'rith International Jewish Monthly
Coalition Close-Up
Cooperation and Conflict: Nordic Journal
    of International Politics
Diplomatic History
The Fletcher Forum
Foreign Affairs
Foreign Policy
Foreign Service Journal
India Quarterly: A Journal of International
    Affairs
International Affairs
International Interactions
International Journal

International Organization
International Perspectives
International Problems
International Studies Notes
International Studies Quarterly
Issues and Studies: A Journal of China
    Studies and International Affairs
Jerusalem Journal of International
    Studies
Journal of Interamerican Studies and
    World Affairs
Journal of International Affairs
Journal of Public and International Affairs
The Journal of Strategic Studies
The Korean Journal of International
    Studies
Millennium: Journal of International
    Studies
Monograph Series in World Affairs
The Nation
National Review
The New International Review
Orbis: A Journal of World Affairs
Pacific Research
Problems of Communism
Review of International Studies
SAIS Review
Socialist Review
South Atlantic Quarterly
Studies in Comparative Communism: An
    International Interdisciplinary Journal
Survey: A Journal of East and West
    Studies
Towson State Journal of International
    Affairs
The Washington Papers
The Washington Quarterly: A Review of
    Strategic and International Issues
World Affairs
World Politics: A Quarterly Journal of
    International Relations
The World Today

Labor Studies/Industrial Relations

British Journal of Industrial Relations
Industrial and Labor Relations Review
Industrial Relations
Industrial Relations/Relations Industrielles
International Labor and Working Class
    History
International Labour Review

Journal of Human Resources
Journal of Labor Research
Labor Studies Journal
Labour, Capital and Society

Latin American Studies, see Area Studies

Law

General

The American Journal of Comparative
Law
American Journal of Jurisprudence
The American Journal of Legal History
The Black Law Journal
California Law Review
Columbia Law Review
Cornell Law Review
Emory Law Journal
Ethics: An International Journal of Social,
Political and Legal Philosophy
George Washington Law Review
Harvard Civil Rights–Civil Liberties Law
Review
Harvard Journal of Legislation
Harvard Law Review
The Journal of Law and Economics
Journal of Legal Studies
Journal of Legislation
Law and Policy Quarterly
Law and Society Review
Legislative Studies Quarterly
Michigan Law Review
Military Law Review
Minnesota Law Review
New York University Law Review
Ottawa Law Journal
Social Action and the Law
Texas Law Review
Transportation Law Journal
Tulane Law Review
UCLA Law Review
The University of Chicago Law Review
University of Colorado Law Review
University of Detroit Journal of Urban
Law
University of Pennsylvania Law Review
Virginia Law Review
Wisconsin Law Review
Women's Rights Law Reporter
The Yale Law Journal

International Law

American Journal of International Law
Boston College International and Com-
parative Law Review
Columbia Journal of Transnational Law
Common Market Law Review
Cornell International Law Journal
Denver Journal of International Law and
Policy
The Fletcher Forum
George Washington Journal of Interna-
tional Law and Economics
Harvard International Law Journal
Hastings International and Comparative
Law Review
The International and Comparative Law
Quarterly
New York University Journal of Interna-
tional Law and Politics
Stanford Journal of International Law
Texas International Law Journal
Vanderbilt Journal of Transnational Law
Virginia Journal of International Law

Middle Eastern Studies, see Area Studies

Military/Strategic Studies, see also International Studies

Armed Forces and Society
The Bulletin of the Atomic Scientists
Coalition Close-up
Comparative Strategy
Conflict: All Warfare Short of War
International Security
International Security Review
Journal of Political and Military Sociology
The Journal of Strategic Studies
Military Law Review
Parameters: Journal of the U.S. Army
War College
Proceedings of the United States Naval
Institute
Royal United Services Institute for De-
fence Studies Journal
Strategic Review
The Washington Quarterly: A Review of
Strategic and International Issues

Peace Studies

Current Research on Peace and Violence
International Interactions
Journal of Conflict Resolution
Journal of Peace Ressearch
Peace and Change: A Journal of Peace
    Research
Peace Research
Peace Research Abstracts Journal
Peace Research Reviews

Philosophy and Science

The Bulletin of the Atomic Scientists
Philosophy and Public Affairs
Philosophy of Science
Proceedings of the American Philosophi-
    cal Society

Policy Studies

Canadian Public Policy
The Cato Journal
Critique: Southern California Public Policy
    and Administration
Denver Journal of International Law and
    Policy
Journal of Contemporary Studies
Journal of Energy and Development
Journal of Human Resources
The Journal of Policy Analysis and
    Management
Journal of Policy Modeling
Journal of Social Policy
Law and Policy Quarterly
Policy and Politics
Policy Review
Policy Sciences
Policy Studies Journal
Policy Studies Review
Public Affairs
Public Affairs Report
Transaction/Society
Women and Politics: A Quarterly Journal
    of Research and Policy Studies

Political Economy, see Political Science

Political Philosophy and Theory, see Political Science

Political Science, see also Government/Politics, International Studies, Social Science

General

American Journal of Political Science
American Opinion
The American Political Science Review
American Politics Quarterly
Australian Journal of Politics and History
British Journal of Political Science
Canadian Journal of Political Science
Canadian Review of Studies in
    Nationalism
Comparative Political Studies
Comparative Politics
European Journal of Political Research
Experimental Study of Politics
Government and Opposition: A Journal
    of Comparative Politics
Indian Journal of Political Science
Indian Journal of Politics
Indian Political Science Review
International Journal of Political
    Education
International Political Science Review
International Review of History and Politi-
    cal Science
Journal of Commonwealth and Compara-
    tive Politics
Journal of Political Science
The Journal of Politics
Micropolitics
Parliamentary Affairs: A Journal of Com-
    parative Politics
Parliamentary Journal
Policy and Politics
Political Behavior
Political Communication and Persuasion
Political Methodology
Political Quarterly
Political Science
Political Science Quarterly
The Political Science Reviewer
Political Studies
Politics and Society
Polity: The Journal of the Northeast Politi-
    cal Science Association
PS
Public Choice
Res Publica
The Review of Politics
Scandinavian Political Studies

Southeastern Political Review
Teaching Political Science
Texas Journal of Political Studies
Western Political Quarterly
West European Politics
Women and Politics: A Quarterly Journal
of Research and Policy Studies

Political Economy

History of Political Economy
Journal of Political Economy
Journal of Social, Political and Economic
Studies
Scottish Journal of Political Economy

Political Philosophy and Theory

Canadian Journal of Political and Social
Theory
Critique: A Journal of Soviet Studies and
Socialist Thought
Ethics: An International Journal of Social,
Political and Legal Philosophy
History of Political Thought
Interpretation: A Journal of Political
Philosophy
Philosophy and Public Affairs
Political Theory: An International Journal
of Political Philosophy
Problems of Communism
Quarterly Journal of Ideology
Radical America
Science and Society
Socialist Review
Studies in Comparative Communism: An
International Interdisciplinary Journal
Studies in Soviet Thought
Telos: Quarterly Journal of Radical
Thought

Public Administration/ Management

Academy of Management Journal
Administration and Society
Administrative Science Quarterly
American Review of Public
Administration
The Bureaucrat
California Management Review
Canadian Public Administration
Critique: Southern California Public Policy
and Administration
Indian Journal of Public Administration

Journal of Policy Analysis and
Management
Management International Review
Management Review
Management Science
Philippine Journal of Public
Administration
Planning and Administration
Public Administration
Public Administration Review
Public Affairs
Public Affairs Report
Public Management
Public Personnel Management
Southern Review of Public Administration

Public Finance and Economics, see Economics

Public Opinion and Survey Research

Public Opinion
Public Opinion Quarterly

Regional Science

The Annals of Regional Science
Growth and Change: A Journal of Re-
gional Development
International Journal of Urban and Re-
gional Research
International Regional Science Review
Journal of Regional Science
Regional Science and Urban Economics

Social Science, see also Behavioral Science, Political Science, Sociology

American Journal of Economics and
Sociology
Centerpoint: A Journal of Interdisciplinary
Studies
Co-Existence
Comparative Studies in Society and
History
General Systems Yearbook
The Humanist
Human Relations
Human Studies
Indian Journal of Social Research
Inquiry: Interdisciplinary Journal of Philos-
ophy and the Social Sciences

International Social Science Journal
International Social Science Review
The Journal of Social Issues
Mathematical Social Sciences
Monthly Review
Plural Societies
Potomac Review
Quality and Quantity: European-American
    Journal of Methodology
Review of Public Data Use
Simulation and Games
Social Action and the Law
Social Forces
Social Policy
Social Research
Social Science
Social Science History
Social Science Information
The Social Science Journal
Social Science Quarterly
Social Science Research
Social Theory and Practice
Socio-Economic Planning Sciences
South Atlantic Quarterly
Studies in Comparative Communism: An
    International Interdisciplinary Journal
Technology and Culture
Theory and Decision: An International
    Journal for Philosophy and Meth-
    odology of the Social Sciences
Theory and Society
The Third World Review
Transaction/Society
WIN Magazine

Sociology, see also Behavioral Science, Social Science

American Journal of Economics and
    Sociology
American Journal of Sociology
American Sociological Review
Journal of Political and Military Sociology
The Journal of Social Issues
Pacific Sociological Review
Plural Societies
Quality and Quantity: European-American
    Journal of Methodology
Social Forces
Sociological Inquiry
The Sociological Quarterly

State and Local Government, see Government/Politics

Terrorism

Terrorism: An International Journal

Transportation, see also Urban Studies

Transportation Journal
Transportation Law Journal
Transportation Research

Urban Studies, see also Government/Politics, Transportation

African Urban Studies
American City and County Magazine
City and Town
Comparative Urban Research
Current Municipal Problems
International Journal of Urban and Re-
    gional Research
Journal of Urban History
Journal of the American Planning Asso-
    ciation
National Civic Review
Regional Science and Urban Economics
Socio-Economic Planning Sciences
University of Detroit Journal of Urban
    Law
Urban Affairs Quarterly
The Urban and Social Change Review
Urban Education
Urban Focus
Urbanism Past and Present
Urban Life
Urban Studies
Western City

Women's Studies

Feminist Studies
Signs: Journal of Women in Culture and
    Society
Women and Politics: A Quarterly Journal
    of Research and Policy Studies
Women Organizing
Women's Rights Law Reporter